EXPLORE
AUSTRALIA

TOP WALKS
IN NEW SOUTH WALES

GW00630891

Ken Eastwood

CONTENTS

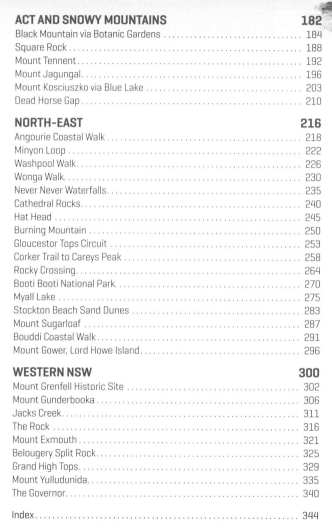

Crimson rosella

TOP BUSHWALKS IN NSW

Walking is one of the best activities you can do to remain healthy. Where better to do it but in nature's lungs, away from the madness of modernity and the pressures and stresses of suburban existence? Suitable for nearly all ages, walking is such a simple activity that requires no real extra skills, and thankfully it is still free.

For some reason, NSW's reputation as Australia's top bushwalking destination has slipped off its once mighty summit. The deep green wilds of Tasmania and Victoria seem to have blinded many to the treasures and wonders of Australia's most populous state.

But along NSW's sparkling 2007 km coastline, and within its rumpled inland folds and the moody mountains of the ACT, an extraordinary range of diverse bushwalks invite people to walk, marvel at and discover the beauty of this land. You can climb high onto bizarre volcanic peaks in the north of the state, or plunge into dark rainforested canyons; you can hike past sapphire-coloured tarns and colourful alpine meadows to the highest peaks on the continent, explore empty beaches on remote stretches of coast, or peer off the sheer sandstone edge of the Blue Mountains escarpment.

Let us never forget that the term bushwalking originated in this state in the early 20th century, when walking clubs began to seriously explore places including the Blue Mountains, Royal National Park and the Warrumbungles.

There is now an abundance of World Heritage–listed sites in NSW, and some of these provide superb bushwalking: the convict sites of the Old Great North Road, the ancient Antarctic beech forests and subalpine plateau in Barrington Tops National Park, the glorious vistas of the Blue Mountains, and the 'island with everything', Lord Howe. But there are other lesser known cultural and natural treasures: extensive Aboriginal art in Gundabooka National Park and the Mt Grenfell Historic Site, huge dunes on Stockton Beach, a mountain that's been burning for 6000 years, and a nature reserve with an exquisite wildflower display that is only open for six weeks a year. While Dorrigo National Park, Ku-ring-gai Chase National Park and Minnamurra Rainforest are well established as beautiful green corridors, other national parks pack surprising knock-out punches, such as Ben Boyd National Park's jewelled coastline and Mount Kaputar National Park's spectacular volcanic landscape, which reaches superlative subalpine heights. Through the great classroom of the bush, we discover the complex web of life around us, intricate layers of geological history, and the footsteps of those who have gone before.

While everyone has their favourite bushwalks, the routes in this book have been chosen precisely because they are inviting, interesting and fun. Although there are some serious challenges that will test even hardened walkers, there are no merciless, off-track bashes through uninteresting scrub, and many of the routes described are suitable for families and mixed-age groups. The emphasis is on walks that will take a few hours to one day, with a few multiday adventures to aspire to.

There are plenty of reasons for loving a particular bushwalk. It may have abundant and interesting wildlife or plant life; it may have views that literally take your breath away. It may draw you to observe the smallest things: glow worms and dragonflies, fungi in forests, or porcelain shells on beaches. It may pose a tough challenge to test your stamina, self-reliance and resolve; or it may just take you to a lovely place of solace, where the journey and the special friends you walk with are more important than the destination.

Whatever your reason for bushwalking, you will find NSW has a track that beckons you to step out and explore.

Tread lightly, breathe deeply and enjoy.
I'll see you on the track.
Ken Eastwood

This book is dedicated to the many Aboriginal people who have walked this land for eons and who know far more of its secrets than I could ever hope to fathom.

A huge thank you to: the special family and friends who accompanied me on many outdoor adventures; the NSW National Parks and Wildlife Service, Australian Capital Tourism and Destination NSW for their assistance; and the Creator for designing such an awesome outdoor playground.

WHAT TO TAKE

Despite outdoor stores trying to sell you all manner of gizmos and gadgets, bushwalking requires very little in the way of gear, particularly if you stick to short or moderate-length walks. Expensive walking poles may help some people with knee problems, but generally a good-old stick will do the same job.

Our society's obsession in recent decades with 'hydrating' has meant that some people won't even go on a half-hour stroll without a water bottle or 'hydration pouch'. But that isn't essential, and it's surprisingly freeing and relaxing to go for a walk in the bush with absolutely nothing: no camera, phone, food or water, just you and nature. However, be warned, on any steep walk, or a walk of more than an hour or so, you should definitely take water, particularly in summer or in humid conditions. It is also worth leaving extra water in the car for your return.

If you are in a group, you may be able to share gear on longer walks.

Here are my recommendations:

Short, easy walk of an hour or so
Nothing

Moderate length walk of a few hours
Daypack with about 1 L of water
High-energy snack, such as muesli bar, banana, nuts or chocolate
Swimmers and towel (optional)
Raincoat and/or extra layer
Camera

Half day, tougher walk
Daypack with 1.5 L of water
High-energy snacks
Lunch
Swimmers and towel (optional)
Raincoat and/or extra layer
Basic medical kit – bandages, bandaids
Compass, map and/or GPS
Camera

Full day, more remote walk
Daypack with at least 2 L of water
High-energy snacks
Lunch
Swimmers and towel (optional)
Raincoat and/or extra two layers; spare thermals, beanie and gloves if in cold weather
Full medical kit and penknife

Heat blanket (these light-weight foil blankets cost just a few dollars and fold up very small, but could help save a life if you are caught out after dark)

Matches

Small torch

Compass, map and/or GPS

Aquatabs or similar – one tablet can purify 1 L of water, which could be life-saving if caught out

Camera

* Tell someone where you are going and when you expect to be back, and what they should do if you don't return by a particular time.

Very remote long walk

All the above

Consider any special requirements, such as a rope (e.g. on The Castle) or snowshoes

Consider taking a personal emergency beacon (can be rented quite cheaply from some national park offices) or satellite phone

Footwear

One of NSW's most famous bushwalking families, the Butlers, are renowned for barefoot bushwalking, and devotees swear by either this or the more recent innovation, the thin-soled 'barefoot shoe' with pockets for individual toes. Not surprisingly, this is unlikely to suit everyone.

The most important thing with footwear is that whatever you choose is comfortable for walking long distances, and that you have walked in them before. Blisters are all too commonly found on those who try out new shoes on a long walk. Even well-fitting shoes or boots can still create blisters over long distances.

For most people, covered shoes should protect your feet from sticks, stones and the risk of rolling an ankle. Hard-soled boots take some getting used to, but protect your feet very well over long distances. Many walkers love wearing hard-soled, thick hiking boots for rough rocky trails, snake country and in wet environments. However, on smooth rock surfaces they seem to turn into roller-skates, and so are not recommended for rock-hopping adventures. Simple sneakers, or trail-runners, are the best for many surfaces.

BUSHWALKERS' CODE

Although it may seem like commonsense, the bushwalkers' code emphasises having minimal impact on the beautiful natural environments you visit. It is still surprising how much rubbish is left in the bush by walkers, that living trees are cut down for firewood, and that areas are polluted by poor sanitation.

Minimal impact practices include keeping your group small, camping in existing campsites and using existing fireplaces, obeying 'no fire' rules, carrying out what you carry in (and often picking up any other rubbish you find), and washing well away from streams to ensure soap, detergents and food scraps don't enter waterways. Toilet holes should be dug at least 20 cm deep and more than 100 m from any water source. Burn used toilet paper in the hole (if it is safe to do so), then bury the remains.

For more tips on minimal impact travel, see the website of Leave No Trace Australia, http://lnt.org.au, or *Australia's Best Eco-Friendly Holidays*, Explore Australia.

Another part of bushwalking management is looking after the welfare of your group. On longer walks this includes: leaving detailed information with a responsible person about where you will be going, when you are expected to return and what to do if you fail to return by a certain time; choosing a walk based on the experience and capabilities of your group; responding wisely to changes in the weather; and caring for injured people.

Bushwalking on your own is a unique pleasure and highly recommended, but you should be completely self-reliant, carry adequate emergency gear to get yourself out of nearly every unforeseen circumstance, and let someone know of your route and expected return.

For more information on bushwalking etiquette, see the website of the Confederation of Bushwalking Clubs NSW, www.bushwalking.org.au. This site also has an extensive list of, and links to, active bushwalking clubs in NSW. They can be a great place to meet like-minded people, develop friendships, gain bushwalking experience in a safe and fun environment, and travel to some out-of-the-way destinations.

HOW TO USE THIS BOOK

Designed to inspire you to get out of the house, and to help you when you are in the bush, this book includes route descriptions, simple maps, plant and wildlife descriptions and advice. In some cases, such as the harder or more remote walks, you will need to carry another more detailed map and compass, or a GPS. However, in most instances it should get you out and back on these routes safely.

DISTANCE

All of the routes in this book require at least a moderate level of effort, as 500 m strolls to a lookout or attraction were not considered 'bushwalks'. Walks can be a loop (returning to the same spot over different terrain), a linear out-and-back style (called a return walk) or a one-way track, requiring transport to return to your starting point.

TIME REQUIRED

This is one of the most controversial parts of designing a bushwalking guide, as everyone walks at different paces on flat ground, let alone while overcoming ascents, descents, tricky terrain, photo stops, weather conditions and track-finding difficulties. Larger groups always move slower than smaller groups of the same skill.

Some national park signs, such as those in the Blue Mountains, suggest times for the slowest of walkers (toddlers, the frail), yet many bushwalkers complete those walks in half the time listed on the signs.

Times in this book are estimated for fit, keen, middle-aged walkers who stop for photos, but take only relatively short food and drink breaks. Many people will take longer than the times written down. On some of the easier walks, or walks where there is much to see and do along the way, times are elongated to account for a more relaxed family-friendly style of walking. Hopefully, fit walkers in small groups should generally find the times accurate.

BEST TIME

Nearly all these walks are suitable for any time of year, but if there are special times when they will be at their best, they are listed.

GRADE

Steep or long climbs, moving over difficult terrain, long distances in remote areas, or tricky navigation will usually score a 'hard' rating; hills, stairs, rough tracks and some scrambling will score a 'moderate', and flatter, more open tracks will generally be rated 'easy'. More information in the route description should help you decide if a walk is suitable for your group.

REFERENCES AND FURTHER READING

www.wildwalks.com/bushwalking-and-hiking-in-nsw
http://ozultimate.com/bushwalking
www.aussiewalks.com
Australia's Best Eco-friendly Holidays, Ken Eastwood, Explore Australia, 2009
Tracking through the South East Forests of New South Wales, Cath Renwick,
    The Beaten Track Press, 2004
Bushwalking in the Budawangs, Ron Doughton, Envirobook, 2004
Hunter Valley Bushwalks, Greg Powell, Kingsclear Books, 2003
120 Walks in New South Wales, Tyrone Thomas, Hill of Content, 2000
Discovering NSW Rainforests, Total Environment Centre and Rainforest Publishing, 1986

X

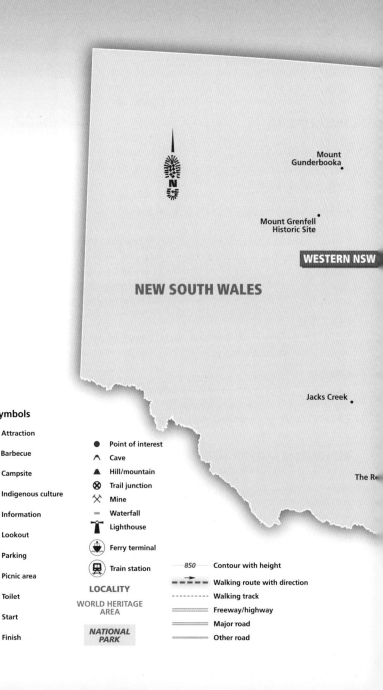

Mount Gunderbooka

Mount Grenfell Historic Site

WESTERN NSW

NEW SOUTH WALES

Jacks Creek

The Re

Map symbols

⊛	Attraction	●	Point of interest
🔥	Barbecue	∧	Cave
△	Campsite	▲	Hill/mountain
🖐	Indigenous culture	⊗	Trail junction
i	Information	✕	Mine
🚶	Lookout	—	Waterfall
P	Parking	🗼	Lighthouse
⊼	Picnic area	⚓	Ferry terminal
🚻	Toilet	🚆	Train station
🚶	Start	**LOCALITY**	
🚶	Finish	WORLD HERITAGE AREA	
		NATIONAL PARK	

850 —— Contour with height
— ▶ Walking route with direction
---------- Walking track
▬▬▬ Freeway/highway
▬▬▬ Major road
▬▬▬ Other road

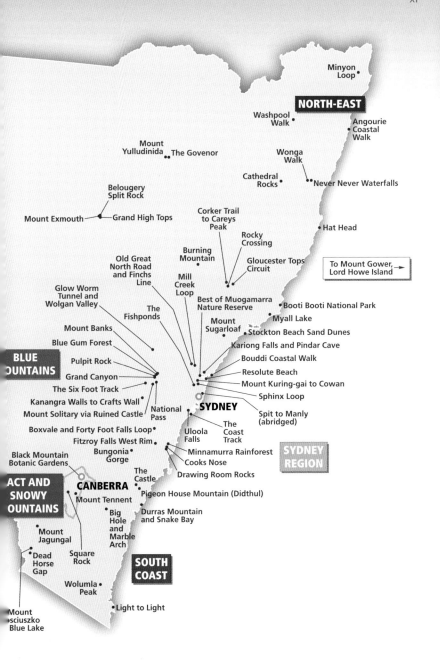

NORTH-EAST

Minyon Loop

Washpool Walk

Angourie Coastal Walk

Mount Yulludinida • The Govenor

Wonga Walk

Cathedral Rocks

Never Never Waterfalls

Belougery Split Rock

Corker Trail to Careys Peak

Mount Exmouth — Grand High Tops

Rocky Crossing

Hat Head

Burning Mountain

Gloucester Tops Circuit

Old Great North Road and Finchs Line

Mill Creek Loop

To Mount Gower, Lord Howe Island →

Glow Worm Tunnel and Wolgan Valley

The Fishponds

Best of Muogamarra Nature Reserve

Booti Booti National Park

Mount Banks

Mount Sugarloaf

Myall Lake

Stockton Beach Sand Dunes

Blue Gum Forest

Kariong Falls and Pindar Cave

BLUE MOUNTAINS

Pulpit Rock

Bouddi Coastal Walk

Grand Canyon

Resolute Beach

The Six Foot Track

Mount Kuring-gai to Cowan

Kanangra Walls to Crafts Wall

Sphinx Loop

Mount Solitary via Ruined Castle

National Pass

SYDNEY

Spit to Manly (abridged)

Boxvale and Forty Foot Falls Loop

Uloola Falls

The Coast Track

Fitzroy Falls West Rim

Black Mountain Botanic Gardens

Bungonia Gorge

Minnamurra Rainforest

Cooks Nose

SYDNEY REGION

ACT AND SNOWY MOUNTAINS

The Castle

Drawing Room Rocks

CANBERRA

Pigeon House Mountain (Didthul)

Mount Tennent

Big Hole and Marble Arch

Durras Mountain and Snake Bay

Mount Jagungal

Dead Horse Gap

Square Rock

SOUTH COAST

Wolumla Peak

Light to Light

Mount Kosciuszko Blue Lake

TABLE OF WALKS

	walk km	walk hours	grade	page
ACT AND SNOWY MOUNTAINS				
Black Mountain via Botanic Gardens	9	3	moderate	184
Square Rock	9	3.5	easy	188
Mount Tennent	15	4	moderate	192
Mount Jagungal	45	2 or 3 days	hard	196
Mount Kosciuszko via Blue Lake	22	9	moderate	203
Dead Horse Gap	9	3.5	moderate	210
NORTH-EAST				
Angourie Coastal Walk	12	3	moderate	218
Minyon Loop	7	2.5	moderate/hard	222
Washpool Walk	8	2	moderate	226
Wonga Walk	6.5	2.5	easy/moderate	230
Never Never Waterfalls	11	4	moderate/hard	235
Cathedral Rocks	6	2.5	moderate	240
Hat Head	11	4	moderate	245
Burning Mountain	4	1	moderate	250
Gloucestor Tops Circuit	7.5	3	moderate	253
Corker Trail to Careys Peak	20	6	hard	258
Rocky Crossing	18	5	easy/moderate	264
Booti Booti National Park	7.5	2	moderate	270
Myall Lake	25	2 days	easy	275
Stockton Beach Sand Dunes	7 [approx.]	2	moderate	283
Mount Sugarloaf	3.5	1.5	easy	287
Bouddi Coastal Walk	9.5	3 or 6	moderate/hard	291
Mount Gower, Lord Howe Island	10	9	moderate/hard	296
WESTERN NSW				
Mount Grenfell Historic Site	5	1.5	moderate	302
Mount Gunderbooka	6	2	moderate	306
Jacks Creek	2.5	1	moderate	311
The Rock	6	2	moderate	316
Mount Exmouth	20	6	hard	321
Belougery Split Rock	4.6	2.5	hard	325
Grand High Tops	16.5	6	hard	329
Mount Yulludunida	4	2.5	hard	335
The Governor	2.5	1	moderate	340

Berowra Waters

CANBERRA

SYDNEY

SYDNEY REGION

Surprisingly for a spread-out city of five million people, Sydney still has excellent bushwalking tracks, particularly in its two major 'lungs', Royal National Park down south and Ku-ring-gai Chase National Park in the north.

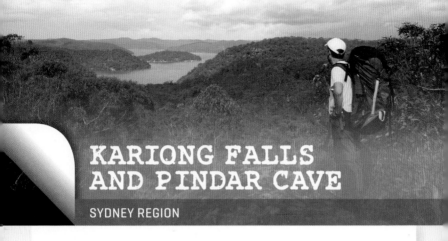

KARIONG FALLS AND PINDAR CAVE

SYDNEY REGION

WALK: 17 km return

TIME REQUIRED: 7 hours or overnight

BEST TIME: Mid-winter to late spring, when the wildflowers are at their best

GRADE: Moderate to hard with some rough stairs

ENVIRONMENT: Hidden waterfall, wildflower-rich heath and woodland, views over quiet Central Coast valley, huge cave

BEST MAP: This book

TOILETS: None

FOOD: None – bring your own

TIPS: Light long pants are recommended as the track to Pindar Cave is overgrown and scratchy

A really interesting day or overnight walk, this includes a stunning hidden waterfall, some great views, a wildflower wonderland and a cave big enough to sleep 50 people. Getting there is a novel experience too; the only way in is by train, to a tiny, remote station by the water.

Several previous bushwalking guides describe the route to Pindar Cave (a route often walked by Scout and Duke of Edinburgh groups), but few seem to add the very enjoyable 5.5 km addition to the beautiful, hidden Kariong Falls. By combining the two, you'll find this walk has plenty to offer.

[above] *View south to the Hawkesbury*

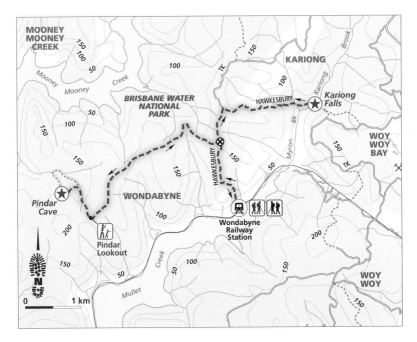

MOONEY MOONEY CREEK

KARIONG

Mooney Mooney Creek

BRISBANE WATER NATIONAL PARK

HAWKESBURY

Kariong Falls

WOY WOY BAY

Pindar Cave

WONDABYNE

Pindar Lookout

Wondabyne Railway Station

Creek

Mullet

WOY WOY

N

0   1 km

There are a wealth of excellent walks immediately on the north side of the Hawkesbury River, and the Big Daddy of them all, the Great North Walk, goes through this area. The best way to access them is via the cute little Wondabyne railway station, which has no vehicular access and a platform not quite big enough for one carriage. It's between Hornsby and Woy Woy, and the train will only stop if you ride in the last carriage and tell the guard that you want to get off at Wondabyne. This all adds to the fun.

Wondabyne itself is little more than a small quarry, that produces very hard, light grey sandstone (some of which was used in St Mary's Cathedral in Sydney and the Australian War Memorial in Canberra). You can see some of the machinery just past the north end of the station.

The walking track begins at the south end of the station, and heads straight up the hill for about 400 m. Catch your breath at the top and you'll enjoy a view of the water back through the trees and over the xanthorrhoeas. From the top of the hill, walk along the fire trail, with a thick, sandy coastal forest on either side. After almost 2 km you'll see a large wooden board with various distances marked on the right-hand side. You are going to turn right here, towards Patonga, along the thin but obvious track that heads downhill. The track meanders around some stunning sandstone features carved by nature, across rock platforms and past some extraordinary scribbly gums: their trunks are almost entirely eaten out by fire but they still support a thriving canopy above.

The bush here is also home to lots of eastern spinebills. This 15 cm long bird has a lovely rufous, black and white area on its tummy and neck and a graceful, curved bill. There are also lots of wildflowers.

The track winds down to a creek crossing, with a little cascade and waterhole. Cross the creek and quickly climb the muddy slope on the other side. You'll then pass a few taller sandstone walls and enter a wet, semi-rainforested area, as you come down towards Kariong Falls. You'll hear the falls before you see them. Be prepared for a big surprise when you come across this beautiful

Kariong Falls

spot where water cascades into a big pool with a sandy bank. Towering off to one side is a large sandstone overhang, with a red hand stencil high on the wall. It's a magic spot to stop a while and enjoy a break, and those desperate for a dip will find a deep area near the falls.

From here, our walk heads back the way you came, 2 km back to the fire trail. Then head left, down the fire trail towards Wondabyne. After 600 m you'll see a sandstone slab on the right-hand side of the track. Cross this, and you'll spot a very obvious, but unmarked, track. This is the route to Pindar Cave. Locating it has bamboozled many young navigators trying out for their Duke of Edinburgh award.

Eastern spinebill

Follow the track for a few hundred metres and it becomes thin and often overgrown. It will take you through thick wildflower-rich heathland that could be quite claustrophobic in the heat of summer, but in winter and spring provides a colourful bouquet to enjoy.

There are plenty of birds through here as well, including another easy-to-spot favourite, the New Holland honeyeater. About the same size as the eastern spinebill, it is a black-and-white bird with yellow wing panels and white tips on its tail feathers that you can see when it darts and dives through the banksia woodland.

Occasionally you'll get great glimpses through to Mooney Mooney Creek or back towards Mullet Creek and the Hawkesbury River, but the best view is at an obvious clear rocky knoll called Pindar Lookout.

From here the track barrels down into the valley, and you'll soon be entering a swampy area that is wet and very muddy after rain. Here you will find lovely Pindar Pool, a surprisingly deep, large-spa-sized ephemeral pool, overhung with banksia, and full of big tadpoles. It could be worth a dip on a hot day.

It's just a few hundred metres from here to massive Pindar Cave. This sandstone overhang is big enough to sleep 50 people, although

Red handprint at Kariong Falls

perfectly flat ground is a little hard to find. It is often used by scouts and other large groups, but if you find it free, it could be a lovely spot to spend the night and enjoy a campfire.

This is your turnaround point, so after you've enjoyed the shelter, you can head back to Wondabyne. Don't forget to flag down the train driver.

New Holland
honeyeater

OLD GREAT NORTH ROAD AND FINCHS LINE

SYDNEY REGION

WALK: 11 km loop

TIME REQUIRED: 3.5 hours

BEST TIME: Any time of year except hot days in the middle of summer

GRADE: Moderate – the ascent is easy, on a wide road with a low gradient, but the descent is on an uneven track

ENVIRONMENT: World Heritage-listed convict sites, sandstone vegetation communities, glorious views over the Hawkesbury River

BEST MAP: Walks around Wisemans Ferry, www.maps.com.au/PDFs/Maps/hawkesb/WalksArWisemans.pdf

TOILETS: Pit toilet near the punt, 800 m from start of walk

FOOD: Wisemans Ferry, a 5-minute drive away (plus punt crossing) has a pub, service station and limited shops

TIPS: If you are coming from the south and there is a huge queue of vehicles waiting to cross Wisemans Ferry, park your car on the southern side of the river and walk onto the punt (there is never a queue for passengers). You will need to walk past the punt station on the other side anyway at the end of the walk. Once across, turn left and walk along the road for 800 m to the start of the Old Great North Rd.

[above] *Wisemans Ferry*

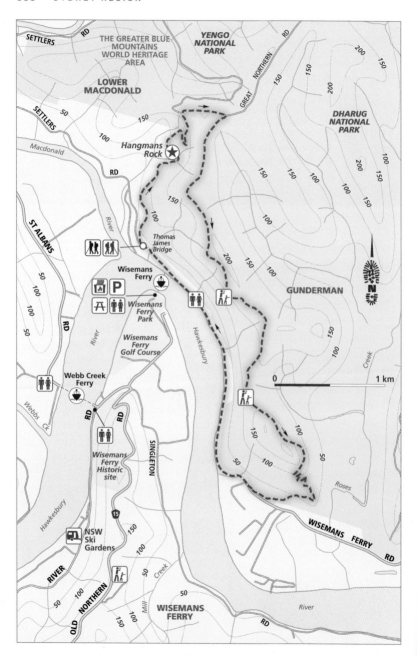

SETTLERS RD

THE GREATER BLUE MOUNTAINS WORLD HERITAGE AREA

YENGO NATIONAL PARK

LOWER MACDONALD

SETTLERS

Macdonald

RD

Hangmans Rock ★

DHARUG NATIONAL PARK

GREAT NORTHERN RD

River

ST ALBANS

Thomas James Bridge

Wisemans Ferry

Wisemans Ferry Park

Wisemans Ferry Golf Course

GUNDERMAN

N

Hawkesbury

Webb Creek Ferry

RD

RD

SINGLETON

0   1 km

Wisemans Ferry Historic site

Webbs CK

Hawkesbury

15

NSW Ski Gardens

Creek

Roses

OLD NORTHERN

River

WISEMANS FERRY

WISEMANS FERRY RD

River

RD

This walk takes you along an incredibly well-preserved part of Australia's convict history – the World Heritage–listed Great North Rd – and then brings you back through great groves of Gymea lilies and thick forests, past rocky outcrops with glorious views of the Hawkesbury River.

In July 2010, 11 Australian convict sites were included on the World Heritage register, including the Old Great North Rd. Only in use for a short period, this section of road is very well preserved, with 12 m high buttressed walls, brilliantly engineered culverts, and convict graffiti. There are multiple excellent information panels that help make this a very interesting walk. The views over the Hawkesbury River in the second half of the walk are an excellent bonus.

In some ways the route (as described here) is like a walk backwards in time. The second half, Finchs Line, was completed first (from 1826) as a main road between Sydney and the agricultural areas of the Hunter Valley. Governor Darling had a particularly scary experience in a horse-drawn wagon going up

Hangmans Rock

Finchs Line, and (not surprisingly) declared it too steep and too narrow. As a result, the much gentler route up Devines Hill was built from 1829. However, even after all that effort, the route was barely used because its lonely path was prone to bushrangers, and coastal steamers soon provided a much quicker means of transport. As a result, rather than becoming developed, it remained quietly sitting in the bush, and has experienced a well-deserved revival of interest in the past decade or so. It's a great day out from Sydney.

From the vehicular punt, on the north side of the Hawkesbury at Wisemans Ferry, turn left and drive (or walk if you have left your vehicle on the other bank) about 800 m. You will cross Thomas James Bridge, built in 1830, which is one of the oldest bridges in Australia still in use. Just past it, there is a small parking area on the left-hand side of the road, opposite the signposted gate to the Old Great North Rd. The route is popular with mountain bikers so parking may be at a premium. There is another small spot to park at the 'Hawkesbury' sign a few hundred metres back down the road.

Head up the wide, smooth Old Great North Rd and you'll immediately be walking over the hard yakka of hundreds of convicts. More than 500 were working on the road at one time, and every pockmark in the sandstone, and every geometrical block, was hacked out by hand at the wrong end of the lash. The work on both sides of the road, as you ascend, is extraordinary in its precision and even beauty, with carved culverts, and towering supporting walls.

The tubby 12 cm long birds you may see on the rocks, with their backs and tails grey and tummies a rich rufous, are rock warblers – the only bird endemic to NSW. They build their nests in culverts and caves.

Two-thirds of the way up the hill, you'll find Hangmans Rock, a cave with a natural hole in its ceiling. Stories that convicts were hanged through the hole are probably unfounded. There are some well-carved stairs and an excellent stone seat to sit and peruse the view for a while, or think of the clink of chains and picks on stone.

At the top of the hill, among some towering Gymea lilies on the left-hand side, you'll come through a gate and across a fork. Turn right, up a rocky fire trail for 500 m, and Finchs Line will appear on

Gymea lilies beside the track

the right-hand side of the track. At this point you are about one-third of the way through the walk, but it's nearly all downhill or flat from here.

Finchs Line makes for very pleasant walking through mixed eucalypt forest, with plenty more Gymea lilies, eggs and bacon bushes and other flowers. At one point where the track turns sharply to the left, a steep little track to the right leads down to a rock lookout, directly above Wisemans Ferry. There are more great rock perches with stunning views over the river during the next kilometre or so and any of them would make an excellent lunch spot.

After gently meandering along the ridge, with views of wetlands over the left side of the track, Finchs Line begins descending sharply over uneven ground, and you'll understand why Governor Darling declared the route so unsatisfactory. It's hard to believe the narrow, steep, rocky path would even have had room for a horse and carriage. It does however provide a fairly quick descent to the valley floor, and the birdsong will soon be replaced by sounds of lowing cattle, whinnying horses, cars and roaring waterski boats on the Hawkesbury.

Once you reach the road, you unfortunately face a 2.8 km walk along the roadside (to the right). Usually it's best when walking along a road with no footpath to face the oncoming traffic (i.e, on the right-hand side), but in this case the only room is on the left side, next to the river.

After a couple of kilometres, you'll be back at the punt (with pit toilets and a small roadside picnic area), and then another 800 m or so past the punt you'll be back at your car.

Gymea lilies at the top of Devines Hill

MILL CREEK LOOP

SYDNEY REGION

WALK: 9 km loop

TIME REQUIRED: 3.5 hours

BEST TIME: Spring

GRADE: Moderate – uneven track and some moderately steep ascents and descents with a few rock scrambles

Flannel flower

ENVIRONMENT: A variety of forest types, including some rainforest and tall eucalypt forest, heathland, valleys, creeks, sandstone features

BEST MAP: Walks around Wisemans Ferry, www.maps. com.au/PDFs/Maps/hawkesb/ WalksArWisemans.pdf

TOILETS: Pit toilet at carpark at the start of the walk

FOOD: Wisemans Ferry, a 5-minute drive away (plus punt crossing) has a pub, service station and limited shops

TIPS: Camp overnight at Mill Creek camping area to get the most out of this special spot

[above] *Creek crossing on the Mill Creek Loop*

*More about enjoying a special area of bushland
than any particular feature, this meandering loop
walk has three ascents and descents, winding
through a variety of forest types and gullies. The area
abounds in wildlife, with wombats, gliders, possums, wallabies
and birds aplenty.*

One keen advocate of this bushwalk describes it as being 'more
about the journey than the destination'. It is commonly listed as an
11 km loop, but comes up on the GPS as just under 9 km. However,
the three sharpish ascents and descents may make it feel a fair
bit longer.

Just north of the mighty Hawkesbury River at Wisemans Ferry is
one of the best camping areas near Sydney. Cross the river to the
north side on the vehicular punt, then turn right and follow the road
along the river for 5.6 km to the turnoff to the Mill Creek Camping
Area. This quiet little spot has about 30 campsites, including space

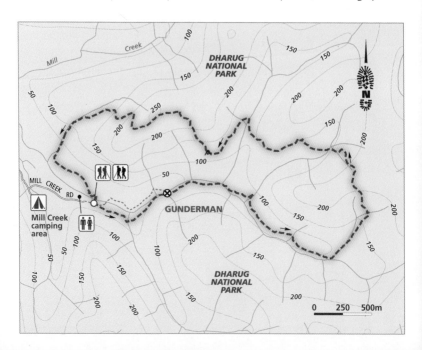

Flowering heathland

for large groups, a pit toilet and individual fireplaces, often with wood supplied. There is no reliable drinking water, but some tank water is usually available. The campsite's position in a valley (away from the river) means it is very sheltered, but can be bitterly cold in winter.

The highlight of the campsite though is the wildlife – in particular a community of common wombats that wander around just after dark. Keeping quiet, and with torches off, take a walk down the dirt road to the picnic and large-group camping area. Turn your torch on when you hear a noise, and you'll almost certainly spot a wombat or two. There are also wallabies, wallaroos, possums galore, great birdlife (including gang-gang, yellow-tailed and glossy black-cockatoos) and populations of squirrel and yellow-bellied gliders, which you can hear at night high in the trees, the sugar gliders yipping and yapping like small dogs.

This walk starts at the picnic area (just past the large-group camping area) where signs advise you to walk anti-clockwise (the ascents are easier and the track is clearer). This means starting with the marked track

Common wombat

Sandstone cave near the end of the walk

in the back right corner of the picnic area. You'll come back across the little bridge at the end of the walk.

The first section is part of the 3 km Grass Tree Circuit, and you can take either of the tracks, as they will meet up in 1.5 km. Birds in this first, lush section include lyrebirds, bellbirds and brush turkeys.

After the two tracks meet, continue in an easterly direction as the track undulates over a steady rise up the valley. There are a couple of beautiful big sandstone overhangs and caves, and flowers including red spider flowers, groves of Gymea lilies, banksias, white hakeas, flannel flowers, wattle and pink boronia. Other plants include pink-trunked angophoras, spiky-haired xanthorrhoeas, and down low the wispy grass-like Grandpa's beard. In Sept–Oct you may also see bright red waratahs.

The track is fairly well defined, with fluoro-orange triangles marking the way at tricky spots. You'll cross creeks a few times.

More than a third of the way through, you'll face the first of the three steeper climbs. Keep an eye out for more birds including grey fantails and honeyeaters.

You'll notice as you descend on the other side of the ridge that you are moving into an area of drier vegetation.

The second ascent is gentler, but the third one – which starts 5 km into the walk – climbs about 150 m in 1.5 km, passing a great cave in a jumble of huge boulders. At the top of the ridge, on the right-hand side of the track, you'll see a lovely large rock platform, with views out to the north.

From the platform, the track rises a little more gently to the highest point. Because of the thick forest there are no great views at the very top. However, a little further along, before the track starts descending steeply, there are a couple of spots with splendid views through the trees out to the west, all the way to the Blue Mountains.

From here there is a slightly tricky descent, with a few rocks to clamber down. Gradually the track returns into lusher forest and past honeycombed sandstone overhangs. The final section features towering white-trunked eucalypts among the bracken, and you'll see the camping and picnic areas on the other side of the creek. Continue along the creek before crossing the bridge back to the carpark.

Towering eucalypts

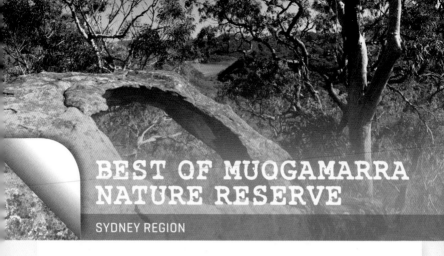

BEST OF MUOGAMARRA NATURE RESERVE

WALK: 11 km loop

TIME REQUIRED: 4 hours

BEST TIME: Muogamarra is only open for 6 weekends in late winter/early spring – the best time for waratahs is towards the end of that period

GRADE: Moderate

ENVIRONMENT: Marked diversity of ecosystems: wildflower-rich woodland, Aboriginal engravings, rare volcanic crater, rainforest, mangroves, extensive views

BEST MAP: This book

TOILETS: Pit toilet near the visitor centre at the start and finish of the walk, flushing toilets at Pie in the Sky at Cowan

FOOD: Pie in the Sky at Cowan is a popular, large pie bakery and cafe with extensive outdoor seating, and is found on the Old Pacific Highway just 50 m north of the turnoff into Muogamarra Nature Reserve: (02) 9985 7018

TIPS: Muogamarra Nature Reserve is a treat for everyone. There are gentle, flat strolls from the visitor centre that are rich with flowers and have great views, mid-length walks, great guided walks (such as the excellent Bird Gully walk) and longer hikes, such as the one described here. Many families and couples would enjoy spending a spring day here, whether or not you choose to do the walk described.

[above] *Sandstone arch and Peats Bight*

*Brimming with wildflower bouquets, and
containing incredibly diverse ecosystems,
this varied loop walk takes you to the best of
Muogamarra's treasures, including a volcanic crater,
Aboriginal engravings, spectacular views, rainforest and the
Hawkesbury River.*

Only open for six weekends a year, Muogamarra Nature is a special
treasure trove on the northern outskirts of Sydney that, since 1935,
has been opening in spring to showcase its wildflower display. The
excellent Discovery Program offers a range of guided walks in the
2500 ha reserve, but you can also do many of the walks on your
own. This walk combines a few of the routes into a great day out.

The turn-off into the reserve is located on the Pacific Highway
3.8 km north of Cowan Railway Station, just before Pie in the Sky
bakery and cafe. On the six Aug/Sept weekends when the reserve
is open, opening hours are 9am to 4.30pm. Volunteers serve at

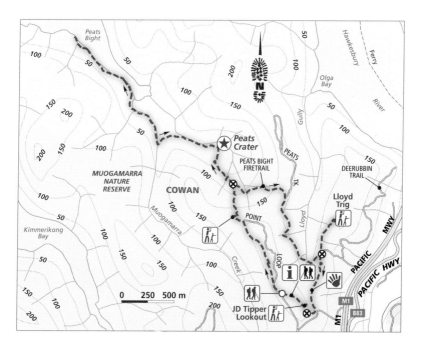

Waratah

the site and collect a fee for entering the reserve (currently $10 per adult and $5 per child).

The visitor centre is 3 km along an unsealed road into the reserve. Drop in there and pick up the extensive laminated track notes, and a map if they have one available. It's also worth checking with the volunteers where the best locations to see waratahs are before you start walking.

Head out on the Point Loop, which starts on the opposite side of the carpark to the visitor centre. Because it is a loop, you can take either the left or right track (perhaps depending where the waratahs are), passing the first of many of the 900 species of flowering plant in the botanically rich reserve. For starters there are Sydney red gums, grey gums, bloodwoods, scribbly gums, drumsticks, banksias, peas, pink waxflowers and boronias. After 500 m or so, the tracks meet near an airy rock platform, with great views down the valley to the Hawkesbury River (where you will be walking) and down to your right where you will see the very distinct vegetation and terrain of Peats Crater.

Lloyd Trig

The next section of the walk is the hardest to follow. About 30 m back from the rock platform, a scramble down some rocks (to the left, facing away from the lookout) leads to a faint track. The footpad ducks and weaves downhill, sometimes with small cairns to mark the way across rock platforms. Volunteers may have trimmed bushes and put some flagging tape in places to help walkers follow this route, but it basically heads downhill almost due north, directly towards Peats Crater, through a wildflower wonderland before disgorging walkers on the Peats Track fire trail. Turn left and downhill.

Most of this road was built in the first half of the 19th century, and you'll see historic dry stone walls and culverts.

Soon you'll hit Peats Crater, one of an estimated 25 diatremes (a breccia-filled volcanic pipe) in the Sydney basin, but one of the most obvious to spot. With particularly rich, volcanic soil, it was highly suitable to cultivation, and so all the original vegetation has been lost, now replaced with introduced grasses, favoured by kangaroos and wallabies; towering Sally wattles, bracken, and a long line of Osage orange trees, which were planted as a hedge between two portions of farming land. These introduced trees are now considered important for their heritage value.

The old road peters out around here. Take the track to Peats Bight that heads out from the left of the crater (downhill again), staying on the same side of the creek. It's here you'll enter a small but lovely cool section of rainforest, with lilly pillies, cabbage tree palms, coachwoods and water gums.

As the track flattens out, you'll begin to see on the right-hand side the start of the mangrove swamp. Prepare to be serenaded by frogs and whipbirds, and look for the stone ruins of a farmhouse, which stood here from 1886 to 1939. The mangroves are quite scenic, and at low tide you'll see the defined channel along which boats once transported goods.

Gradually the views of the Hawkesbury River improve, and you'll reach a point just beyond the mangrove trees with the remains of an old stone jetty and an uninterrupted vista across the water. It's a great spot to sit and take a break before heading back.

On the way back, however, don't take the steep, ill-defined track back up to the lookout, but continue along the Peats Track fire trail past the crater for a few more kilometres. The fire trail is stony in places and a little hard on the feet, but the gradient is never particularly severe. Among the rocks and flowers, keep an eye out for goannas, snakes and other reptiles.

At a T-junction at the top of a rise, the Peats Track fire trail hits the Bight Fire Trail or Deerubbin Extension Walk. Turn left, and almost immediately, a small marked track on the left leads up to Lloyd Trig. This delightful little side trip will take you up to 230 m above sea level, with splendid views down to Brooklyn, Long Island Nature Reserve, and across Pittwater to the Barrenjoey Lighthouse. It's a great spot for lunch.

The final stretch is back down the Lloyd Trig track, then turn right and up the fire trail, which is likely to be quite busy with other walkers. There are Aboriginal engravings and sharpening grooves along a long series of sandstone platforms, most of which are best revealed and explained on the guided walks. However, a large engraving of a whale on the right-hand side of the track (marked off with ropes) is certainly worth admiring.

Not far past this, a small marked track to the right leads up to the flat JD Tipper Loop and back to the visitor centre. Turn right when you hit this loop and you'll quickly find the JD Tipper Lookout, with some more brilliant views over the Hawkesbury, out to Brooklyn Bridge and beyond.

A very short stroll along this track leads back to the visitor centre and a picnic area with proper tables and bench seats.

RESOLUTE BEACH

SYDNEY REGION

WALK: 4 km loop

TIME REQUIRED: 2 hours

BEST TIME: Spring or summer

GRADE: Moderate – there are lots of stairs

ENVIRONMENT: Sydney sandstone, beautiful coastline, rainforest gullies, heathland

BEST MAP: Ku-ring-gai Chase National Park, NSW Land and Property Information

TOILETS: At the Resolute Picnic Area, but NOT at West Head

FOOD: Shops at Terrey Hills, 6 km before the park entrance, or at the expensive, but otherwise excellent, licensed Cottage Point Kiosk, a half-hour drive from West Head

TIPS: Bring your swimmers

Saw banksia

[above] *Barrenjoey Headland*

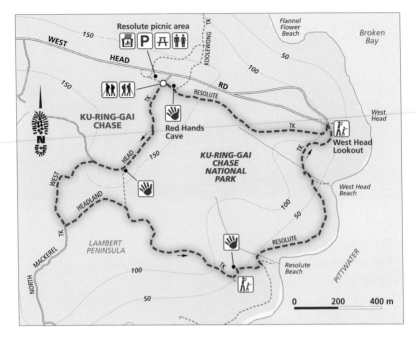

This is a cracking walk with Indigenous art sites and some quiet little beaches, that culminates in probably the best view in all of Sydney.

At the end of West Head Rd, in Ku-ring-gai Chase National Park, you are pretty much at the most northerly point in greater Sydney. Here you will find a superb lookout and picnic area which you'll get to enjoy three-quarters of the way through this walk.

The serpentine drive into the national park begins on McCarrs Creek Rd out of Terrey Hills or Church Pt. Then swing into West Head Rd. If you have time, make sure you do some of the other great short walks that branch off West Head Rd, such as the tracks to America Bay [2.2 km return] or Flint and Steel Beach [2 km], or the Willunga Track to the highest point in the park [1.4 km]. You'll travel 12 km past the park gate before getting to the Resolute Picnic Area and the start of the walk.

Lovely pink smooth-barked apples, brush turkeys, butterflies and goannas will probably greet you at the picnic area (which has gas barbecues and toilets, but no view). Head straight down the fire trail at the back of the picnic area towards Resolute Beach, ignoring the turn left to West Head or Red Hands Cave (you'll see them on the way back). In spring, this area is a lovely wildflower garden.

After a few hundred metres, there are clearly signposted Aboriginal carvings to the left of the track, including a male figure, fish and eels, but in the middle of the day in summer they are quite hard to see. From the back of the rock platform, take the small, signposted Headland Track. It can be overgrown and scratchy, but it's worth getting off the fire trail for 200 m. When you rejoin the fire trail, turn left and wander through an attractive forest of scribbly gums, bloodwoods, stringybark, banksias and bottlebrush.

Brush turkey

About 250 m after rejoining the fire trail, take the steep track to the left signposted 'Resolute'. It passes a lovely cliff line with cabbage palms and a large rock shelter that was used by

West Head Lookout

Isopogon flowers – better known as drumsticks

Aboriginal people for millenia, before it hits a T-junction. Turn left towards Resolute Beach (the other way goes around the headland to Mackerel Beach). Where the track forks again, it's well worth popping down the 100 stairs or so to the right to the beautiful little Resolute Beach. Less than 100 m long, it is secluded and sandy, and one of Sydney's best hidden beaches. There's little to no shade, but it is great for a quiet dip.

After cooling off, it's back up the 100 stairs, then continue right, through lovely cool rainforest gullies and along the coast. After a few hundred metres there's a track down to West Head Beach, but this beach is more rocky than Resolute, so not as enticing for a swim.

Start the steep but mercifully short climb up the hill. Just 50 m before the West Head picnic area – which can have coach-loads of people – it's worth stopping at the large rock platform on the right-hand side for a look back across Pittwater. Then continue up to West Head, and enjoy sensational 270-degree views over Lion Island to the Central Coast, out to Barranjoey Lighthouse and along the whole Palm Beach isthmus.

When you are ready to move on, find the little track that heads left (when facing uphill) marked 'Red Hands Cave'. It's only 850 m back to the car at this stage, and pretty flat. Listen out for the sound of cracking nuts high in the sheoak trees and you may be lucky to spy glossy black-cockatoos, with their fire-engine-red tails.

Just 250 m from the end of the walk, you'll find Red Hands Cave, with some of the only accessible Aboriginal ochre art in Sydney. Some has faded, but one hand in particular is still very clear. It's a peaceful and contemplative spot to spend a few minutes before heading back to the car.

Views of Barrenjoey Lighthouse and the Palm Beach isthmus

MOUNT KURING-GAI TO COWAN

SYDNEY REGION

WALK: 17 km one-way

TIME REQUIRED: 2 days is best, but can be completed over a full day

BEST TIME: Spring

GRADE: Moderate to hard – this walk has several steep ascents and descents

ENVIRONMENT: Rainforest, Sydney sandstone, woodland, beautiful river, mangroves, heathland and saltmarsh

BEST MAP: The Great North Walk, maps 2 and 3, Land & Water Conservation

TOILETS: At Mount Kuring-gai Station or Mount Kuring-gai shops near the start of walk, at Berowra Waters (halfway through walk) and at Cowan shops, 200 m north of the end of the walk

TRANSPORT: Starts and finishes at railway stations; however trains from Cowan are infrequent, changing trains at Berowra to get back to Mount Kuring-gai may be required: www.cityrail.info/timetables

FOOD: Halfway through the walk, across the river on the punt, is the Berowra Waters Fish Cafe, with excellent burgers, fish and chips, salads, coffee and cold drinks: (02) 9456 4665; www.berowrawaters.net/fish_cafe.asp

TIPS: Although an enjoyable day-walk, this is better tackled as an overnight walk, with great, isolated campsites by Cowan Creek that will make you feel a long way from anywhere, even though you are still in greater Sydney

[above] *Thickly forested ridges above Berowra Creek*

Starting with a gorgeous little rainforest gully, then powering beside and above the gloriously secluded Berowra Creek, and finishing with some rugged ascents and descents in valleys of wildflowers, this is a gem of an overnight walk within the northern outskirts of Sydney. There are no facilities at the isolated camping sites, but that's part of their attraction. There is also an opportunity to take a ride on a river punt and enjoy a cafe meal halfway through the walk.

It is often surprising what treasures lie under our noses, and the start of this walk, Lyrebird Gully, falls into that category. The bubbling creek, with alternating emerald pools, cascades and boulders covered in bright green moss, is the thread that runs through the gully, linking caves and overhangs, beautiful forest and rich birdlife.

After Lyrebird Gully, this route joins the Great North Walk, the well-marked 250 km trek from Sydney to Newcastle.

This route can be walked either direction. If you are camping out, you just need to work out where you want the campsite to fall. Unfortunately there are no campsites right in the middle of the walk. The text that follows describes the walk from south to north. This results in a very easy first day and then a quite tough second day.

DAY ONE: 6 KM
If you are coming by train, cross the Pacific Highway as you exit Mount Kuring-gai Station and head south about 200 m. The start of the walk is clearly marked near the intersection of Glenview Rd and the highway. It begins with a very steep descent down a sealed track then dives into Lyrebird Gully along a narrow footpath. Fifteen minutes after starting, you'll feel like you are kilometres from anywhere.

The palette of colours are a feast for the eyes, with orange banksia flowers, pink and crimson angophora trunks, yellow and gold wattles, lime-green bracken and mosses, and pink boronia and spider flowers.

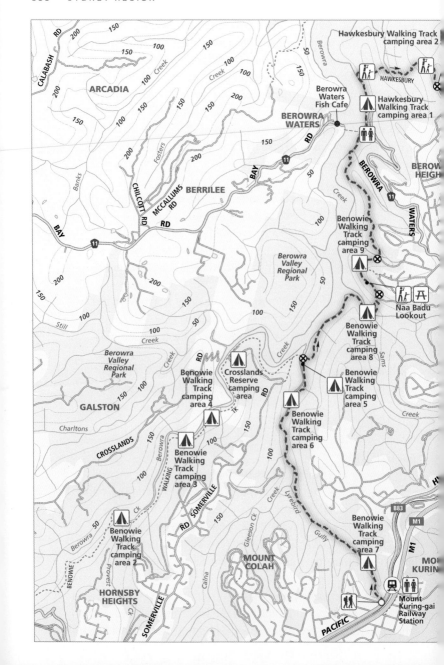

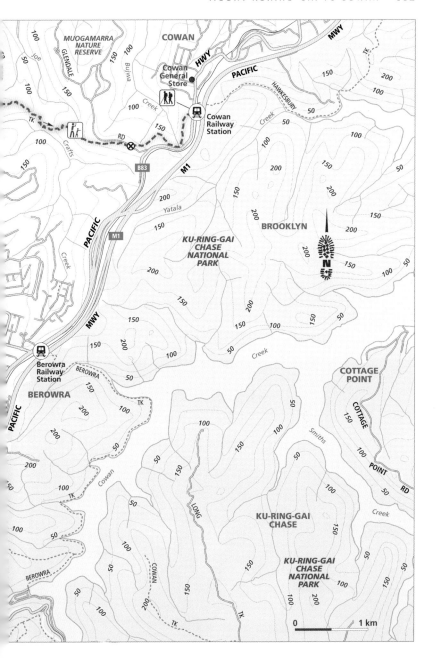

Golden wattle

With the constant accompaniment of the gurgling Lyrebird Gully Creek as it cascades over small drops and around rocks, you'll hear a symphony of sounds, including frogs and an avian choir of wrens, cockatoos, rainbow lorikeets and whipbirds. As the name suggests, there are also lyrebirds in the gully, and perhaps the prettiest of NSW's small birds, the spotted pardalote.

The track meanders through the riparian rainforest (a rainforest beside a river) with coachwoods, sassafras and pittosporums, past some lovely sandstone overhangs, and crosses the creek several times on steps and flattened areas that have been hewn out of the stone. Use these, because the rocks can be treacherous in other spots.

It's a long, gradual descent down the gully before the forest opens up. Here you'll find a couple of basic campsites beside the creek. Some 4.5 km after starting, you'll spot a bouncing bridge across the creek to your left, and a sign pointing to Crosslands – a

Brightly coloured sandstone beside Berowra Creek

popular picnic and boating area. The deep area around the bridge is a great place to have a dip on a hot day.

Our route does not cross the bridge, but now follows the signs to Berowra Waters through an interesting saltmarsh area and then along Berowra Creek (which is tidal at this point). After a couple of kilometres it rises slightly up a knoll, and there is a little campsite in the lee of a large boulder. A slightly better campsite is just 100 m down the hill; however, campers at this site must pitch tents well back from the water's edge, and up a slight rise if possible, as the tide often sneaks up and covers the flat ground. There are no facilities at the campsite, and drinking water from the creeks is not recommended.

Spotted pardalote

DAY TWO: 11 KM

A real workout for the lungs and legs, this day has three big ascents and two big descents, going from almost sea level up to 200 m in elevation each time.

The first climb starts within a few hundred metres of leaving camp, after following the side creek upstream, then (in the only confusing spot on this walk) crossing it and heading to the left across boulders to some stairs.

At the top of the steep ascent, turn left onto the Link Track, a fire trail. If you turn right here, it's a 2.5 km walk to Berowra Station, which could make this a much shorter day walk.

Just along the Link Track is the much-needed break of Naa Badu Lookout, with a picnic table, bench seat and sensational views over the wild upper reaches of Berowra Creek. Keep following the Link Track for a few hundred metres after this, and then the Great North Walk (your route) dives off to the left on a narrow track.

Along this next section, the track becomes quite eroded and difficult in places (particularly if you are carrying a large pack) as you meander along the top of the ridge, and then steeply down to Berowra Waters. But there are wildflowers aplenty and occasional views down onto the creek that make up for it.

Flowering heathland on the ridgetop

As you come into the settlement of Berowra Waters, you'll notice a profusion of houseboats and other vessels, and some riverside cottages. When you reach the bitumen, there are public toilets just across the road (the only place to refill water bottles, but the small basins make it quite hard to do so).

The best thing to do here is to catch the punt across the river (no charge), and recharge yourself at the excellent Berowra Waters Fish Cafe, in anticipation of the two big climbs to come.

When you are ready to move on, initially travel along the road heading north along the flat on the eastern bank of the river (the same side that you have been walking on). A few hundred metres past the end of the road the track heads very steeply up the hill, with rough rock stairs and some steep constructed stairways. Strong metal loops inserted in the rocks provide extra footholds at some points.

At the very top of this hill, on the right-hand side, is a glorious rock eyrie with great views back to Berowra Creek. It is the last view you will get of the water, so it's worth savouring.

From here the track heads across some valleys, descends for a little bit, crosses a lovely little creek, then ascends sharply again. At the top of the next rise is a short

Rainbow lorikeet

flat section that should be quite quick to move through, before descending, one last time, all the way down to a large waterhole on Joe Crafts Creek. It is steep again up the other side, and there are a couple of tight rock chutes to squeeze through, before getting to the last section – a flat 2 km to Cowan Station. You'll cross Glendale Rd (unsealed) and will gradually be welcomed back to civilisation with noise of the train line and the highway nearby, before passing behind some houses and being disgorged from the bush opposite Cowan Station. Toilets and water are at the general store up the road (north) about 200 m.

THE FISHPONDS

SYDNEY REGION

WALK: 7 km loop

TIME REQUIRED: At least 3 hours with little legs

BEST TIME: Spring

GRADE: Moderate

ENVIRONMENT: Blue gum forest, Sydney sandstone, creeks, parkland and a small amount of street walking

BEST MAP: The Great North Walk map 2, Benowie Walking Track, Land & Water Conservation

TRANSPORT: The Shorelink 587 bus takes 15 minutes to reach the start and end point of the walk from Normanhurst Station: www.shorelink.com.au

TOILETS: The nearest toilets are at Ruddock Park, Westleigh, on Quarter Sessions Rd – there are no toilets on the route

FOOD: Pennant Hills Rd, 5 km from the start

TIPS: Allow a bit of extra time to explore the fascinating rock features, cascades and waterholes along the creek. The area around here is so nice it's worth exploring some of the other tracks.

[above] *Pools and channels sculpted by water*

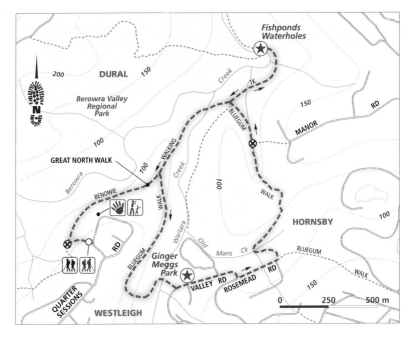

A surprisingly beautiful area of bushland not far from civilisation, this walk is great for families with primary school-aged kids who like exploring little caves and creeks.

The Great North Walk is one of Australia's most renowned long walks. It stretches 250 km from Sydney to Newcastle and the Hunter Valley, and it's a worthy goal if you can find a couple of weeks to spare. But as most of us can't, it's cleverly designed with lots of places to hop on and off. This loop combines parts of the Great North Walk, Benowie Walking Track, the Bluegum Walk and the more recently established Ginger Meggs Walk to make a cracking half-day route suitable for families. In the mornings, you are almost guaranteed to see interesting wildlife: swamp wallabies, echidnas, large diamond pythons, crimson rosellas, blue-tongue lizards or goannas.

There are plenty of places to access the Great North Walk in this part of Sydney, but for this loop the best spot is next to 294 Quarter

Sessions Rd, Thornleigh. Before starting the walk, deviate down to 280 Quarter Sessions Rd, where some Aboriginal rock art sits right beside a house. Many carvings have been lost in European times, but there are some more nearby in the bush for those with the eyes to spot them. Also, just past the carvings is a very nice natural lookout over the valley that you'll be walking in.

Return to number 294 and walk down the fire trail for about 100 m past some scribbly gums. Then you'll see the narrow track signposted off to the right. Follow this over some lovely rock slabs, and you'll meet the Great North Walk in another 60 m or so. Turn right.

The narrow track initially winds through some lovely rock features, including a sandstone wave, cavelets, boulders and some larger cliffs with large rock skinks peeking out of the crevices. It then curves behind some houses above the cliffs, and around a lovely creek with large tree-ferns.

You will soon come to an obvious fork. The way to the left is the way you'll come back. Although it doesn't really matter, it's recommended to go right first as the route is slightly clearer. This is the start of the Bluegum Walk, and over the next couple of kilometres, it passes through some gorgeous forest, with 40 m high Sydney blue gums and other tall trees, standing like masts amid a sea of lime-green bracken. You'll no doubt hear raucous sulphur-crested cockatoos and kookaburras through this section.

Sandstone and banksia

Some of the Bluegum Walk signs may be missing, so once the small track reaches a fire trail, it may seem confusing, but it isn't really. Head left downhill, and then left again, continue downhill, then veer to the right and cross Waitara Creek over a concrete causeway. You'll be temporarily heading out of the bushland into suburbia.

Straight away on your left you'll see a playground and picnic area (with a bubbler), called Ginger Meggs Park. Jimmy Bancks, the creator of the classic Aussie cartoon, spent time as a kid here. Unfortunately there is no toilet, but young walkers might appreciate the playground.

From the park, turn left onto Valley Rd, through a lovely forested suburban area, then turn left again into Rosemead Rd. At the end of this road, there is another open picnic area with a fire trail that veers off to the left. Follow this trail and cross Old Mans Creek on stepping stones.

Again, you'll be surprised at the beauty and serenity of the forest here, even though you are little more than a stone's throw from houses.

At the next junction, a fire trail veers left, but your track goes straight ahead, jumping down roughly. Off to the right you'll see an alternative route around a rifle range (on some days you'll hear the gunfire), but keep on the steep track down towards the Fishponds. At the track junction near Berowra Creek, head right, and then down to the stepping stones at the Fishponds.

The Fishponds are a series of gloriously inviting waterholes. Signs warn against swimming and, in particular, diving, so if you do take a dip, do so with great care and, because of the risk of pollution, it is probably advisable to keep your head out of the water.

On the other side of the creek, a thin track follows the water for 100 m or so, and it's well worth a detour, before getting back on the Great North Walk.

The main track will pop past xanthorrheas, flannel flowers, wattles, banksias and other wildflowers, and creep past caves and cliffs, before descending again to Berowra Creek and a narrow wooden bridge. Here the water flows over cascades and through tunnels, forming whirlpools and lovely rock holes with thick green

Diamond python

mosses on the sides. It is a truly beautiful place for the next couple of hundred metres or so.

It is at about this point that most groups should think about heading back (the Great North Walk goes up steeply from here), but it is such an absolutely gorgeous section of bushland, that you will probably be tempted to keep going. Those with stamina (or a car at the other end) can go the extra 6 km through to Galston Gorge.

However, to make a reluctant start back, return over the little wooden bridge and the stepping stones at the Fishponds, and then right along the creek (not up the steep track you came down). This is also a beautiful section of bush with another glorious set of rock features where the water bubbles through, carving smooth holes into the sandstone. Those with extra energy or time for adventure can keep exploring up Berowra Creek here, but the route back crosses Waitara Creek and zigzags up the other side through some tricky little rock sections. In spring, take your time moving up the hill and enjoy the wildflowers. The creek is about 55 m above sea level, and your car is at 170 m, so you have more than 100 m to climb.

As you walk along a ridge, you'll soon pass the Bluegum Walk that you took earlier off to the left. Continue right, back along the track, past the tree-ferns and past the houses. Just be careful near the interesting rock features (remember that sandstone wave) as you don't want to miss the route upwards to the left to your car.

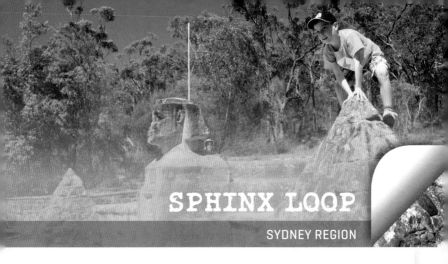

SPHINX LOOP

WALK: *10.5 km loop*

TIME REQUIRED: *3 hours*

BEST TIME: *Spring*

GRADE: *Moderate*

ENVIRONMENT: *Dry and wet sclerophyll forest, Sydney sandstone, creeks, banksia woodland*

BEST MAP: *Ku-ring-gai Chase National Park, NSW Land and Property Information*

TRANSPORT: *The Shorelink 577 bus takes about 15 minutes to reach the park entrance from Turramurra Station: www.shorelink.com.au*

TOILETS: *Flushing toilets at the cafe, halfway through walk, or at Bobbin Head, also near the halfway point*

FOOD: *North Turramurra shops, 2 km from the start of the walk, has cafes and a supermarket*

TIPS: *Avoid doing this loop walk in the middle of a summer's day, as the fire trail return can be stifling*

[above] *Sphinx memorial*

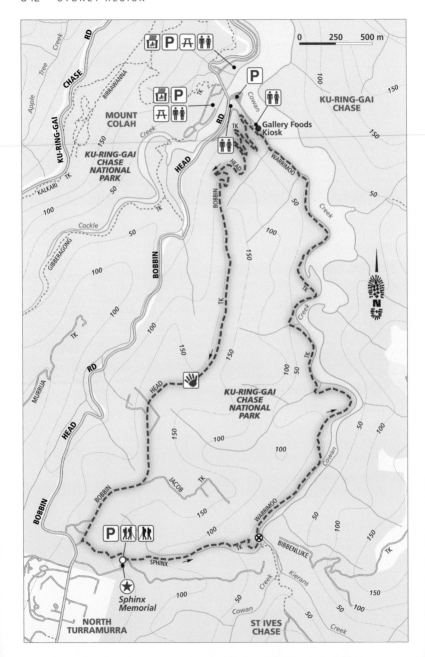

With a mix of easy access, interesting history, some lovely bushland and a quiet river, this is a pleasant and very manageable loop for families. In the middle there is the bonus of a cafe and one of Sydney's best picnic areas.

Ku-ring-gai Chase National Park is one of the living, breathing, forested lungs on the outskirts of Sydney that provides fresh air and serenity to the inhabitants of such a large city.

The park has several sections and various entry points. The start of this walk is right near the entrance gate on Bobbin Head Rd, North Turramurra. If you do not have a national parks sticker and don't want to pay the day-use fees, you can park outside the gates and walk in.

If driving in, take the first little road to your right immediately after the gate, and in a couple of hundred metres you'll be at the carpark.

Immediately you will see the Sphinx Memorial, after which the first part of this route was named. One-eighth the size of the Sphinx in Egypt, it was hewn over 1.5 years in the late 1920s by William Shirley as an unusual memorial to his fallen comrades in the Australian Imperial Force in WWI. Shirley himself had suffered from gas inhalation and tuberculosis on the Western Front, and died not long after completing the memorial.

There is drinking water available at the start of the walk here, but no toilet facilities.

The walk starts just downhill of the memorial, and quickly involves a dog-leg right and left across a fire trail (along which you'll return), but the track downhill is clearly marked.

Quite rough at the beginning, the track descends about 100 vertical metres, through dry sclerophyll forest with banksias, wattle, xanthorrhoeas and Sydney redgum. In spring you'll see a host of smaller flowers, including pink boronia and spider flowers. To the left of the track a creek tinkles down the hill, and at one point you'll have to step across it. There are some lovely little cavelets and moss-covered rocks. Early in the mornings in this top section you may see swamp wallabies and the area sings with a lot of birdlife.

After walking downhill for just over 2 km you'll come to the bracken intersection with the Warrimoo Track, beside the large, wide and peaceful Cowan Creek. The creek is tidal at this point, and at high tide can offer some special swimming spots. At low tide its colourful blend of deep green pools and yellow sands provides a striking natural palette beside the track.

Head left along the Warrimoo Track, and you'll pass through a combination of wet, riparian rainforest vegetation, and areas of mangroves. Wading birds such as the elegant white-faced herons, with their very sharply pointed beaks, are often seen along here. There are a few little creeks to cross and after heavy rain some of these crossings may be tricky.

After about an hour of walking, you'll find a fairly large and colourful sandstone overhang right next to a broad sweeping bend on the river. It's a good spot for a quick rest. Note the oysters on the rocks, the birds flitting across the river and the beautifully shaped dome of a mountain on the other side of the creek.

From this point on, keep a watchful eye out for the many middens the track crosses. These are ancient piles of discarded

Cowan Creek

shellfish created by Aboriginal people over many thousands of years. Some of these middens are many metres deep.

You also have a great chance of seeing goannas, or lace monitors in this section. Large lizards, they can look scary to the uninitiated, and can deliver a nasty bite, but they are not at all aggressive if you leave them alone and just watch them scamper up trees, or waddle along the track.

You'll soon spot many boats moored at Bobbin Head. If you're lucky, you may see one of the historic wooden Halvorsen boats, built 1925–80 (many at Bobbin Head) by the world-famous Halvorsen family.

The return track heads sharply uphill to the left, but before taking that, continue along the flat, behind the marina and the boat repair area, to the Gallery Foods kiosk on the marina. There are also clean toilet facilities here (with a sign asking that you not remove leeches in the toilet block). You can take a seat at the kiosk and watch the large schools of bream waiting for scraps in the water.

The second half of this loop is not as interesting as the first and young legs might not want to walk up the steep hill from the marina. They may be more interested in continuing along the water, past the marina, to the Bobbin Head picnic area which has a large playground. This popular picnic spot has an information centre, barbecues and plenty of shade. Someone will need to walk 4.5 km and get the car, but once they have it they can easily drive the few kilometres down Bobbin Head road to meet the rest of the group.

Those up for the walk should head back along the river about 100 m from the kiosk to the track that heads uphill. The first section is steep, with big steps, but there are a couple of great spots to stop and enjoy the view. The track soon joins a wide fire trail, and you will keep heading uphill, to the left, as it zigzags through scribbly gum forest.

The bulk of the fire trail is through thick forest, with little to view, but the rich banksias attract a lot of birdlife, such as wattlebirds, honeyeaters and firetails, so it may be worth keeping a pair of binoculars at the ready.

Waratah (Telopea speciosissima) – the NSW floral emblem

Almost exactly halfway back along the fire trail, you'll see an unsignposted area immediately to the right of the track, with a couple of large logs around a cleared rock face. Ku-ring-gai Chase National Park is rich with Aboriginal artwork (there are hundreds of known sites) and this spot provides some examples. The rock engravings are rapidly wearing out, and it may take some time and patience to see them clearly (it's easiest in winter or when the sun is low in the sky, or after rain), but spend some time and you'll pick out an echidna, a human-like spirit figure or two, and a series of mundoes, which are four-toed footprints (left by the creational ancestral heroes). It's actually a lovely spot to just sit quietly in the bush for a while and enjoy the silence.

The last section back to the carpark is a bit of a slog, and on the weekend you may be accompanied by mountain bikers whizzing along the track. Not long before you reach the park gate, you will see the fire trail veer sharply to the left. Follow this downhill for a couple of hundred metres, and you'll soon be back at the start of your walk, with the Sphinx Memorial and carpark on your right.

SPIT TO MANLY (ABRIDGED)

WALK: 8 km return, approximately – longer or shorter depending on where you turn around

TIME REQUIRED: 3 hours

BEST TIME: A blue-sky day

GRADE: Easy

ENVIRONMENT: Outstanding views of Sydney Harbour, banksia heathland, angophora woodland and Sydney sandstone

BEST MAP: Walking Tracks of the Middle Harbour Valley and Northern Sydney Harbour Foreshore Sheets 3 & 4, STEP Inc

TRANSPORT: Several bus routes can deliver you to the south end of Beatrice Street, Clontarf; a short walk from the beach: www.131500.com.au

TOILETS: At Clontarf Reserve at the start of the walk

FOOD: Seaforth shops, 2 km from Clontarf; Clontarf beach has a kiosk

TIPS: In summer, bring your swimmers and a snorkel and mask

[above] *View out to the heads*

This delightful route goes through one of the largest intact areas of bush on Sydney Harbour, offering some truly stupendous views over North and South heads, Aboriginal engravings and some delightfully quiet stretches of sand.

There are a few lovely spots on Sydney Harbour where the bushland has survived relatively unscathed – places such as Balls Head, Kelly's Bush and Berry Island. In some places Aboriginal engravings can be seen. The area between Clontarf and Forty Baskets beaches has one of the largest remaining sections of bushland. It is part of the very popular Spit to Manly walk, which is a wonderful 10 km classic and heavily used on weekends.

This slightly shorter version picks the eyes out of that walk, starting and finishing at peaceful Clontarf Beach (with adequate parking, toilets, a picnic area, playground and pleasant swimming), and includes a diversion to a 100-year-old lighthouse.

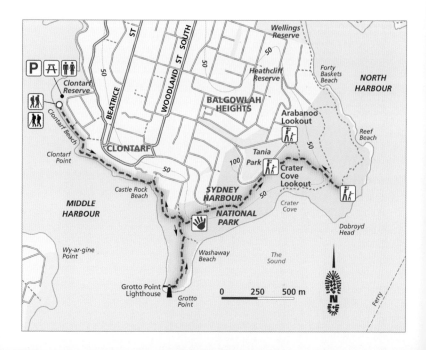

Facing the water at Clontarf Reserve, head left along the beach. At high tide, you may have to wade past a few waterside houses, or backtrack and walk along the parallel road. There is room to walk past when the tide goes out.

At the end of the sand, the track goes uphill at Clontarf Pt, past a series of lichen-stained sandstone boulders, overhangs, creeks and ferns. The vegetation is a little weedy through here, but don't be disheartened, there are some lovely sections to come. A few tracks

Angophoras or smooth-barked apples

head off to the right to scraps of sand, and if the water is clear, there can be some excellent snorkelling around some of the little headlands and coves. A few other small tracks head off up steps to the left, but most of these just end at houses, so stay on the obvious route.

The only confusing part of the route is near Castle Rock Beach, when you come to a T-intersection, with unclear signage. Going left will take you uphill to a road. Instead, dogleg right towards the beach, then left after 20 m to continue on the route. You can also pop down to the water to enjoy the little beach.

The next section is lovely. Called the Castle Rock Track, it features large sandstone caves, and some gorgeous smooth-barked apple trees, or angophoras. These common Sydney trees, sometimes also called Sydney redgums, have vibrant pink or orange trunks and often have contrasting lime-green bracken growing around their bases, which seems to bring out their colours even more.

At the next track intersection (after a little jig uphill), deviate from the Spit to Manly Walk by turning right and following the rugged 500 m track, through banksia tunnels and angophora woodland, down to the stumpy white lighthouse at Grotto Pt. It was built in 1910–11. Some quite friendly eastern water dragons inhabit the rocks and bushland around the lighthouse, and it's quite easy to get a close look at them.

Eastern water dragon

After a break, head two-thirds of the way back up the Grotto Pt side track, and take the unmarked track off to the right. It heads east, down steeply for 100 m or so to an unfenced cliffline, above waves crashing onto Washaway Beach. It's a lovely little-visited spot to sit and observe the sailboat races and the splendour of the harbour opening.

From here head back up and right onto the main track and after another couple of hundred metres you'll see the Grotto Pt Aboriginal engravings on the right-hand side. There are kangaroos, fish, boomerangs and spirit figures to pick out – although in the middle of a summer's day they may be hard to spot (most fainter Aboriginal engravings are easier to see when the sun is low in the sky or after rain).

Continue uphill, through some lovely bushland with boardwalks installed to protect the coastal wetlands. You can keep your eye out for flannel flowers, fairy-wrens and firetails, but it might be hard to focus on these when the views of the harbour get better and better. At one point a rock platform gives an ideal eyrie to view the water, and a little further on you'll find the fenced Crater Cove Lookout. Near the very top of the hill a track heads off to the left to Arabanoo Lookout, but the views there really aren't any better than Crater Cove. Continue along the main track a little further. It starts to go downhill and soon you'll reach another lovely rock platform with widespread views over Dobroyd Head, Manly and North Head. The track keeps going downhill, to more delights such as Reef Beach and eventually Forty Baskets Beach, but this is as good a place as any to turn around if you want to get back to Clontarf. Just head back the same way you came, without the detour to Grotto Pt Lighthouse, and enjoy a final swim at Clontarf. The rest of the Spit to Manly walk can wait for another day.

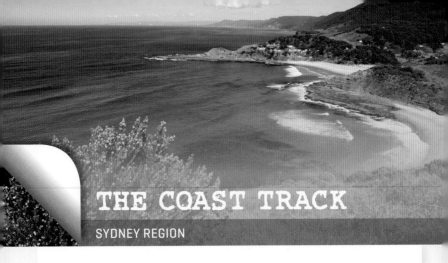

THE COAST TRACK

SYDNEY REGION

WALK: 27 km one-way

TIME REQUIRED: 2 days (best) or 1 full day

BEST TIME: All year

GRADE: Moderate

ENVIRONMENT: High sea cliffs, remote wild beaches, coastal heath, rainforest

BEST MAP: Royal National Park, Australian Geographic

TOILETS: At Otford Station at the start of walk, North Era, Garie, Wattamolla and Bundeena Wharf at the end of the walk

FOOD: Heathcote, a half-hour drive from both ends of the walk, has a string of shops including cafes and takeaways; there is a cafe and takeaway located about 500 m south of the start of the walk on Lady Wakehurst Dr – weekends and public holidays only

TRANSPORT: This walk is serviced by public transport at both ends: Cronulla Ferries (02) 9523 2990, www.cronullaferries.com.au/ferries-to-bundeena; Cityrail 131 500, www.131500.com.au

TIPS: If you are keen to walk this popular route in one day and are using public transport, study the timetables carefully as ferries from Bundeena to Cronulla cease running in the early evening, and trains from Otford can be infrequent.

You are required to book and pay a fee in advance before camping at North Era. Contact the national parks office: (02) 9542 0683, 10.30am to 1.30pm Monday to Friday only.

[above] *Otford Lookout*

Justifiably one of the most popular bushwalks in the country, in one of the oldest national parks in the world, this classic walk cruises along a stunning stretch of coast, with plunging sea cliffs, remote beaches, rainforest and wildflower-rich coastal heath. It makes for a very pleasant overnight trek, or a cracker of a long day walk.

DAY ONE: 9 KM

As it is popular with scouts and other large groups, this walk is best done during school term, and on weekdays if possible. It's a classic walk and worth having to yourself as much as possible.

Starting at Otford Railway station, walk up the stairs, then left along the fire trail and right down Fanshawe Rd, towards the coast. After about 300 m you'll hit Lady Wakehurst Drive. Cross the road carefully to Otford Lookout, turn left and walk for 100 m to the signposted start of the walk. If travelling by car, there is parking at the track head.

The track starts with a little climb up to the ridgetop, through a pleasant forest, to a turn-off to Werrong Beach. This is a 'swimsuit

Anglers by surging seas

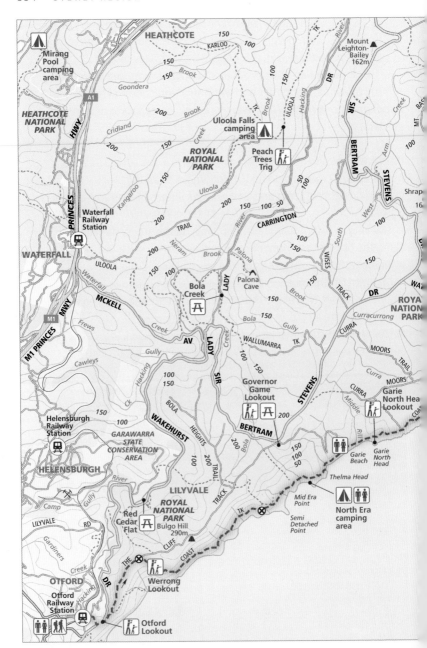

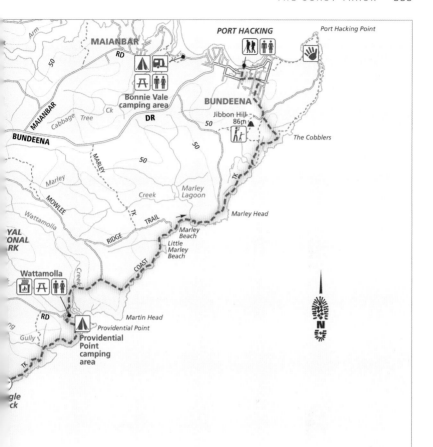

TASMAN   SEA

0   2   4 km

optional' (read 'nudist') beach, but quite a steep detour this early on unless you are super keen to get your gear off.

The Cliff Track continues through some lovely thick forest, with giant Gymea lilies flowering on the edge of the escarpment, the ocean smashing into rocks beneath them. About 2 km after leaving Otford Lookout you'll take a turn off to the right, and then you are on the Coast Track proper, as it teeters along the escarpment, with an unfenced lookout or two on the edge of the cliff.

The track then plunges into a lovely section of dark green rainforest, with figs, native cherries, bangalays, cabbage tree palms, epiphytes and tree ferns. At times the fallen palm fronds in the so-called Palm Jungle can make it hard to distinguish the main track, but most of the braided alternative routes end up in the same place.

Coming across grasslands into Burning Palms and South Era, you'll see some of the 200 small cabins erected in the park. Most of these were built 1930–50, and are kept privately under renewable licences. Nearly all the cabins are maintained only through people carrying in supplies and equipment. There is no public drinking water available.

The track continues up sharply from South Era and over another ridge to North Era, which has one of the largest Aboriginal shell middens in the Sydney region. The camping area is spacious and has a couple of pit toilets.

A stay here is a superb stop in the wilderness near Sydney. You may be visited in the evening by wallabies and kangaroos, or even one of the park's feral Rusa deer, and be serenaded at night by the resident frogs.

Permits are required to camp. See walk introduction for details.

DAY TWO: 18 KM

It isn't far from the camping area across to the shacks of Little Garie and then along the shoreline to Garie Beach (which is accessible by road, and has a Surf Lifesaving Club, and toilets, but no drinking water on tap).

At the end of Garie Beach, the track once again climbs steeply to a colourful heathland of banksias, hakeas, mallee, coastal

Gymea lily above Werrong Beach

A quiet day at Wattamolla

rosemary and native iris. After a few kilometres, it descends to Curracurrong Creek, and on the edge of the cliff a large, flat-topped raptor-looking rock is appropriately dubbed Eagle Rock.

Halfway through this day's walk (about 7 km past Garie Beach), you'll reach the hugely popular picnic area of Wattamolla. It's a beautiful spot and in summer there will probably be swarms of people jumping off rocks, swimming and splashing in the lagoon and under Wattamolla Falls, picnicking and playing loud music. There are barbecues and toilets here.

Cross the carpark and a rock slab above the falls, and the track continues through a little bit of heathland – with firetails and honeyeaters darting through the scrub – past a cute little dam, and then up to an intersection. Turn right towards 'Marley Beaches' and you'll soon be on the edge of some spectacularly precarious cliffs, some of which are completely overhung with only thin bits of sandstone on top. It can make it quite spooky when you get to the edge and look across at the rest of cliff, realising that there is very little stopping any of it from plunging into the heaving sea far below.

A little further on are the delightful Little Marley and Marley beaches. The surf can be dangerous at Marley, and you are a long way from help, so take particular care if you swim here.

As you ascend the ridge on the other side of Marley Beach, side tracks will beckon you to explore the rock slabs on the right-hand (ocean) side of the track, and this is well worth doing. Although not marked, there are some excellent Aboriginal engravings here.

The next section of the route has an unusual feature: high cliffs with sand dunes on top. These are relics from about 10 000 years ago, when the sea level was much higher than it is today.

After crossing another creek, called The Waterrun, the track heads inland. Ignore a short track to the right, and continue on the main track, which will lead to the end of Beachcomber Ave. Follow it to the end, then turn left on Scarborough St, follow it to the end, then right down Brighton St, which will take you to Bundeena Wharf.

Heathland blossom along the top of the cliffs

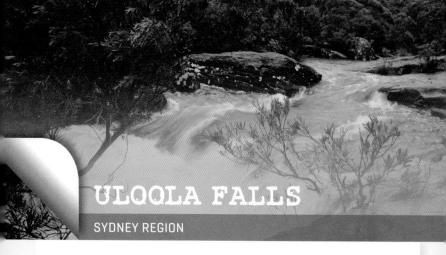

ULOOLA FALLS

SYDNEY REGION

WALK: 15 km loop

TIME REQUIRED: 6 hours

BEST TIME: After or during rain

GRADE: Moderate

ENVIRONMENT: Dense heathland, scribbly gum forest, creeks

BEST MAP: Royal National Park, Australian Geographic

TOILETS: Near start of walk at Heathcote Station, at Uloola Falls campground and at the picnic area, Audley

FOOD: Heathcote has shops and cafes; also the Weir Cafe in Audley, Lady Carrington Drive: (02) 9542 6222; www.weircafe. com.au

TIPS: Bring your swimmers

Native fuschia

[above] *Cascading creeks are a feature of this walk*

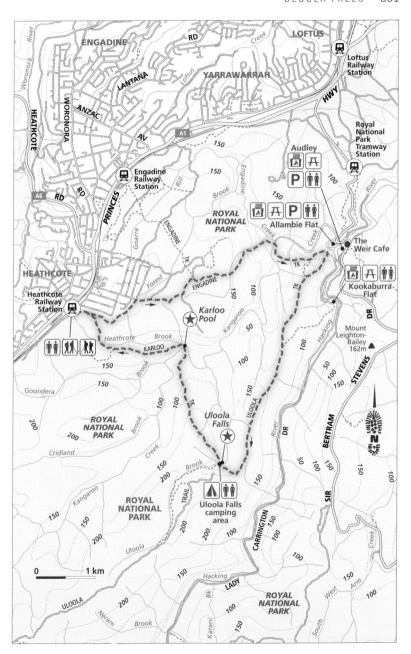

Top of Uloola Falls

On parts of this wild walk you'll feel like you are in the middle of nowhere, and at others you can look over Botany Bay towards the Sydney skyline, or enjoy a cappuccino.

Why sit indoors on a rainy Sydney day, when this cracker of a wild walk is awaiting you on the southern outskirts? If the rain is heavy or constant, you'll be wading across gushing creeks and seeing Uloola Falls at its best. If you catch it on a hotter, drier day, there are pools to cool off and have a swim. And best of all, you can even grab a decent coffee, or a full sit-down meal, half way through the walk at the Weir Cafe at Audley.

Begin at the eastern side of Heathcote Railway Station, and walk to the right of the fire station on the opposite side of the road. Turn left (to the east), and follow the track behind the fire station. Follow this track behind a row of houses. Several tracks will tempt you into the bush, including the track you will return on (marked 'Karloo Pool'), but stay on the fire trail along the cleared grass area for about a kilometre until you reach the cul-de-sac at the end of Bottle Forest Rd. Take the fire trail to your right, marked 'Bottle Forest' and follow this past a few bike tracks, ignoring the first major track to the left (which is the Loop Track, but probably not marked as such). About 1 km after leaving the end of Bottle Forest Rd, you'll come to another intersection, which should be signposted as 'Audley' to the left. Take this fire trail for another 400 m to a clearing with several tracks, and then a right onto the walking track that is also signposted 'Audley'.

You'll now pass through some lovely closed forest, with large angophoras and plenty of huge Gymea lilies. The track tootles beside Tuckawa Rill, which bubbles and burbles down beside you, and there are mountain devils and other flowering delights.

After a couple of kays you'll reach Kangaroo Creek, which may be flowing so ferociously that the way across is hidden, but the stepping stones are directly in front of the track. If it is warm, this is a good place to cool down for a while.

The track goes up some steel stairs and then along a ridge, past some of the most impressive scribbly gums you'll find anywhere before it joins a loop track called Robertsons Roundabout. If you want to avoid Audley and cut about 1 km off your route, turn right at the first intersection, but if you have time it is worth going down to the large picnic area, where there are coots, moorhens, ducks, kayakers, picnickers and a great cafe (a short stroll across the bridge).

After reviving, start back up the track you came down and then take the first track to the left (the other half of Robertsons Roundabout). This is the steepest part of the walk. At the top of

Rock spine with views over the extensive heath

the hill, just before it joins another track and forks, make a short detour to the rocky knoll on the right, which has views over Audley weir, Botany Bay and the city in the distance. A little dip in the rock is perfectly shaped as a comfy natural chair.

At the fork in the track, go left. There is a lovely wide rock platform with expansive views after a few hundred metres. Ignore another track to the left marked 'Wattle forest'.

Keep following the track through thick, tall heathland that in places almost completely covers the track. It may be worth putting on long sleeves and gaiters, as the going is pretty tough. Thankfully there are rock platforms every few hundred metres where you can take a breather from the claustrophobic atmosphere of the heath. Follow the yellow arrows painted on the rocks and you can be sure that you are on track. There are lots of wildflowers through this section, including eggs and bacon, spider flowers and banksias. In spring the waratahs flower which adds to the floral interest.

About 5 km from Audley, you'll come to Uloola Falls. The best view is from a rock ledge on the side of the falls from which you are approaching. There is a basic campground with pit toilet behind the falls at the junction with the Uloola Track, which comes in from the south. Ignore this track, and cross Uloola Brook just above the falls, heading north-west on Karloo Track to Karloo Pool. This track will gradually become wider and offers a few great views across a wild and seemingly remote valley.

Tea-tree flowers

Native cockroach

Karloo Pool, when you reach it, is deep and perfect for a swim before your last 3 km back to Heathcote. If it has been raining hard, you may have to wade across the creek to your left. The rocks may be slippery so take care.

There is a sharp climb up from the creek, so take a breather at a small clearing at the top of the ridge to the left of the track, where there are beautiful overhangs covered in a carpet of thick moss, and draped with pink and white bells of native fuchsia.

Then it's back up Karloo Track, once again through lush eucalypt forest, until you come to the fire trail at the back of the houses. Turn left and soon you'll be back at the station.

National Pass

CANBERRA

SYDNEY

BLUE MOUNTAINS

The World Heritage–listed Blue Mountains, Sydney's wild backyard playground, is deservedly the traditional home of bushwalking in Australia. Routes ranging from short strolls to multiday epics that go deep into its forested ravines; dance along its precipitous orange sandstone cliffs; and explore the wonder of its waterfalls, wildflowers and wildlife.

MOUNT BANKS

BLUE MOUNTAINS

WALK: 10 km loop and return

TIME REQUIRED: 3 hours

BEST TIME: Crisp and clear winter or spring morning

GRADE: Mostly easy to moderate, with a few steps and steep sections

ENVIRONMENT: Glorious Blue Mountains views over valleys and cliffs, eucalypt forest and woodland

BEST MAP: 1:25 000 Mt Wilson, NSW Land and Property Information

TOILETS: Pit toilet in the picnic ground at the start of the walk

FOOD: Bells Line of Road has a sprinkling of roadside cafes, bakeries and fresh fruit and veg stores further east

TIPS: Walls Lookout is another great spot along Bells Line of Road, with a much shorter walk to get to the breathtaking, precipitous cliff line

With a gloriously heart-stopping unfenced cliff line looking over the Grose Valley and a pleasant walk through eucalypt forest, this is a great mid-length Blue Mountains walk away from the maddening crowds.

Unlike the Great Western Highway – a mostly four-lane road that goes through the almost continually developed Blue Mountains urban strip – the Bells Line of Road is a driver's delight. With a single lane each way for

[above] *Grose Valley cliffs*

most of the distance, it winds along isolated ridges; and through orchards, thick patches of forest with ferns and blue gums, and steep sandstone cuttings. Accompanied by the tinkle of bellbirds, drivers pass some of the best wild canyon country in Australia and the beautiful Blue Mountains Botanic Garden, Mt Tomah, which is a particular delight in spring and in autumn when many of the leaves change colour. Bushwalks off Bells Line of Road are wilder, often off-track, more remote and less visited than those off the Great Western Highway, and that just adds to their attraction.

Almost exactly 9 km drive west of the turnoff to the Botanic Garden, the Mt Banks picnic area is signposted on the left when coming from Sydney. You'll see the dome shape of 1072 m Mt Banks on your left. (There is no warning that the picnic area turnoff is approaching until you see the sign.)

The 2 km track to the picnic area and carpark is rough, but can still be driven carefully in a sedan. The picnic area has no view, a few tired picnic tables, a barbecue area and a pit toilet. There is no water.

From here though, things get better and better. Start by taking the obvious (gated) fire trail that heads away from the picnic area. On some weekends you'll find this is a popular track for mountain bikers. The undulating track winds through some interesting heathland with wattles and drumsticks, and – quite aptly – banksias. There are more than 70 species of banksia in Australia, all named after Joseph Banks, the botanist on Captain James Cook's vessel, HMS *Endeavour*. Mt Banks was named in his honour by explorer George Caley, who climbed the mountain in 1804 and freaked out, deciding he couldn't cross the Blue Mountains when he saw the stupendously rugged Grose Valley opening out before him.

As you walk along the fire trail, you'll occasionally get views towards the wild canyon country to your left. On most weekends in summer, experienced canyoners will be out in that area, exploring canyons such as the classic Claustral Canyon, which involves tricky abseils down waterfalls in dark caves. Your route is much easier!

After 2.5 km of easy walking, you'll see a large track coming down from the right. Signage here is a bit confusing, but you will

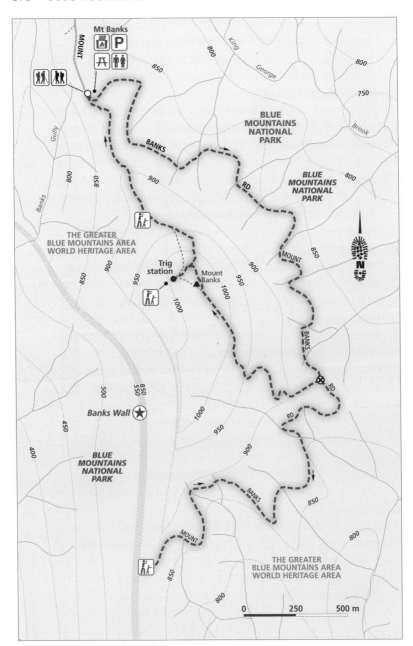

eventually take this track to the summit. First, keep going along the fire trail towards Banks Walls. At a moderately fast pace it is another half-hour walk along the fire trail, mainly through dry woodland and some moister areas of forest as the track skirts below a low cliff and descends to a creek.

Just past an ugly concrete tank on the left-hand side, the fire trail reaches its closest point to the cliff edge, and you'll see a small track heading off to the right. Be warned: the cliffs here are heart-stoppingly high and there are no safety fences. Way across the valley you may be able to see Horseshoe Falls and Bridal Veil Falls, and the town of Blackheath further back. Straight down and slightly to the left, far, far below, is the Blue Gum Forest and the Grose River. On a still day, the roar of the river is carried upwards to this quiet eyrie.

It's worth stopping and spending a while here. Be sure to take the little detour along the track over to the right, where you'll see the long sandstone cliffs called Banks Wall.

The fire trail keeps going for several kilometres past this point, but it's best to turn around here, and go back 2.5 km to the intersection you passed earlier. Head up the other track, which gradually becomes steeper and narrower, and quite overgrown

Multicoloured sandstone cliffs

in parts. In the thickest parts, the birdlife will probably be quite prolific, and you're likely to hear and see whipbirds, wattlebirds, honeyeaters and white-browed scrubwrens. Towards the top of the climb, you'll encounter some lovely forest, with blackwoods and other tall eucalypts with an understorey of bracken and ferns. (The upper part of Mt Banks is basalt, not sandstone, so the vegetation is comparatively lusher.)

You'll come to a marked fork in the track. The downhill track leads to the carpark and picnic area but you should veer left and power up the last little bit to the trig station. Because of the tall trees, there isn't a great view at the very top, but if you follow a thin track past

Mt Banks summit

*Flowering mountain devil (**Lambertia formosa**)*

the other side of the trig station for about 50 m, there are a couple of very small grass areas at the edge of the trees, perfect for a couple of bottoms to take a break and enjoy the extensive views and the solitude. From this spot it's quite easy to see Pulpit Rock on the other side of the valley.

Head back down the short summit track you came up, and then continue straight at the fork down the steep ridge track. There are a few tricky spots on this narrow path, so take care. Gradually the views will open up. As well as the fire trail you originally walked on, you'll see some lovely features, including weird sandstone formations, heathland full of wildflowers, and a lone gum tree growing out of a rock ledge. A small side track leads about 40 m off to the left, to another lovely viewpoint that provides a good spot for a break.

Keep following the ridge track down, and it will soon lead you right back to the picnic area, coming in next to the fire trail.

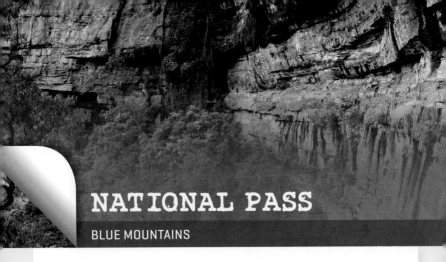

NATIONAL PASS

BLUE MOUNTAINS

WALK: 6 km round trip

TIME REQUIRED: 3 hours

BEST TIME: Any time – the bottom half of the walk stays relatively cool, with water trickling down and there are opportunities for cooling off

GRADE: Moderate

ENVIRONMENT: Rainforest gullies, stupendous cliffs, waterfalls

BEST MAP: The best map is on large signs at the start of the route and at major intersections, but it doesn't seem to be available in print form. Instead, use the National Parks map Walking Tracks – Wentworth Falls and Valley of the Waters available from national parks offices.

TOILETS: At Wentworth Falls Picnic Area at the start of the walk and Conservation Hut two-thirds of the way through it

FOOD: Wentworth Falls shopping area on the Great Western Highway

TIPS: In summer bring a cozzie for a dip under the falls

[above] *Dramatic Blue Mountains cliffs*

This classic bushwalk was established in 1908 and was celebrated for its excellent design. The track hovers beside cliff edges and drifts under waterfalls, the bulk of it halfway up the cliff. Extensive track work was done during the centenary, and it is now better than ever, with historic photos displayed along the way.

Most people start and finish this exciting loop at Conservation Hut, but starting at Wentworth Falls Picnic Area gives you more options at the end of the walk, including shortcuts back to the start, or those with little or tired legs can stop in the cafe at the hut while someone gets the car. It also puts the big uphill section in the middle of the walk, rather than at the end. The picnic area carpark can be very busy in the afternoons, so it's best to start this walk in the morning.

From the carpark at the end of Falls Rd, take an initial look at the Kedumba Valley from Jamison Lookout. You won't need to

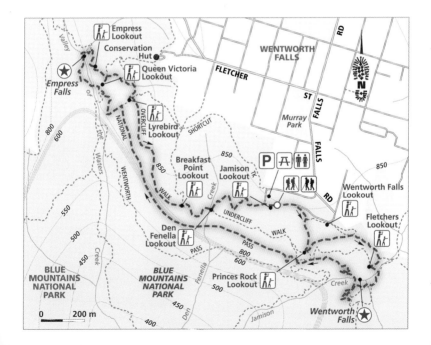

hover here too long, as the views only get better. Head left along the roadside footpath and then take the first track down the stairs to Princes Lookout. This stunning spot provides a great view of Wentworth Falls, which plummets about 200 m over three drops to the valley floor. Take a look also across the falls to the cliff on the other side, and you should be able to see your track going along the cliff and steeply down.

Despite the busy lookout area, you may still be lucky enough to see lyrebirds and scrub wrens in the bushes, and hear the cries of black and white cockatoos. From the lookout, don't take the tempting little unmarked track that appears to head towards the falls – it will leave you stranded about 4 m above the track you want to be on. Instead, look along the opposite side of the track and walk a few more metres up the hill to the marked 'Undercliff Track' which begins by (seemingly) travelling in the wrong direction. Within 100 m it forks, and you can swing around to the left, under the Princes Lookout towards the falls. Ignore the extra nature loop and head to Fletchers Lookout (with a heart-stopping vertical view over the falls) and then on past the cascades to the stepping stones at the top of the falls.

The next section of track is one of the best spots in the Blue Mountains, with the track going across a narrow sandstone ledge

Overcliff Track

Crimson rosella

that juts out precariously over the falls, giving you a great sense of the height as you gaze across the Jamison Valley towards Ruined Castle and Mt Solitary.

Head down the steep stairs, which will probably be wet and slippery – use the handrails – until you get to the bridges across the pools at the bottom of the main falls. In summer, this is a lovely spot to rest a while and play in the cool water, but be careful as some of the rocks are very slippery.

After a break, continue along the National Pass on the other side of the falls. Unless it is particularly dry, water from various other falls will sprinkle down from high above. Specially adapted plants live in the wet zone on the cliffs, including a dwarf pine, no more than 1 m high, that is found only in the vicinity of this walk. Ignore the track down Slacks Stairs (unless you want to take the longer Wentworth Pass walk) and you will pass through forests with colourful birds such as king parrots, rosellas and kookaburras, and the lovely little rock warbler.

After a couple of kilometres, you will head down slightly to the upper reaches of the Valley of the Waters, and then the start of the long uphill climb. Take your time as you make your way up through a cool rainforest gully with cascading water bubbling beside you, and a lovely green blend of mosses, ferns and lichens all around. At the bottom of Empress Falls there is another opportunity for a dip, but keep an eye out for canyoners who may throw their ropes into the pool from the top of the waterfall.

Near the top of the walk up, ignore the track left marked 'Nature Trail to Leura' and head right. Just after Queen Victoria Lookout, the track splits again. The most rewarding experience is to be had by taking the track that heads to the right to the 'Overcliff/Undercliff Track'. Tired legs can opt to take the track that heads straight up to the cafe in the Conservation Hut, and wait to be picked up, or can take the Short Cut Track from the hut back to the carpark.

Taking the Overcliff Track, however, you will pass by several hanging swamps (making the rough track quite damp in places) with rich birdlife. There are several more awesome lookouts before you come to the fork just after Den Fenella Lookout. Take the right fork and then after a few hundred metres there is a marked track to the left that takes you back to the bottom of the carpark. Or if you still haven't had enough of the glorious views, continue on the Undercliff Track for a few more hundred metres and take the next fork back up to Princes Lookout.

The dramatic walk beside Wentworth Falls

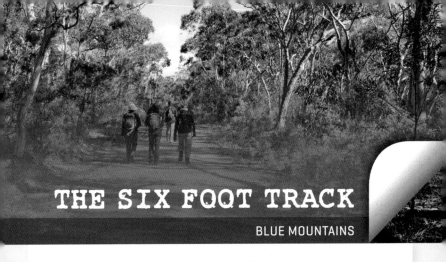

THE SIX FOOT TRACK

BLUE MOUNTAINS

WALK: 44 km one way

TIME REQUIRED: 3 days

BEST TIME: Spring and autumn, as it can get very hot in summer (40°C or more) or very cold in winter (with snow on the Black Range)

GRADE: Hard, but achievable for fit 10 year olds and 70 year olds alike

ENVIRONMENT: Rainforest gullies, farmland, woodland, mountains

BEST MAP: Six Foot Track by the NSW Land and Property Information – it includes detailed track notes, history, flora, fauna and safety tips: (02) 9236 7720.

GUIDED OPTIONS: If you don't feel prepared to walk this route on your own, you can walk with the security of a guide, either carrying all your own gear, or – the most luxurious option – having your heavy pack transported for you by car, with your tent set up and a welcoming hot meal and drinks prepared at the end of each day. All you need to do is carry a camera and some lunch, and enjoy!

Life's an Adventure:
www.lifesanadventure.com.au

TRANSPORT: Blue Mountains Trolley Tours runs a bus every day from Katoomba to Jenolan Caves, which is your best transport option. It leaves Katoomba at 9.45am, and leaves Jenolan Caves at 3pm. www.trolleytours.com.au.

TOILETS: The closest toilets to the start of the walk are probably at Katoomba Train Station.

FOOD: Katoomba has great cafes and large supermarkets.

TIPS: The guided tour in which your gear is carried for you is a great way to experience this classic walk and highly recommended, particularly if you are not experienced in carrying a pack.

Hardened walkers training for the Kokoda Track in Papua New Guinea often do this walk in both directions, as it is about the same distance.

[above] *Easy walking, day 1*

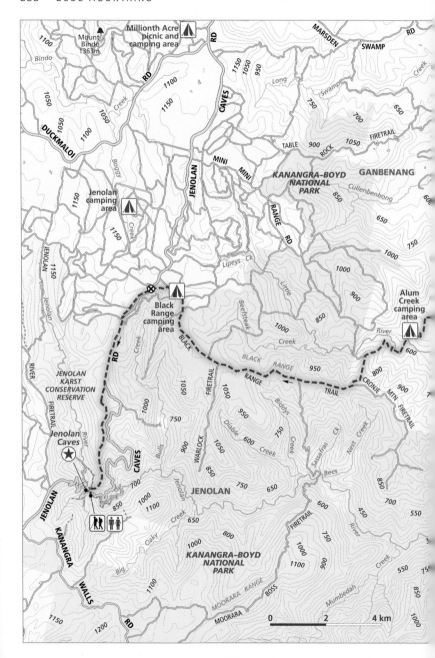

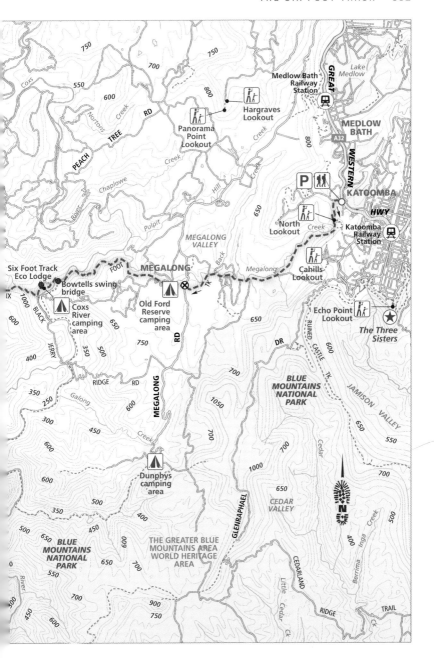

One of the most varied walks you can do in the Blue Mountains, this historic route crosses through almost all the terrain the mountains offer. There are resplendent sandstone cliffs, cold creeks, rainforest gullies, thick woodlands, rolling farmland with Angus cattle and vineyards, and one of the best swing bridges in the country. Most people walk it from Katoomba to Jenolan Caves (as described here), which means a taxing 12 km uphill grind to the top of the Black Range on day 2. The walk finishes at some of the best limestone show caves in the world.

In the late 19th century, promoters of the increasingly popular Jenolan Caves blazed a new horse route from Katoomba to the caves to aid tourism. Previously, some sections, such as the initial steep descent into the valley, were considered almost impassable.

The resulting route, the Six Foot Track, could be ridden in eight hours, but it also became a supply route for farms in the Megalong Valley. A small village opened up along the route at Megalong where miners at the nearby kerosene shale mine could find housing and buy provisions. It included huts, a school, hall and a 13-room hotel. Mining ceased in 1897 and nothing substantial is left at the site today, so don't expect a corner store and an ice-cream!

For many years, the Six Foot Track fell into disuse and disrepair until 1985, 100 years after it was first blazed, when the route was reestablished and signposted. Today, as well as being a legendary three-day hike, it is the site of Australia's biggest off-track marathon, attracting nearly 1000 runners each year who run the track in just a few hours.

The two main campsites are spacious and have pit toilets. There is also the option to spend a night or two at the Six Foot Track Eco Lodge, 15 km into the route. It has bunk beds in communal rooms, drinking water and cooking facilities: www.6fttracklodge.com.

DAY ONE: 15 KM

The walk starts at the Explorers Tree parking area, 3 km west of Katoomba on the Great Western Highway. Leave your car here

or alternatively park in Katoomba and get a taxi to the start of
the walk.

Near the start of the walk you'll find the precipitous North
Lookout offering a view on the horizon of the Black Range, which
you will climb on day two. It's well worth appreciating what you are
going to achieve, before starting on the descent into the valley.

The first couple of kilometres go steeply downhill, with large
uneven stairs. This is Nellies Glen, a beautiful damp rainforest
gully. Take your time through this section to savour the lush ferns,
coachwood, sassafras, ribbon gums and black wattle.

At the bottom, you'll find yourself in a beautiful forest where
large angophora trees radiate pink and orange trunks through
the greenery.

Gradually, the forest thins and you'll begin to see horses, and
occasionally cattle grazing in large paddocks. At times the track
takes you through paddocks, past vineyards and over stiles. It is
well defined, signposted and easy to follow.

Towards the end of day one, you'll come to the Cox's River. If it is
a hot day, it is easy to find some beautiful waterholes and natural
spas to swim and soak in. The water can be icy-cold though, so take
care not to cramp.

Banksia beside a creek crossing

Thick forest, day 2

The best way to cross the river is the 40 m long suspension bridge, 15 m above the river. Only one person can cross at a time, and as it sways substantially, it is usually necessary to hang on. It's a fun way to cap off the day.

Just 800 m further on is the Eco Lodge, and the large camping area is a few hundred metres past that. Water may not be available from the tank at the campsite, and it is advisable to boil and/or treat water from the river.

Greater glider

DAY TWO: 19 KM

Day two starts with a climb over the Mini Mini Saddle. Most of this day's walk is on a dirt road, and although the road isn't busy, it is used by cars, trailbikes and horses. This is also the day you will ascend 1000 m, from the Cox's River campsite at 300 m to the Black Range campsite at 1300 m. After a short downhill then flat section near the Little River, the walk continues ever upwards, with little respite, although it is rarely steep. Surprisingly, there are few opportunities for views, so instead learn to appreciate the forest around you as it changes from Sydney peppermints to Blue Mountains ash, brown barrel, stringybark, banksias, tea trees and hakeas. The observant will notice wildlife such as bellbirds, rosellas, wallabies, kookaburras, eels and occasionally snakes. There might also be echidnas, wombats or even platypus.

Finally you will climb far enough out of the forest to have a great view back towards Katoomba, and this is probably your best option to break for lunch. After that the track heads into the forest along the top of Black Range for 6–7 km before you get near the campsite, where wallaroos thump around and gliders fill the night with their barking calls. You will know the campsite is near when the track begins to go through managed pine forests.

DAY THREE: 10 KM

Day three is an easier day, with some lovely lush forests and a flat section beside Jenolan Caves Rd, although some steep descents near the end could test sore leg muscles!

As you come into Jenolan Caves, pass by Carlotta Arch and then walk down the concrete path to arrive just opposite Caves House and the very welcome bistro and cafe.

If you haven't been here before and there is still some energy left in those legs, make sure you stay and do a cave tour or two … but bear in mind the bus leaves at 3pm. An alternative is to wander through the Grand Arch to the little walk around stunning Blue Pool, where platypus are often seen during the day.

Bowtells Swing Bridge can only be crossed by one person at a time

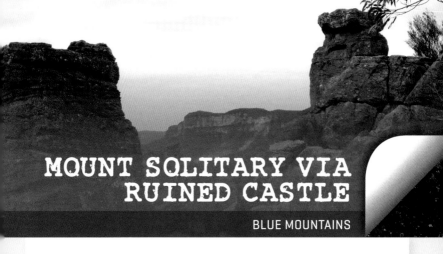

MOUNT SOLITARY VIA RUINED CASTLE

WALK: 16 km return

TIME REQUIRED: 2 days, or 1 long day

BEST TIME: Milder weather in spring or autumn is best; winter can be very cold with snow possible; weeks after decent rainfall are ideal because there is likely to be water in Chinaman's Gully

GRADE: Very hard

ENVIRONMENT: Steep cliffs, grand views, rock eyries, rainforest and woodland

BEST MAP: 1:25 000 Jamison and 1:25 000 Katoomba, NSW Land and Property Information

TOILETS: There are no toilets on the walk; Scenic World, in Katoomba, is the closest

FOOD: Katoomba has supermarkets, great cafes and restaurants

TIPS: Do not be turned off by the description of the slog up Mt Solitary. Instead, just aim to do a day walk to Ruined Castle – an outstanding walk on its own, with sensational views.

By descending and ascending the cliff line via the Scenic Railway at Katoomba, you will add a few extra kilometres, but can avoid the strenuous Golden Stairway.

[above] *Top of the Ruined Castle, looking towards Mt Solitary*

Although not particularly long, this is a very tough walk with several gruelling climbs that will knock the stuffing out of most walkers – especially those carrying a full backpack. But the views and splendour of this part of the Blue Mountains are worth every drop of sweat. You'll see beautiful rainforest, towering cliffs and enjoy camping on one of the Blue Mountains' grandest features. This is highly recommended for experienced walkers.

Before driving to the start of this absolute cracker of a walk, stop at the hustle and bustle of Echo Pt at Katoomba. Once you've admired some of the best views of the iconic Three Sisters, look directly out across the valley, and you'll see the incredible route you're about to take. Directly out in front of you is a large mountain in the middle of the valley. That's Mt Solitary. To the right of it, on the top of a pointy hill, is what looks like a ruined castle. It's actually a jumble of rocks, with some prominent sandstone spires sticking up like turrets. Your walk will start on the top of the cliff line to your right, called Narrow Neck, descend into the valley, then go up and over Ruined Castle, then up Mt Solitary. The main campsites are where the top of the mountain dips down a little into a sheltered gully.

Mt Solitary, near the campsite

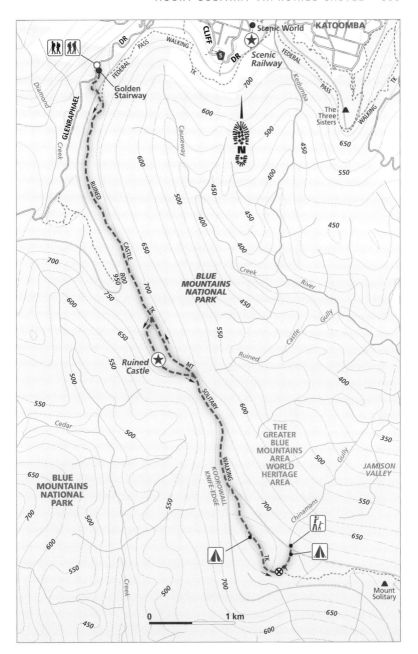

Drive out along Cliff Drive past Scenic World, and then left onto the rough dirt track signposted 'Narrow Neck'. Full of big potholes, ditches and sharp corners, and with plunging cliffs either side, it is a track you'll need to take slowly. After 1.7 km, you'll come to the top of the Golden Stairway (signposted on the left-hand side) where there is room for a few cars to park. On weekends, parking will be difficult, with cars crammed back along the track and past the Golden Stairway trackhead.

The well-marked track heads steeply downhill, sometimes on steel stairs, and other times on eroded tracks and roughly hewn rocks, through some lush rainforest alive with birds. A small lookout offers views back across to the Three Sisters. You'll also see Mt Solitary, which still seems impossibly far away.

At the bottom of this descent (you will have dropped some 200 m), you'll come to the Federal Pass track. To your left the track heads back to Katoomba and the Scenic Railway, but our route turns right, through more beautiful rainforest dominated by blackwood. It can be quite cold and moody through this dark forest, and muddy after rain, though you may enjoy rare shafts of sunlight where a tree has fallen.

Mainly flat, the track then takes you through some wet forest, with tall tree ferns, lime-green bracken galore and towering eucalypts. About 3 km after the start of the walk you will reach the turnoff to Ruined Castle on your right. The main track to Mt Solitary continues straight, but the Ruined Castle walk provides an interesting (if steep) detour that links up again with the main track. If the weather has closed in and you won't get views from the Ruined Castle, then it is probably better to bypass it at this point and try again on the way out. But if you can manage it the first day, when your legs are fresher, it will make for a more relaxed second day.

The climb up to Ruined Castle is short, but quite taxing, and the track is eroded.

The turrets are unmistakable. They can all be climbed for outstanding views over the valley, but the easiest and safest one to climb is the tallest, which is the third one along. Leave your big

Descending Mt Solitary, towards Ruined Castle

packs somewhere at the bottom, take some lunch, and enjoy this divine spot in the clouds. Ascending the second turret is also quite fun, with a tricky scramble through a tunnel of rock. There are no barricades or protection, so take great care on all climbs.

After a well-earned rest, the hardest part of the walk begins. Continue on the narrow track along the Ruined Castle ridge towards Mt Solitary. At the end of this little ridge the route may appear to head left, but keep going straight off the end of the ridge down a tricky, steep, slippery and eroded track.

You will soon re-encounter the main track where you should turn right towards Mt Solitary. Passing through some pleasant angophora forest, you will see a few little campsites on the right-hand side of the track before the start of the big climb.

The climb itself is one of those deceptive mirages, where the summit repeatedly seems to be much closer than it is. You will crest a rise, thinking you are there, but then find another hill to climb. At times the walk up the fabled Koorowall Knife-edge becomes more like a rock-climb, with tricky ascents up boulders and small rock walls. All of this is made much more difficult with a heavy pack, of course, whereas fit day walkers with smaller packs won't find it nearly as taxing.

As you ascend, you will find some great rock ledges on which to rest and enjoy the view back over Ruined Castle to Narrow Neck. Take your time and enjoy it! Pink dots, arrows and occasional engravings mark the way up. Avoid detouring to the right or left too much, as the track generally goes up the middle of the ridge.

On the exposed ridge, you'll find xanthorrheas and some delightful flowers snuggled into the cliff.

Towards the top, when you think you must be there, the track maddeningly drifts right and drops down again, before a last, strenuous, steep and slippery ascent up a gully bristling with casuarina needles. Thankfully there are quite a few robust trees to hang onto to ensure you get to the top.

Finally, breaking onto the casuarina forest on top of the mountain, you'll stumble across a great campsite in the trees. This top spot can be exposed in cold weather, whereas the campsites less than 1 km away are much better protected. Continue along the track until it drops down into a saddle. There are some campsites right by the main track here. Alternatively, take the side track to the left and head down into an area called Chinamans Gully which has some excellent, large rock overhangs on the right-hand side and flat areas for camping. If it is not a total fire ban, campfires are permitted in this area.

If you keep following the track down, you will find more sheltered campsites, and – if you have timed your trip after big rains – there may be water in the ephemeral creek as you get close to the cliff edge. National Parks staff warn you NOT to rely on there being water in this creek, and will also advise if there is likely to be any. If there is water, you are advised to treat or boil it because of the campsites upstream.

The thin track follows the creek downstream and after a few hundred metres reaches the stunning unfenced cliff on the edge of Mt Solitary. You can sit here and soak up the surroundings for hours – you've definitely earned the break!

Enjoying the views from Mt Solitary

The route back to the car is almost the same. Take extreme care on the descent from Mt Solitary – it is advised to do many of the climbing sections facing into the cliff. Hang on firmly and step down carefully. At the junction of the track to Ruined Castle, go straight ahead, ignoring the steep climb back up the extra peak, and continue merrily along the valley floor, saving your strength for the sapping final climb up the Golden Stairs.

This is indeed a tough walk, but one of the best routes in the Blueys if you are up to the challenge.

Arrows mark the track up Mt Solitary

GRAND CANYON

WALK: 5 km loop

TIME REQUIRED: 2.5 hours

BEST TIME: Winter, when the air is bitingly fresh and you don't overheat on the big climb

GRADE: Moderate

ENVIRONMENT: Moist canyon with sandstone overhangs, forest, waterfalls, grand views

BEST MAP: 1:25 000 Katoomba, NSW Land and Property Information

TOILETS: Evans Lookout

FOOD: Blackheath has some lovely cafes and pubs

TIPS: If you have friends who are experienced canyoners and want to try canyoning with them, there is a short canyon section of the Grand Canyon walk that involves one abseil into a dark hole and a few swims, before rejoining the main track. It only adds an hour or so to the trip and is a great first canyon. Some adventure companies occasionally run guided trips through it.

[above] *Grose Valley, from Evans Lookout*

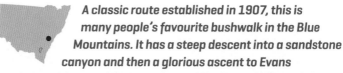

A classic route established in 1907, this is many people's favourite bushwalk in the Blue Mountains. It has a steep descent into a sandstone canyon and then a glorious ascent to Evans Lookout, with one of the best views of the Grose Valley. It is long enough that you know you've had a walk, but not too long for most people.

The full loop involves a relatively boring 1.5 km walk beside Evans Lookout Rd, Blackheath, between Evans Lookout and the Neates Glen carpark. There are some nice flowering mountain devils and other bushes in this section, but most people will find it an unnecessary evil. So, the fittest person in the party can drop everyone off at Neates Glen carpark, then park the car at Evans Lookout, before hot-footing it back along the track, or alternatively, park at Neates Glen carpark and pop up to pick up the car at the end of the walk while everyone else recovers from

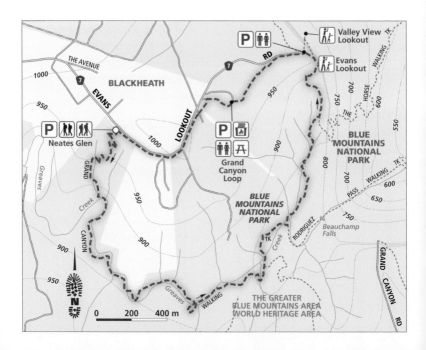

Moss- and lichen-cloaked trees

the climb at Evans Lookout. There is also a carpark halfway along this section.

From the Neates Glen carpark, the walk descends almost straight away, with a series of switchbacks and some stone stairs. The track is very well defined and walked by many, many people. Enjoy the changing vegetation as you descend through stringybark forest and dry sclerophyll to increasingly moist and darkened forest with mossy trunks. A creek burbles and bubbles its way down beside the track, with multiple tree-ferns and lush ferns lining the banks. Birds include rufous fantails, splaying their tail feathers, and eastern yellow robins with their bright chests and grey backs. If you're lucky you'll also spy yellow-tailed black-cockatoos in the drier forests, their calls sometimes sounding like squeaky iron gates.

After crossing the creek, there is a lovely section with large sandstone overhangs, a short natural tunnel, and a waterfall to walk behind (or under). At one overhang, chains have been attached to rock on the left side of the track. This is the anchor point for canyoners to abseil into the black hole beyond, which takes them straight down to water level. They then follow the watercourse 50 m or so below the walking track before rejoining it later, and you may even hear them whooping or clinking along in their abseil gear. As it only has one abseil and is relatively short with little chance of getting lost, it is considered one of the safer canyons in the Blue Mountains, but should still only be attempted in groups with experienced canyoners.

At times along the walking track, you'll get glimpses of the creek far below. Once the track reaches creek level, an especially large overhang offers a lovely spot for a break. The track then continues down the valley, crossing over the creek several times.

The last time it crosses, another track – to Rodrigeuz Pass – comes in at an oblique angle on the right. You may not even notice it if you are focused on the crossing. Those after an extra stroll could duck along this less-used track for 1 km or so to the lovely hidden Beauchamp Falls.

Back on the main track though, you now begin the long and at times taxing ascent to Evans Lookout, which is about 200 m above the creek. There are multiple sections with steep stairs, but the track is well maintained and if you take it easy, enjoying the ferns, the bubbling creek and the changing forest, the top will appear mercifully quickly. It opens out into the wide open lookout, which is bound to be full of people, offering stunning views down the valley to the Grose River far below, over plunging orange cliffs, and to Mt Banks on the other side of the valley. Stop for a while, recover your breath, wait for the rest of your group, and enjoy this truly splendorous sight.

Evans Lookout

PULPIT ROCK

BLUE MOUNTAINS

WALK: *13 km return*

TIME REQUIRED: *4.5 hours*

BEST TIME: *Sept–Oct is the best time to see waratahs*

GRADE: *Moderate*

ENVIRONMENT: *Spectacular cliffs and waterfalls, hanging swamps, eucalypt forest*

BEST MAP: *1:25 000 Katoomba and Mt Wilson maps, NSW Land and Property Information*

TOILETS: *Eco-toilet at Evans Lookout, Govetts Leap has flushing toilets*

FOOD: *Blackheath has some excellent cafes, pubs and shops*

TIPS: *If you start this walk in the middle – at Govetts Leap – then your party can walk the shorter distance to Pulpit Rock, and then decide whether to do the extra walk to Evans Lookout. Govetts Leap is an excellent spot to watch the sun set, as it lights up Mt Banks.*

[above] *Dramatic lookouts on Pulpit Rock*

Virtually one continual lookout, the Cliff Top Walk from Evans Lookout to Pulpit Rock is breathtaking in its scope, and includes some awesome sandstone features, two of the Blue Mountains' tallest waterfalls, and an opportunity to see the NSW floral emblem, the waratah.

You're in for a visual treat on this walk, so make sure you pick a clear day. However, be aware that in the mountains the weather can change quickly – it's usually advised to carry a raincoat, which can double as protection from wind and cold.

This is almost the tale of two walks, as the section from Evans Lookout to Govetts Leap is very different to the further section to Pulpit Rock.

From the Evans Lookout carpark (at the end of Evans Lookout Rd, Blackheath), head north, past the toilets, along the clearly marked Cliff Top Track. Although the track always remains atop the cliff, this first section has a few descents and ascents of up to 100 m that will remind you that you are actually walking and sucking in clean air. As you go, you'll be passing through open forests of ash and peppermint trees; heathlands with banksias, drumsticks and the pink and red hanging epacris bells; swampy areas with spiky hakea and buttongrass; and protected gullies with mountain ash. Blue Mountains National Park has some 1300 plant species, and some signs will help you identify a few along the way.

Waratah (Telopea speciosissima) – the NSW floral emblem

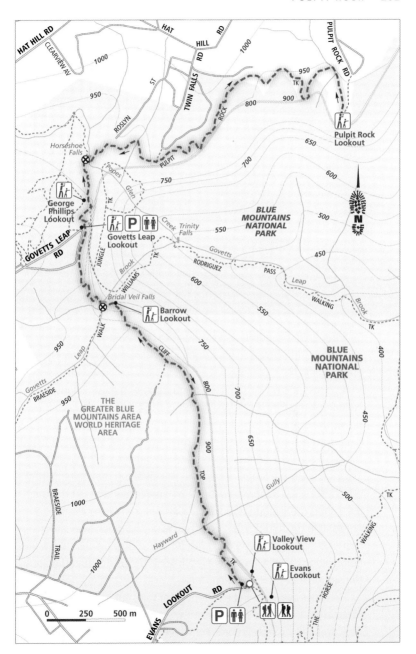

Pulpit Rock

Through the vegetation you'll see the changing vista of the extensive Grose Valley to your right, and dramatic plunging orange cliffs.

A couple of kays into this walk, you'll come to an excellent lookout overlooking Bridal Veil Falls. As these falls plummet off the top of the cliff, they form a mist that waters a hanging garden of bladderworts, sundews and ferns on the cliff. Just after this lookout, the Braeside Walk comes in from the left, and you will cross the creek on concrete stepping stones. The climb up the stairs on the other side will probably slow-up most people, but once at the top, it's a short stroll along to Govetts Leap. This popular spot can be crowded in the middle of the day and is on the must-see list for tourist coaches, so if you don't like crowds it may be best to keep going along the cliff, past the carpark and the toilets, and then onto the signposted track to Pulpit Rock.

This next section can be muddy after rain, but in a few hundred metres you'll be away from the crowds and will get an incredible view over the curved cliff area for which Horseshoe Falls is named.

Again, the route will descend steeply (and more roughly) about 60 m down to the creek. Popes Glen Track continues straight ahead, but your route crosses the creek. The crossing can be tricky, but if you look for the best point, your feet should stay dry. Before crossing though, duck 50 m or so up the Popes Glen Track to a lovely little cascade, trickling onto a sandy beach.

After crossing the creek, head up the uneven and eroded track on the other side. At the top of the little rise, you will get one of the many great views on this walk – looking across Horseshoe Falls in the foreground to Bridal Veil Falls. Often the sun will play with the mist off Bridal Veil Falls, causing a rainbow to fill the valley.

The next 2 km through to Pulpit Rock is your best chance to see waratahs on this walk. With bright red blooms in spring about the size of a cup and saucer, standing on 1–2 m tall stems, they really are an impressive sight (in fact, their Latin name *Telopea* means 'seen from a distance'). The difference between the blooms being fully open or closed can be just a couple of weeks, depending on the weather. It is illegal to pick wildflowers or tamper with vegetation in a national park so, please, just admire them.

The track deviates away from the cliffline, just when the dramatic feature of Pulpit Rock seems to be getting closer. But don't fear: after passing by some lovely sandstone caves, and crossing through some wet gullies and past hanging swamps and more wildflower wonderlands, you'll reach the sign pointing down to Pulpit Rock or up to the Pulpit Rock carpark.

Pulpit Rock itself is a delightful surprise, with some exciting viewing stations perched on three levels, and the valley far, far below.

Enjoy the spectacle and the solace, and then enjoy doing it all again on the way back to Evans Lookout.

BLUE GUM FOREST

BLUE MOUNTAINS

WALK: 7 km return

TIME REQUIRED: 3 hours

BEST TIME: Winter mornings

GRADE: Hard

ENVIRONMENT: Stunning blue gum forest, steep gullies, cliffs

BEST MAP: 1:25 000 Mt Wilson, NSW Land and Property Information

TOILETS: Eco-toilet in the camping ground at the start of the walk

FOOD: Blackheath, 8 km away, has great cafes, pubs, takeaways and a deli

TIPS: When about to head steeply uphill, or halfway up a hill, raise your blood sugar levels with a few lollies, chocolate, muesli bar or fruit drink. It can help the mountain seem smaller and less steep. Also, even if it is bitterly cold at the top, be prepared to change into something much cooler for the climb out.

There are many ways into the legendary Blue Gum Forest, and this is the shortest – and the steepest. It will test even the fittest walkers.

Often called the cradle of conservation in Australia, Blue Gum Forest was protected by a large group of bushwalkers way back in 1931 – the first time that the Australian bushwalking community managed to permanently conserve something of natural beauty.

[above] *Mountain blue gums in Blue Gum Forest*

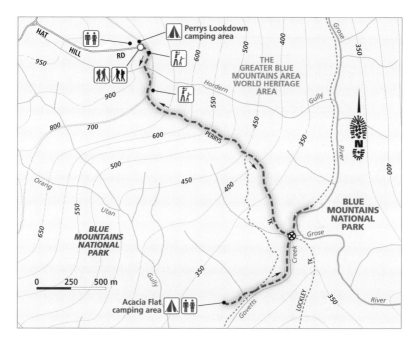

At that stage, the forest, which has a rich stand of huge mountain blue gums, standing with their tall, straight and smooth white and cream trunks above bracken and green grass, was being grazed, and the farmer was determined to cut the trees down. Bushwalkers from the Sydney Bushwalkers and Mountain Trails Club banded together to buy the plot, for the steep price of £130, and it was turned into a conservation reserve in 1932.

The glorious mountain blue gum (a close relative of the Sydney blue gum) favours sheltered valleys like this one. There are other places to see them in the mountains, but nowhere else has such a rich and glorious display. The blue gum's Latin name (*Eucalyptus deanei*) was given in honour of an amateur botanist, Henry Deane, who was a Blue Mountains railway engineer by day during the late 19th century.

It isn't easy to get to the forest, and most access routes are long. Overnight campers (who stay at Acacia Flat near the forest – campfires not permitted) are generally advised to go in by one of the gentler, but longer routes (from Pierces Pass or Lockleys Pylon) or the more exciting route via Victoria Falls. This route, from Perry's Lookdown, is steep and dramatic, and can have you there and back in a few hours – if you are up for the challenge.

Heading north-west on the Great Western Highway out of Blackheath, take Hat Hill Rd, which is clearly marked to Perry's Lookdown. Travel 8 km down this road, the last 5 km on a fairly rough dirt road. At the end is a pleasant campground, with a clean toilet, frequented by superb lyrebirds. Park here and begin the long descent. The first few hundred metres are deceptively easy, with a couple of lookouts. The last of these has a memorial to four schoolboys who died in the area (not from the steep walk out, but from a bushfire).

From here the route drops sharply and nastily – you will descend about 600 m in not much more than 1.5 km. The stairs are uneven and unrelenting, and like many, you may discover that going down jagged and rough stairs, sometimes with drops of a metre, is actually harder on the thighs and knees than going up. It is particularly hard if you are carrying a pack, or a child on your back.

Around you the marvellous and massive Blue Mountains amphitheatre of Mt Banks, Mt Hay, Lockleys Pylon and other peaks joined by orange cliffs, tempt you to stop and gaze, but you'll have plenty of time for that on the way up. For now, focus on your feet and getting down safely.

About halfway down, the gradient substantially decreases, and the vegetation changes – you'll see ironbarks and pink angophoras – and the birdlife dramatically increases. Listen for the tinkle of bellbirds, the cheeky chatter of rainbow lorikeets, the scratchy calls of yellow-tailed black-cockatoos and sulphur-crested cockies and the more subtle sounds of other species.

If it has been raining, the clay track in the next section can become quite slippery. The undergrowth here is a little overgrown with weeds, but soon you'll come into the Blue Gum Forest, with the unmistakable 40 m tall blue gums. You'll see other trees of course, including ironbarks, turpentine, banksias, casuarinas, paperbarks

Blue gums reaching into the blue sky

and wattle, and the birdlife can be quite prolific. At a steady pace, it will have probably taken a little less than an hour to get here.

Right at the bottom, not far from the Grose River, the track comes to a four-way intersection, where an excellent information sign provides a detailed history of the area. From here you can explore in any direction, allowing yourself enough time to go back the way you came.

Turn to the right and after about 500 m, you'll come to the Acacia Flats camping area, where there is a pit toilet.

Straight ahead, you'll quickly come down to the Grose River, which is a lovely spot to have a break before the brutal climb back up.

And to the left is the bulk of the Blue Gum Forest, so it's definitely worth wandering in this direction for several hundred metres. The track keeps going, so just make a decision to turn back to the intersection when you are ready. The blue gums continue for quite some distance, but their density decreases the further you go along the alluvial flat.

The Grose River – a great place for lunch before the tough climb out

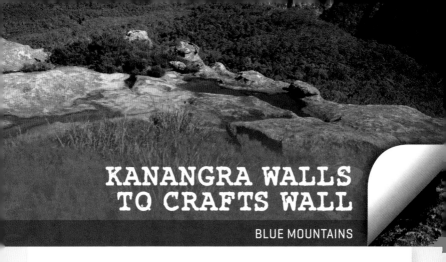

KANANGRA WALLS TO CRAFTS WALL

WALK: *12 km return*

TIME REQUIRED: *4.5 hours*

BEST TIME: *Cool, crisp and clear days in autumn, winter or spring*

GRADE: *Moderate to hard – navigation skills are required, but there is no huge change in elevation, so most of the walking isn't too strenuous.*

ENVIRONMENT: *Some of the deepest, most impressive gorges in the Blue Mountains, plunging cliffs, heathland and eucalypt forest*

BEST MAP: *1:25 000 Kanangra, NSW Land and Property Information*

TOILETS: *Eco-toilet at start of walk*

FOOD: *Oberon, an hour's drive away, has cafes, bakeries, pubs and supermarkets*

TIPS: *The drive to Kanangra Walls will take at least 1.5 hours from Blackheath, and you will pass Jenolan Caves. If the trip is part of a holiday, make sure you spend some time exploring the exquisite limestone caves. You can stay at Jenolan or Oberon, or at a host of B&Bs nearby.*

[above] *Pools on the escarpment*

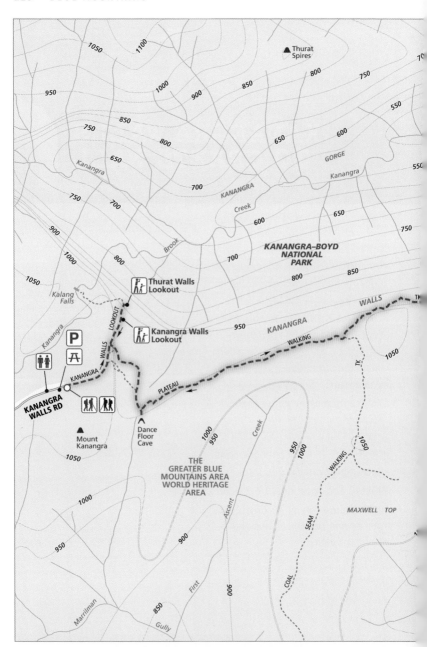

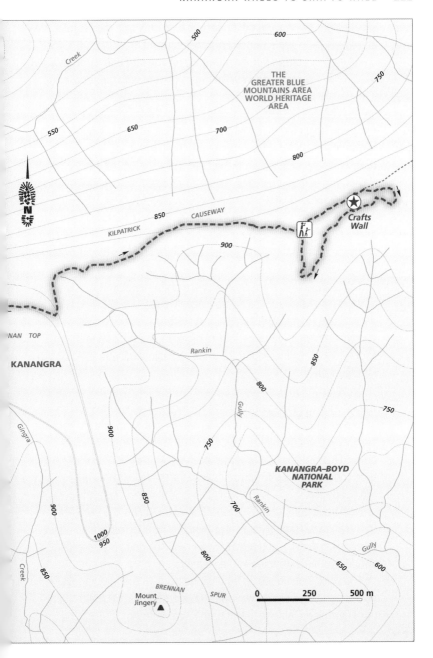

A wild, adventurous hike on unmarked tracks, this walk dances precariously on dramatic unfenced cliffs, before plunging off the cliff line through quiet forests, and surfacing at the castellated feature of Crafts Wall.

Although adjoining Blue Mountains National Park, Kanangra–Boyd National Park is away from the usual tourist trail and is generally much wilder and quieter. On the 30 km dirt-road drive from Jenolan Caves, you're likely to see hordes of kangaroos and wallabies, and even the occasional wombat.

There are only a couple of very short, marked bushwalking routes at the end of Kanangra Walls Rd. This is more typically the starting point for longer bushwalks undertaken by experienced walkers who enjoy exploring this remote wilderness.

This walk is one of the best ways to get a taste of what Kanangra has to offer. Navigation is comparatively easy, but you should take a topographic map and compass. It takes you to the doorstep of some of the best-named mountains in the country: Mt High and Mighty, Mt Stormbreaker, Roar Knoll, Rumble Knoll and the 1164 m Mt Cloudmaker.

To begin, head from the carpark towards the lookouts. Ignore for the moment the Plateau Track to the right. There is an abundance of birdlife here – particularly honeyeaters and wattlebirds. From the lookout you should see to your right the line of Kanangra Walls, and beyond it (to the left) a lower area, called Kilpatrick Causeway, and then the castle-like structure called Crafts Wall, where you are headed.

Now head back to the Plateau Track, and follow the steps down to the historic Dance Floor Cave (which was used as a dance hall by early settlers). If you are lucky, you will see one of the resident superb lyrebirds dancing in the vicinity.

The walk then heads up an obvious track to the plateau. You'll notice almost straight away that the plateau has no trees – it is pure heathland, able to stand both freezing temperatures and

Steep and relentless Kanangra country

long, hot, dry summers. Plants include waist-high shrubs such as drumsticks and low-growing triggerplants.

The track along the plateau links rock platforms, and you may feel at times you have lost the route, but it generally goes in the same direction, a stone's throw from the cliff edge. Little side tracks keep popping out to the precipice, and it's hard to resist checking out every one. Keep an eye out for wedge-tailed eagles or other raptors riding the thermals.

Towards the end of the plateau, a large rock platform offers great views of stunning waterfalls both back across the gorge and deep below. Near here, a well-defined track heads right, quickly swinging around to the south. This is the track to Maxwell Top, but it's not the way you want to go. Your route takes you fairly consistently east-nor-east, staying near the edge of the cliff line (on the left). At times the track will seem to disappear between the rock platforms, but keep the faith and you'll pick it up again.

At the end of the plateau, you'll hop across a deep crevice in a rock. This crevice turns into a gully and ravine that you will soon be climbing down. To access it, first continue for another 60 m or so through a casuarina forest on the left-hand side of the gully. If you reach the end of the cliff line, with an impossible drop, backtrack a few metres, and you'll find a way to carefully clamber down into the gully.

Follow the rocks downhill at the bottom of the steep descent, and a narrow track will appear drifting off to the left. This will lead you down and then up and along Kilpatrick Causeway, along the top of the ridge. The track at times is quite indistinct, but the heading stays pretty consistent.

About 2 km after exiting the gully, you'll climb a short slope and the orange rampart of Crafts Wall will appear above you. You will reach it at the north-west corner, where there is a small cave and a visitors book. The main track (which goes on to Mt Cloudmaker) continues straight, along the north side of Crafts Wall, but it's worth

Wedge-tailed
eagle

Heathland vegetation with Kanangra Walls in the distance

going all the way around and over Crafts Wall, so start by heading right. In a couple of hundred metres, you'll find some easy ramps up onto the top (marked with cairns), and then a fairly well-defined track will take you to a perch on top of the northern cliffs, with great views. After a break, head back down the ramps, and continue a circumnavigation of Crafts Wall. On the sheltered, southern side, you'll find lots and lots of caves and some thick forest. There is no decent track, so the going can be slow, but just keep the cliffs on your left, and in less than an hour, you should be all the way around. Note the track continuing to Mt Cloudmaker from the north-east corner of Crafts Wall, and also note the 'leaning forest' on the north side, with all the trees reaching sideways to the sun.

Once you've completed the circumnavigation of Crafts Wall, head back the way you came, stopping at a few more of those great vantage points on the edge of the cliff.

GLOW WORM TUNNEL AND WOLGAN VALLEY

BLUE MOUNTAINS

WALK: *9 km loop*

TIME REQUIRED: *3 hours*

BEST TIME: *Weekdays any season, out of school holidays so you can get the tunnel to yourself*

GRADE: *Easy to moderate*

ENVIRONMENT: *Historic glow worm tunnel, tree-fern valley, eucalypt forest, expansive views, remote pagoda country*

BEST MAP: http://ozultimate.com/bushwalking

TOILETS: *Eco-toilet at start of walk*

FOOD: *Lithgow, 35 km away, has cafes, bakeries, pubs and supermarkets*

TIPS: *There are several ways onto this loop walk, but the Glow Worm Tunnel carpark is the best*

With the longest glow worm tunnel in NSW, a lovely gentle loop walk through beautiful forest and expansive views over the Wolgan Valley, this is a fun, family-friendly route.

There are plenty of places to see glow worms in NSW, and a few so-called glow worm tunnels (including one near Bowral), but this is justifiably the most famous. More than 300 m long, and completely dark in the middle, the historic railway tunnel (constructed 1907) is a brilliant place to turn

[above] *Exiting the Glow Worm Tunnel into a grove of tree-ferns*

the torches off for a while and watch the glow worms come out like twinkling stars.

Just getting out here into the vast Wollemi National Park feels like a bit of an adventure. It's a 30 km drive along increasingly rough dirt tracks north-east of Lithgow, with very few signs.

From central Lithgow, head down Bridge St and follow the tourist signs to Glow Worm Tunnel, which will lead you out of town on the State Mine Gully Rd. Plenty of forest tracks and other tracks lead off this road, but keep following the main track, through pine and native forests (beware of roos at dusk and dawn). You should be able to travel reasonably quickly in a sedan along the first 20 km or so (being careful of logging trucks) but make sure you reduce speed as the track becomes rougher. There are deep hidden ditches, cavernous potholes and dangerous grooves, but as long as you slow down to about 40 km/h for the last section, you should make it easily in a sedan.

You enter a section of Gardens of Stone National Park about 10 km before reaching the carpark (the tunnel is located in the adjoining Wollemi National Park). The road forks, with Old Coach Rd going to the right. This is leads to an alternative approach to the tunnel, but the better option is to stay on Glow Worm Tunnel Rd, as it will soon take you through the 'Number 1 tunnel'. This is NOT the

Number 1 tunnel

Honeycomb sandstone

glow worm tunnel. Take care as you drive through it. Another couple of careful kays after the tunnel, you'll finally reach the carpark at the end of the road. There is an eco-toilet here but no drinking water.

From the carpark, the track heads down a valley, across a bridge and through hand-hewn stone clefts, towards the tunnel. A short distance before you reach the tunnel you'll see the Pagoda Track on the right-hand side. This is the way you'll be coming back. Keep eyes and ears alert for lyrebirds along this section of the walk. Their calls, among the loudest bird calls in the world, mimic the calls of up to 27 other birds, as well as their own beautiful songs.

Before you reach the tunnel, you'll see, down low on the left-hand side, a dark cave into which the creek flows. If you have a good torch, an adventurous spirit and don't mind getting wet feet, you can enter this little canyon, called Bells Grotto. However, it bypasses the actual glow worm tunnel, so if you do duck down into this, you may have to double back to get back on track.

The glow worm tunnel itself has large tree ferns either side of its dark recesses. It is rough inside and usually has water trickling through it, so it is essential that you have a torch. However, in the

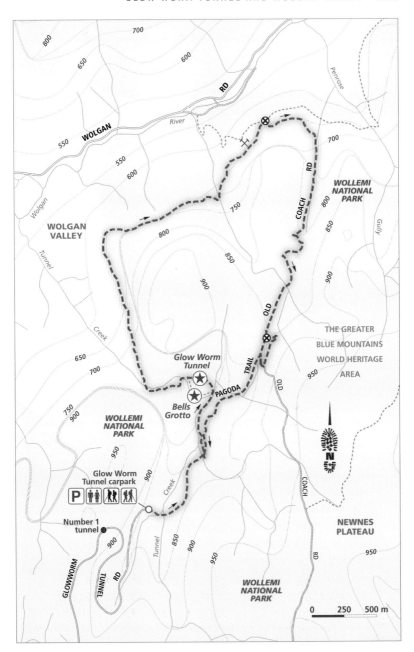

centre of the tunnel, when you can't see either end, turn off your torch for a few minutes, let your eyes (and the fly larvae) adjust, and soon you'll see greenish glows on the ceiling, and high on the walls.

You will exit the tunnel into a stunning tree-fern glen. Take the marked track to the right, past some lovely caves, and then along the left-hand side of the creek. You will cross the creek and follow the cliff line after 100 m or so, but don't be tempted to cross too early – keep going until you see some iron girders. After rain, this section of the track will be very wet.

As you follow the towering orange, yellow and red sandstone cliff line around to the right, you'll get great views out over the Wolgan Valley. Because it follows the old railway line, the track stays relatively flat through the next few kilometres. You'll pass old culverts, sleepers, rock walls and other evidence of the century-old route.

Keep going through some lovely eucalypt forest and after a pleasant stroll, you'll reach a major junction. A small track to Newnes continues straight ahead, a larger fire trail heads left down to Wolgan Rd, while the route you want, the Old Coach Rd, heads up to the right. It is a long, gradual ascent through a lovely hidden valley with bell birds and sculpted rock walls with colours of honeycomb, sienna, ochre, gold and red. This area is renowned for its many beautiful stone features formed by erosion over an estimated 200 million years. Some of the best-known features are the 'pagodas' or 'beehive' formations – multilayered, ledge-frilled structures reaching to the sky.

The forests through here are alive with birds. As well as more lyrebirds, you are likely to see treecreepers, fairy wrens, yellow-tailed black-cockatoos and other species. Koalas have also been spotted.

A couple of kilometres past the junction, a clearly marked narrow track, called the Pagoda Track, heads off to the right. This track (the roughest section of the loop, but still pretty easy going) squeezes past some lovely pagodas and cave formations. The adventurous might like to get up on top of one of the pagodas for a view across the pagodas to distant mountains. One of the safest to climb is on the left-hand side after about 100 m (just be careful

Pagodas

as the sandstone ledges can give way]. Alternatively, you can treat yourself to a view without rock climbing by continuing along the Old Coach Rd up the hill for an extra 400 m or so, past a gate, before returning to the start of the Pagoda Track.

Less than 1 km along the Pagoda Track, the route spills out onto the track you started on, not far from the Glow Worm Tunnel. Turn left and you'll soon be back at the carpark.

Beach tracks on the Light to Light walk

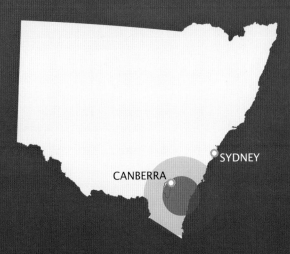

CANBERRA

SYDNEY

SOUTH COAST

Less travelled than the NSW North Coast, the South
Coast has many delightful treasures for walkers
to uncover: from the much-loved Minnamurra
Rainforest, to the massive wild features of Morton
National Park and the Budawangs, and the
resplendent multicoloured vistas of the Sapphire
Coast at the southern end of the state.

BOXVALE AND FORTY FOOT FALLS LOOP

SOUTH COAST

WALK: 12.5 km loop

TIME REQUIRED: 4.5 hours

BEST TIME: Winter mornings, when the Southern Highlands are at their crisp best

GRADE: Hard; the first section, however, is easy

ENVIRONMENT: Rainforest, scribbly gum and banksia woodland, tunnels, historic old tramway, Nattai River gorge

BEST MAP: Bushwalks around Mittagong in the Mt Alexandra Reserve, from the Mittagong Visitor Information Centre, 62–70 Main St, Mittagong: 1300 657 559 or (02) 4871 2888

TOILETS: At the big shopping centre in Mittagong, about 3 km from the start of the walk

FOOD: The large shopping centre in Mittagong has everything you could need

TIPS: Many people do the easy walk along the Boxvale Track, but the extra loop down into the canyon and along it to Forty Foot Falls is well worth it if you are up for the challenge

[above] *Forty Foot Falls*

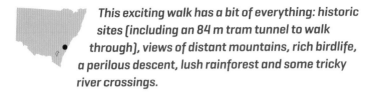

This exciting walk has a bit of everything: historic sites (including an 84 m tram tunnel to walk through), views of distant mountains, rich birdlife, a perilous descent, lush rainforest and some tricky river crossings.

Mittagong is a lovely town in the Southern Highlands, only a 1.5-hour drive from Sydney. This walk makes for a great day trip from the state capital, or a solid half-day if you are staying in the area.

From Mittagong, head west along the Old Hume Highway for about 3 km until you cross over the freeway. Just after crossing the freeway, turn right onto Boxvale Rd, then almost immediately left down a rough dirt track, marked 'Boxvale Walk'. In 100 m or so, the rough track ends in a parking and picnic area in a pleasant scribbly gum and banksia woodland. There are no toilets or drinking water, and signs warn throughout the walk not to drink from the creeks or river.

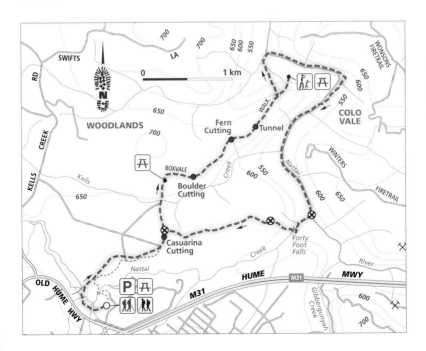

Fern Cutting

The Boxvale tramway was constructed in 1888 for a colliery that closed in 1896. Ninety years later the route was reopened as a walking track. Like many tramways, it provides an excellent walking or even mountain-biking track, with a generally flat gradient and smooth surface. The tramway-track labourers chiselled, drilled and blasted their way through a handful of rock cuttings, which now provide interesting spots along the walk, particularly as plants overtake them, and the dark tunnel is a joy to walk through.

Be careful at the beginning of this walk, as there is a confusing network of tracks and fire trails going to historic and other sites. The Boxvale walk starts down to the left of the carpark, near the large, covered information board that has a helpful map on one side. At the start of the walk, stick to the narrow, tramway-width track, marked with red squares, rather than getting distracted by any of the fire trails.

The track initially crosses a small creek. Then on the left-hand side you'll pass a large reservoir built in 1930 to increase Mittagong's water supply. Keep an eye out during this early stage for a variety of fauna: red-necked wallabies, wombats, a variety of cockatoos (including yellow-tailed blacks, glossy blacks and the fairly quiet gang-gang cockatoos) and – allegedly – koalas in the grey gums and broad-leafed peppermints. The plant life in the woodland is interesting too, including waratahs, yellow-flowering broad-leaved drumsticks and dotted sun orchids. Don't be discouraged in this first section if you can still hear the freeway – soon the noise will recede and you'll feel like you're miles from anywhere.

Walking on an old tramway is some of the easiest walking you can do, and you'll make fairly quick time to the turn-off to Forty Foot Falls on your right, with farmland on your left. If all goes well, the track to your right is the way you'll come back.

For now, keep heading straight, through a section where you can see the clever way in which the tramway track was built up above the surrounding woodland. You'll pass through various rock cuttings too, which have all been given names. Some have collapsed slightly, and others are covered in a rainbow of lichens. The best is 'Fern Cutting', where towering tree-ferns have taken up residence.

No torch is needed when you reach the attractive 84 m tunnel, but you'll need to take a little bit of care as the ground is quite uneven. Not long past the tunnel, you'll reach the end of the line where the box carts were loaded. Take the track that heads down to the right. After 600 m, you'll reach a large lookout area, with two picnic tables (no toilets or water). Up the valley to the left you can see right up to the Blue Mountains, with Mt Cloudmaker clearly visible. Unfortunately, the lookout has been built so far back from the cliff edge that adventurous souls who want to look down into the gorge need to carefully scoot past the fence on the right-hand side, and clamber down to the edge of the drop, where you can see the Nattai River far below.

The walk up to this point is very easy, and some of your party may choose to sit here a while before returning the same gentle way.

Those up for the fun challenge of completing the loop will head back up to the intersection, then left past the old cart loading area, and to the start of the 'incline'. This treacherous and tricky descent plummets 170 m in just 500 m. Its combination of water-polished bedrock, casuarina needles and loose boulders, means great care needs to be taken, and its quite sobering to watch the dislodged boulders tumble down below you. A cable has been provided for a handrail, but it is poorly designed and is generally too low to the ground to be useful. Just take your time.

At the bottom of the incline, the tall eucalypt woodland is alive with myriad birds. The next section of the track is overgrown and the hardest section to follow. It is better labelled for those travelling the other direction so, if in doubt, look backwards. At first it heads to the right along a small creek. Once the creek reaches the Nattai River, keep an eye out almost straight away for large white painted arrows on logs that point to a log bridge across the river. It's really just a massive tree that has fallen. It is slightly rounded on top, and quite slimy, so take care when crossing. On the other side are some overgrown and flood-damaged signs and the route is hard to trace. As you search for it, be careful of stinging nettles, particularly if you are wearing shorts.

The route heads to the right up the gorge, but it actually starts by heading left immediately after the log bridge, then hooking around to the right. Initially it is quite overgrown by bracken, but stick with it, as it should become clearer after 50 m or so.

This next 3 km section, along the river, is mainly through thick, dark rainforest, with mosses and lichens growing over every surface. Everything is slippery, there will be fallen trees over the track, and the going will be slow – expect to take at least an hour along the gorge – but it is quite beautiful, and the observant might notice superb lyrebirds and brush turkeys in the forest, and ducks and other waterbirds on the river.

After a while you'll pass through a natural rock arch, and not long after that, the track heads right down to the river's edge where there are a series of large boulders. At this point you need to cross the river again. There is a sign hidden in the undergrowth, but you may not spot it. If the track has completely petered out though, you may have missed it! On the crossing, many of the large boulders are incredibly slippery and you will need to be cautious.

Once on the other side, the track continues along the river, occasionally going up the hillside a little. It may become slightly hard to follow at times, as it doesn't receive much traffic. You will

Fallen flowers on the forest floor

cross two creeks. The second, Nattai Creek, is where you will find a well-marked intersection. The track straight ahead leads back to Mittagong. You should turn right onto the Forty Foot Falls Track which you will find much more trafficked.

Cross the creek at the obvious flat rock area, and then up the steel ladders and stairs. Unfortunately the track seems to avoid the best views of the falls. So, before scaling the last bit of the cliff line, detour off the track and follow the cliff line down to the bottom of the falls. Because the rock is quite undercut, you can stand right underneath the falls with the water going overhead.

Back on the track, head up the steep stairs and ladder to the top of the falls, and again, divert off the track for a lovely lunch spot on rocks near where the water drops off the edge. Even if you don't have lunch here, it's worth having a drink and a snack, to give you a burst of energy for the next 1 km uphill.

Up the hill, you'll encounter the maze of tracks again, but keep following the red markers. Turn left at the first fire trail (there is a picnic table there), then left again. You will walk along for almost another kilometre before reaching an unmarked intersection – turn right here to take you back to the original track near the farmland. Turn left along your original route and head back to the start.

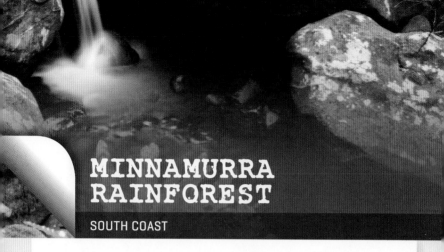

MINNAMURRA RAINFOREST

SOUTH COAST

WALK: 4 km loop plus return walk to Minnamurra Falls

TIME REQUIRED: 1.5 hours

BEST TIME: As soon as the area opens, at 9am each morning

GRADE: Easy with a couple of uphill slopes

ENVIRONMENT: Temperate rainforest, creeks, waterfalls

BEST MAP: This book

TOILETS: Flushing toilets at the visitor centre at the start and finish of the walk

FOOD: There is a small cafe at the visitor centre

TIPS: Take some binoculars to look for rainforest birds as you meander slowly around the gentle loop walk

One of the most easily accessible temperate rainforests in the state, Minnamurra has wide and gentle boardwalks suitable for strollers and wheelchairs for the first few hundred metres.

This walk is split into two sections – a very gentle 1.6 km rainforest loop walk, and a slightly more energetic walk to the Minnamurra Falls.

The Minnamurra Rainforest area, in Budderoo National Park, is well signposted at the end of Minnamurra Falls Rd, just 10 minutes from the small historic town of Jamberoo, about a two-hour drive south of Sydney. You will need to pay for parking, or have a national parks sticker.

[above] *Cascading creek*

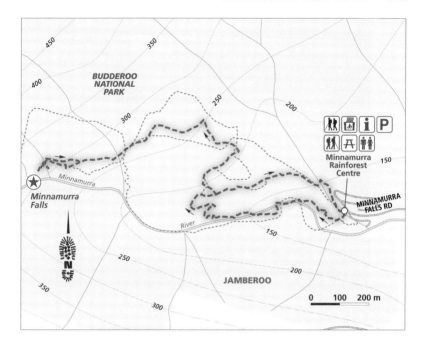

The visitor centre, and the start of the walk, is just opposite the carpark, but it is worth popping down to the picnic area by the river. This area, and in the vicinity of the visitor centre, can be one of the easiest places to spot superb lyrebirds in the wild. These chook-sized birds are some of the best vocal imitators in the avian world, and often sing a loud song that includes half a dozen different bird calls. The male lyrebird has a long, ornate tail with curved feathers that look a little like a lyre when it goes through its elaborate breeding display, between June and Aug.

The loop walk starts just outside the visitor centre and is well marked. All visitors are encouraged to walk in the same direction. It is a simple boardwalk, with zero chance of getting lost, and the gentle grading makes it suitable for wheelchairs and strollers. Kids will enjoy the two suspension bridges.

Many of the trees are labelled, and you'll soon be recognising them as your eyes adjust to the reduced light in the rainforest: sandpaper figs, brown beech, red cedar, bloodwood, coachwood,

Minnamurra Falls, higher section

lilly pilly, sassafras and brush cherry. There are a few bench seats to rest on, including one near a huge strangler fig. Keep a particular eye out for the giant stinging trees (labelled). They have lime-green leaves that look a little like a heart.

Minnamurra itself is an Aboriginal word said to mean 'lots of fish', and although you might not spot many as you walk along the bubbling river, you might see eastern water dragons or even swamp wallabies. But most of the wildlife here is feathered. Gentle, brown cuckoo-doves often nibble fruit by the path, but you may also see, or hear, wonga pigeons, king parrots, satin bowerbirds and the distinctive whip-like call of the eastern whipbird. The green catbird makes one of the most bizarre calls, a bit like a baby screaming.

Not long after the walk rises from the river up a series of switchbacks, a paved track comes in on the left. Take this for the extra 2.4 return walk to Minnamurra Falls. (Very little or tired legs could go straight back to the visitor centre along the main loop track.)

The Minnamurra Falls walk heads uphill for a couple of hundred metres. There are a few benches provided for rests but most people should make it up with no problems. On the right of the track you'll see one of the scourges of the Australian bush – lantana. Introduced into Australia in the 1840s as a hedge, this invasive weed has thorny stems and takes over large areas.

Lantana aside, there is plenty to like on the rest of this walk, including cabbage tree palms, ferns and Illawarra flame trees. There is a slight downhill towards the very small and gentle Lyrebird Falls, and then a very small uphill again at the end of the track to Minnamurra.

Superb lyrebird

The falls are split into two sections. The higher section is at the end of the track, and is in a pleasant part of the valley. The lower section is more dramatic, and plunges down a thin, dark canyon. You can see the falls disappearing into the canyon from a lookout area about 60 m back from the end of the track.

Take the track back to the main loop track, and turn left. In about 10 minutes you'll be back at the visitor centre.

Minnamurra Falls, lower section

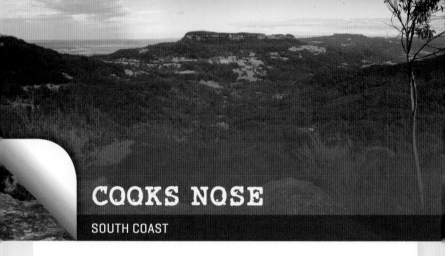

COOKS NOSE

SOUTH COAST

WALK: *8 km return*

TIME REQUIRED: *2 hours*

BEST TIME: *Early on a spring morning*

GRADE: *Easy*

ENVIRONMENT: *Heathland, thick scrub, forest and cliffs*

BEST MAP: *On the sign at the carpark*

TOILETS: *Pit toilet in the picnic area at the start of the walk*

FOOD: *The little towns of Jamberoo and Robertson have good pubs and some shops*

TIPS: *Like much of Australia's wildlife, birds are best seen in the first few hours after dawn and the last few hours of the day*

This is an easy stroll through a reserve abundant with birds, culminating in a lovely lunch spot overlooking the Kangaroo Valley.

There are only a few places in NSW where you won't feel like a nong walking around with a pair of binoculars looking for birds, because nearly everyone else is doing the same. This is one of them.

Barren Grounds, on the winding road between the towns of Robertson and Jamberoo, was first gazetted as a reserve in 1957, primarily because

[above] *View over Kangaroo Valley*

it is vital habitat for two rare birds: the eastern bristlebird, a grey-brown bird with prominent whiskers; and the lovely green grass parrot. Both of these birds are still regularly seen in the 2200 ha reserve, along with 180 other species of bird, some 20 mammal species (including swamp wallabies and wombats), 40 reptile and frog species, and more than 500 plant species. There are flowers all year round, but in spring Barren Grounds blooms particularly nicely with Christmas bells, pink tea tree, boronia, native fuchsia and yellow peas.

There are several linked walks through the reserve, and you could easily spend a day or so on the wide trails. Much of the reserve may appear fairly plain to those not so interested in the plants and animals, but the advantage of the relatively flat walk to Cooks Nose is that it culminates in a lovely cliff-top vantage point overlooking Kangaroo Valley. It's also a perfect-length walk for those who just want to stretch their legs for a couple of hours.

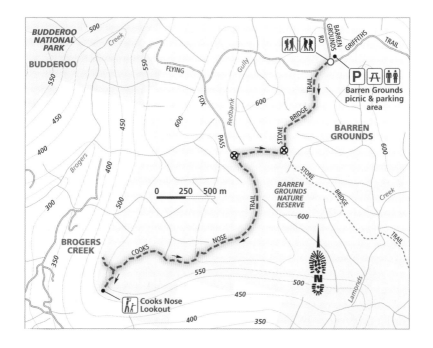

Cooks Nose

From the Barren Grounds picnic and parking area (about 1 km off the road) tracks head off in two directions. Take the one heading south, past the bunkhouse, marked 'Cooks Nose'. The wide fire trail starts off across exposed open country, with some views across the heathland. The plateau here is unusual in that it is an elevated heath swamp, about 600 m above sea level, which is one of the reasons it is such good habitat for so many bird species. The track also winds through thick thickets of hakea and banksia, with wattles and a profusion of coral ferns growing thickly beside the track, and tiny flowers in amongst it all. Honeyeaters, wattlebirds and plenty of other species will dart across the track in front of you, while square-tailed kites soar overhead. The tracks are well-marked, and you'll take the second turn-off on the left, slightly uphill, signposted to Cooks Nose. Keep following this track (ignoring a couple of minor fire trails that come in)

Native fuchsia

for another couple of kilometres as it falls gently down the slope. Towards the end it will split, with a thin track heading right, and another disappearing straight ahead, down into a more overgrown section. The track on the right goes to a rock platform near the edge of the cliff, but the views are not great. Instead, plunge down the hill straight ahead, and in a few hundred metres you'll arrive at Cooks Nose, with a big rock platform on the edge of the cliff. The views of the Kangaroo Valley and surrounding mountains are superb, and it's a great spot for lunch.

Return the way you came, or deviate along any of the other tracks for a longer walk.

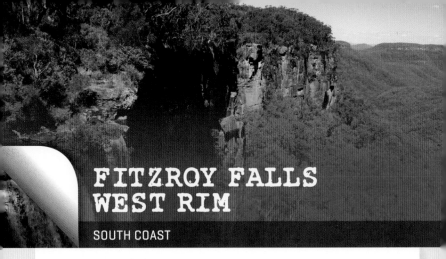

FITZROY FALLS WEST RIM

SOUTH COAST

WALK: 4.5 km return

TIME REQUIRED: 1.5 hours

BEST TIME: Winter, autumn or spring afternoons, after rain

GRADE: Easy, but a few stairs

ENVIRONMENT: Waterfalls pouring off sandstone cliffs, forest

BEST MAP: Available from the visitor centre

TOILETS: Outside the visitor centre at the start of the walk

FOOD: Cafe at visitor centre

TIPS: The East Rim walk is pleasant too, but the West Rim walk offers more dramatic views and some bonus waterfalls

Fitzroy Falls is one of the loveliest waterfalls in NSW and this relatively flat, easy walk shows it off nicely, with multiple lookouts on the edge of a spectacular escarpment, just a few hundred metres apart. The falls are lit by the sun in mid-late afternoon.

Most of the vast Morton National Park is a declared wilderness area rich with stunning cliffs, waterfalls, valleys, rainforest gullies, sandstone features and forests. The section around the Fitzroy Falls Visitor Centre provides a great introduction to this wonderland, on well defined and very well signposted tracks.

[above] *View from Fitzroy Falls Lookout*

The visitor centre, just off Kangaroo Valley Rd, between Moss Vale and Kangaroo Valley, has a cafe and some excellent displays of some of the plants and animals found in the park. There is also a picnic area with coin-operated barbecues.

One obvious track leads from the visitor centre past Yarrunga Creek where you may see platypus. The track then forks, the East Rim walk goes across a bridge, while the West Rim walk continues to the first of a string of breathtaking lookouts. The first of these perches right near the edge of Fitzroy Falls which plunges some 80 m off the cliff. If the falls are pumping, you can watch the water pour right down the Yarrunga Valley.

Keep following the obvious track, past a series of helpful signs pointing out vegetation, and describing lyrebirds and wombats. The track occasionally runs into a fire trail that parallels the walking track, but usually only for a few metres, and it is always well signposted and clear where to go. You'll pass some robust and quite beautiful Sydney peppermints, creamy scribbly gums and solid

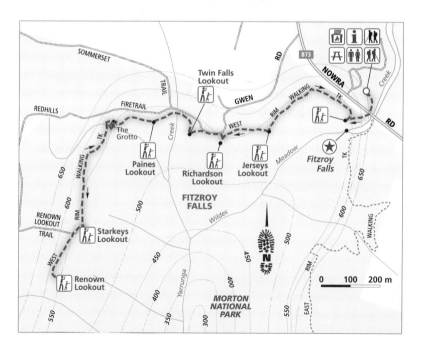

ironbarks, with a thick understorey of mountain devils, honeyflowers, hakeas, banksias and pittosporums. The observant (and the quiet) should notice myriad small birds through this quite lovely forest, including thornbills, eastern spinebills, crimson rosellas and honeyeaters. There may even be lyrebirds.

High in the gum trees you may also notice vibrant green clumps along the branches. These are likely to be mistletoe, a parasitic species spread by the delightful mistletoe bird, the male of which has a bright red chest.

New Holland honeyeater

Twin Falls Lookout offers a couple more delightful waterfalls to admire, before the track continues over a small bridge and you begin to get long views back towards Fitzroy Falls. After ducking under a few overhangs, and a small wetter, rainforest section, a small deviation to The Grotto is marked on the left-hand side. The track here is steep and involves ducking under a few more rocks, but is worth it to get to a lovely damp spot where the water rushes past on its way towards the big cliff.

The last lookout in the string of absolute pearlers is Renown Lookout, which offers a splendid long view back, not just of Fitzroy Falls, but of the river as it plunges down various other falls on its way down the valley.

The return journey will probably be quicker because you will be less inclined to stop. If you haven't had enough walking, cross the bridge near the start and continue along the East Rim Wildflower Walk, which could take another couple of hours.

Twin Falls Lookout

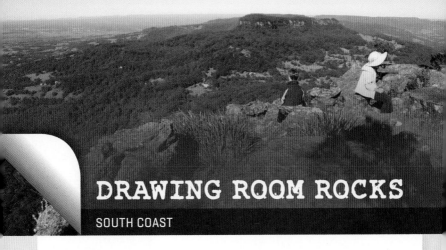

DRAWING ROOM ROCKS

SOUTH COAST

WALK: 3 km return

TIME REQUIRED: 1.5 hours

BEST TIME: A clear morning in autumn, winter or spring

GRADE: Easy to moderate

ENVIRONMENT: Farmland, splendid coastal views, heathland, cliffs and sandstone formations

BEST MAP: This book

TOILETS: None – try Berry

FOOD: Berry, 7 km drive from the trackhead, has delightful cafes, a bakery and ice creamery with lollies galore

TIPS: Track is initially hard to find, but the walk is obvious once you are on it

The zenith of this walk is a cliff edge with stunning 200-degree views. Perched on the edge are sandstone features that could well be nature's chairs and tables.

A bit of a local secret, Drawing Room Rocks doesn't appear in tourist brochures or local walking guides. Even many locals don't know where it is. There are no signposts to help you find the track head, but once you find it, the walking is relatively easy, and on a clear day the effort is definitely worth it.

From the Princes Highway, take Woodhill Mountain Rd just past the eastern (Sydney) end of Berry's shopping strip. Follow it for about 6 km, until you reach a saddle and an intersection with Wattamolla Rd coming

[above] *South Coast secret: Drawing Room Rocks*

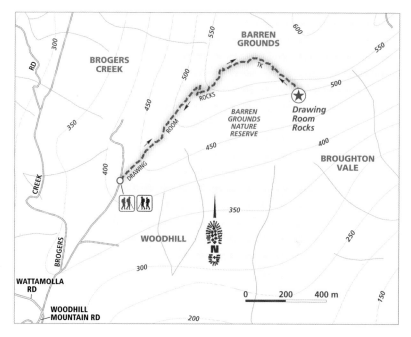

in from the left. Continue straight on to Brogers Creek Rd. In under 200 m, the road will fork again, with the main (tarmac) road heading to the left and down the hill, and a private gravel road on the right going straight ahead. This may appear to be nothing more than a driveway with a letterbox beside it (number 20). Take this gravel track straight ahead, and it will take you steeply uphill. After about 650 m, you'll pass a small parking area on the right-hand side that could fit three cars at a pinch. Another 200 m further is a cattle grid and gate, and the start of the walk. It may have a sign at this point saying 'Drawing Room Rocks Bushwalk', but even if not, don't drive beyond the cattle grid. Park here (there is just enough room for two cars). If there is no parking here or at the small parking area down the hill, then drop off passengers and backtrack to the intersection on the road, where there is a wide area with plenty of room. All people parking near the top are advised to back in, to make it easier to leave if the other spots are taken.

Natural chairs and tables formed by erosion

The track starts by following a barbed wire fence uphill. You should have some lovely early views over the surrounding farmland. All up, this walk ascends 200 m from the cattle grid, reaching an elevation of just over 600 m, but the rise is steady and gentle, with the walk rambling its way up the hill.

After a few hundred metres you'll reach a sign declaring the 'Barren Grounds Nature Reserve'. The bulk of this important bird habitat reserve is accessed off Jamberoo Mountain Rd, which is almost an hour's drive from here, but this is the only walking track to Drawing Room Rocks.

The track is easy to follow, although it becomes a little rugged at times. You'll pass a string of sandstone cliff lines, painted in a rainbow of orange, red, yellow and with the addition of green algae. Vegetation includes ironbarks and other gums, and an understory of banksias, hakeas, bracken in places and the red-flowering bells of fuchsia heath. You'll have several views to your left. Where the sandstone cliff line finishes, a small track heads off to the right. It really isn't worth exploring any of the deviations to your right as the view at the end is better than them all.

About halfway up the hill, the track enters a thick banksia and tea-tree tunnel and the views disappear almost entirely. You may however, spy black cockatoos and other small birds through this section. After the banksia, towards the summit, the track goes through thick heathland. Long sleeves are recommended for this section because the track becomes quite narrow while it ploughs through the dense avenue of scratchy plants. Keep an eye out for more flowers though, including yellow drumsticks, white coral heath and pink trigger plants.

The track opens up just before the impressive cliff line, and the 200-degree views that stretch over sandstone ramparts to the south-west and the valley beyond; the cloaked slopes to the north covered in thick green gums; and over the lush rolling farmland to the east to the wide blue expanse of the Pacific Ocean. It really is a splendid sight.

Just a few metres to the right of the first cliff you come to, you'll find nature's drawing room on the cliff edge, with sandstone chairs and tables laid out for a picnic. One perfect bottom-sized chair sits precariously on the edge of the cliff, and you can admire the view with your feet hanging off into space.

It's worth having a picnic, or at least an extended break here, to enjoy the view, before heading back down the way you came.

Skink

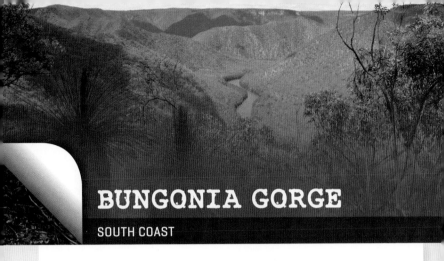

BUNGONIA GORGE

SOUTH COAST

WALK: *7 km loop*

TIME REQUIRED: *4 hours*

BEST TIME: *Spring, summer and autumn, but not after or during big rains*

GRADE: *Hard; some simple off-track navigation is required*

ENVIRONMENT: *Very steep gorge, river boulders, open forest, waterholes*

BEST MAP: *1:25 000 Caoura, NSW Land and Property Information*

TRANSPORT: *Car needed to reach Bungonia National Park, about 20 minutes drive east of Goulburn*

TOILETS: *At the David Reid carpark near Bungonia Lookdown, at the start of the walk*

FOOD: *Goulburn shops or the Marulan roadhouse*

TIPS: *Bring plenty of your own water. It is recommended that you boil the available water at the start of the walk before drinking it, but the uphill section is very steep and you will need plenty.*

[above] **View from Mt Ayre**

With some of the most beautiful, secluded swimming holes in the country, in dramatic gorge country, this walk should be a classic. Don't be fooled by the relatively small distance, as it is a tough walk. It takes in Mt Ayre, the Shoalhaven River, and links two marked trails with an off-track section along the creek.

Park at the David Reid carpark, near Bungonia Lookdown in Bungonia National Park. Take the marked white track (combined with the red track at this stage), which leaves from the lower right side of the carpark as you face towards the cliff. The track meanders toward Mt Ayre and you will see some square white and red markers on some trees. Pay attention to these, as you will need to recognise them later.

Before reaching Mt Ayre, the red track deviates sharply down to the left. Ignore that and stay on the path straight ahead and you'll soon see views over the Shoalhaven. The track skirts around the

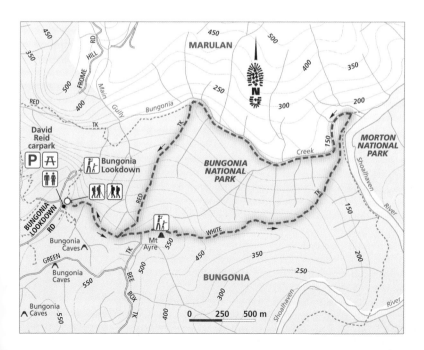

very top of Mt Ayre (don't deviate off the path as the view is better on the track) before reaching an unfenced lookout with grass trees and a bench. It's just 2 km to the river from here, but the going immediately gets tough, with a steep and slippery scree slope. At times you may need to walk down sideways. You'll walk down a ridgeline with kookaburras in old gum trees, termite mounds, and the tinkle of bellbirds in the air.

Another steep descent follows, after which you follow the Shoalhaven along a narrow ridge with great views of some of the Bungonia Creek's waterholes on the left. The minerals in the limestone have made the pools a stunning emerald colour. At the end of the White Track, deviate right for 50 m to stand on the edge of the Shoalhaven.

Now the off-track section starts taking you up Bungonia Creek. The going is fairly easy, particularly on the flat section on the other side of the creek, but the river boulders can be slippery and can move, so watch your step. You don't want a twisted ankle down here.

Take the time to enjoy the deeper pools with a swim or two, and keep an eye out for azure kingfishers, large goannas and eastern grey kangaroos coming down to the creek for a drink. After about 1 km, or half an hour's rock-hopping, you will find a large, beautiful

The first of several gorgeous swimming holes in Bungonia Creek

Steep descent among xanthorrhoea

swimming hole with a large rock slab on the left-hand side: a perfect place for a break and another swim.

Ten minutes further upstream, start sticking to the left-hand side of the creek and you will see large signs warning of rock falls from quarry blasting. The creek takes a large left-hand bend, and just after that you will see red markers on the rocks, and a signpost with an arrow, indicating the way up on the Red Track. This is the way to go.

As you have not at this stage seen the main section of the gorge, you may be tempted to travel further up the creek. This is not recommended, as the going gets tougher and tougher with boulders the size of houses. If you would like to see that section, you are better off doing the entire Red Track in the other direction – do not attempt it travelling upstream as the other end of the track is hard to find.

Instead, follow the Red Track slowly upwards to the left, taking plenty of breaks to admire the view. Eventually the track becomes less steep and rejoins the start of the White Track. Turn right and in a few hundred metres you'll be back at the car.

PIGEON HOUSE MOUNTAIN (DIDTHUL)

SOUTH COAST

WALK: 6 km return

TIME REQUIRED: 2.5 hours

BEST TIME: Cooler months

GRADE: Hard

ENVIRONMENT: Stunning panoramic views over mountains and valleys, eucalypt forest

BEST MAP: 1:25 000 Milton, NSW Land and Property Information

TOILETS: Pit toilet in the picnic area at the start of the walk

FOOD: Milton, 40 minutes drive away, has cafes, pubs and supermarket

TIPS: Pick up a walking stick to make the steep ascent and descent a little easier

A steep walk with some exciting steel ladders at the end, takes you to the top of this iconic mountain, with stupendous views over Morton National Park and the South Coast.

The most distinctive mountain on the South Coast, with a summit 720 m above sea level, Pigeon House can be seen for many kilometres around. To Captain James Cook, the peak looked like a square pigeon house, but those who notice its breast-like shape with pointed nipple, will not be surprised to learn that it was a special Aboriginal women's place, called Didthul.

Follow the signs from Croobyar Rd out of Milton, or if coming from further south, look for signposted turnoffs from the Princes Highway.

[above] *The distinctive Pigeon House Mountain, or Didthul*

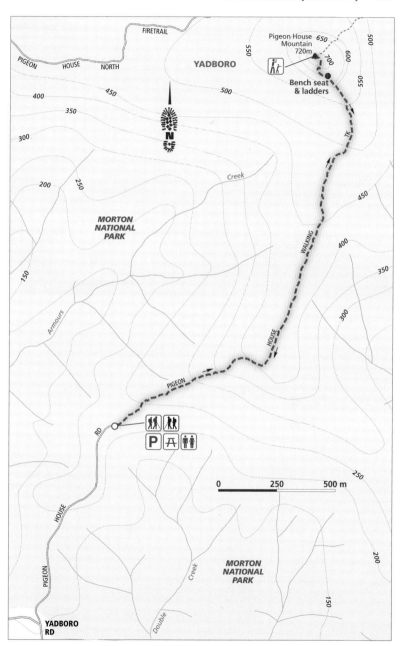

Trig station, with views over Byangee Mountain and The Castle

The unsealed roads are generally fairly good, but can contain some surprise potholes, and could be quite slippery after rain. Allow about 40 minutes drive from Milton to reach the signposted carpark, which has a pit toilet and shaded picnic area.

The walk has four sections. First, there is a steep climb out of the carpark, up an eroded, wide track, gaining about 200 vertical metres. It is fairly unrelenting, but there is a pleasant black and silvertop ash forest on either side. At the top of this section there is a rock platform on the right side of the track that offers some great views out to the coast, and provides a chance to catch your breath. You'll also see the summit of the mountain to the north.

The second section runs almost flat along the ridgetop through some forest and heathland, with wattles, hakeas, banksias, epacris and other native flowers. In mist it is moody and beautiful, and in clear weather it is a gentle and very enjoyable part of the walk.

A series of stairs marks the start of the third section, which climbs steadily through taller and wetter forests of woollybutts, stringybarks and sedges, finishing at the base of the summit cliffs, where there is a bench seat and the first of the steel ladders.

For many years, the final section had just a couple of basic steel ladders and a tricky rock scramble between them, but now there is a brilliantly engineered steel structure, joining steep stairs and ladders. Children and those with a poor head for heights may still struggle as the structure is see-through, and as the view opens up around you, it feels quite exposed.

At the top, the track winds across the summit to the lookout, which provides stunning views over flat-topped Byangee Mountain and The Castle beyond it, and into the deep valleys of the Budawangs. From elsewhere on the summit, you'll see the ocean, and views in every direction. Take note too of the eucalyptus that dominates the summit. It is a rare Pigeon House ash.

After a break, return to the car along the same track.

THE CASTLE

SOUTH COAST

WALK: 13 km return

TIME REQUIRED: 10 hours

BEST TIME: Clear, mild weather; winter is best for the steep ascent, but with short days, there is great potential to be caught out in the dark, so you will need to carry torches; in summer it could be ferociously hot

GRADE: Very hard: this is for experienced walkers only, it involves steep climbing with ropes and the potential to become dangerously lost

ENVIRONMENT: Dramatic wilderness, unfenced cliffs, steep mountains, caves, deep valleys, river crossing

BEST MAP: 1:25 000 Corang, NSW Land and Property Information

TOILETS: Pit toilets in the camping area and the carpark at the start of the walk

FOOD: Milton, an hour's drive away, has cafes, pubs and a supermarket

TIPS: Do not underestimate this walk – only well-prepared, experienced walkers should undertake it; bring a 20 m length of rope and some survival gear

[above] *Summit view over Byangee Mountain, Pigeon House and the ocean beyond*

The stuff of legends, the walk to The Castle is one of the best in the state. It is gruelling and potentially dangerous, but incredibly rewarding, with stupendous views of the Budawang Wilderness that have been described as some of the best in the state.

Talk with bushwalkers in Australia for long enough, and you'll soon hear some scary stories about ascents of The Castle. People have been caught high on its impenetrable walls in storms, have been forced to bivouac overnight, or become hopelessly lost in the maze of tracks. Even a straightforward ascent, where everything goes right, includes some tricky and exposed climbing, a gruelling ascent, a squeeze through a tunnel and a long, long day. Make no mistake, this is a serious undertaking, but an incredibly rewarding one and should be included on any bushwalker's bucket list.

The Castle lies deep in the area known as the Budawang Wilderness, on the border between Morton National Park and Budawang National Park. This area, explored by experienced, well-prepared bushwalkers, includes such legendary places as Monolith Valley.

Because time is fairly critical on this walk and you will want an early start, it is best to camp near the start of the walk – either at the simple Long Gully campground (off Long Gully Rd), or the Yadboro campground a few kilometres further back on Yadboro Rd.

Exposed walking, off the main route, on the eastern side

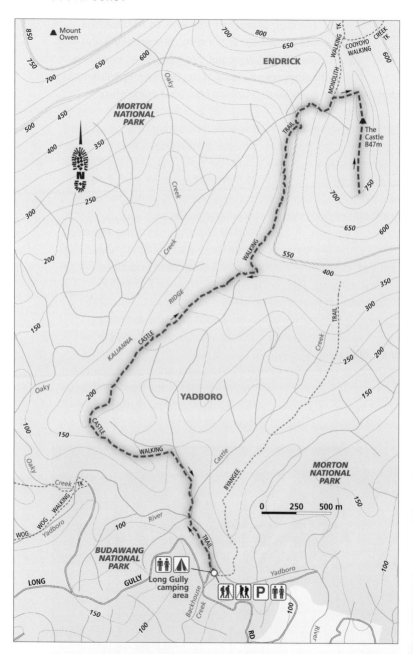

The walk starts in the day parking area near the Long Gully Campground, which is a 40 km drive from Milton, mainly on unsealed roads. The Castle looms menacingly above the campground, its steep walls daring you to storm them.

The area abounds with a rich variety of birds, including bowerbirds, wrens, quietly delightful gang-gang cockatoos, and screeching catbirds. There are also wombats, kangaroos and wallabies, and in summer the area comes alive with snakes, including tiger and brown snakes.

Many of the most epic tales of people getting lost on The Castle walk were in a time before the track became better maintained and defined, but there are still plenty of opportunities to take a wrong turn.

From the day parking area, the track follows the river for about 200 m before crossing over to the other side. Depending on the level of the river, there may be a combination of stepping stones and logs, or you may just have to get your feet wet. On the other side, the track dips in and out of a creekline in the moist forest before steadily climbing up Kalianna Ridge. The track is fairly easy to walk on and generally keeps to a steady gradient, so you should make fairly quick time on this section.

After an hour you'll be near the first rock slab which has a chain installed to help walkers up. From here you can get a sense of the height you have already gained and enjoy the first great views of the walk.

Once you reach the cliff line proper, the walk skirts awkwardly along the west (left) side. At times it ducks down steeply into the forest, and then curves back up to clamber over rocks at the base of the cliffs. Progress will be fairly slow. In one section – Rooty Hill – you'll walk almost entirely above the ground on the eroded roots of hardy mallees. All the time the cliff towers above, with its bronze and orange faces pocked with caves and other features.

Towards the end of the cliffline, you'll come across a fairly deep cave (a great place for a rest break in bad weather), before the track goes up another level. Within a few hundred metres, a conglomerate platform appears on the left of the track, with grand

Scaling fixed ropes to the summit

views over the Oaky Creek valley, Mt Nibelung and Mt Owen. A nearby rock spire looks a little like an Easter Island statue.

From here the track climbs sharply again, but now on stairs and cut logs installed by the national parks service.

The track forks at a triangular-shaped slightly cleared area (no signposts), with a small track veering up to the right (towards the cliffs) while the main track continues up the ridge towards the saddle and Monolith Valley beyond. You can climb The Castle from either track, but this text describes the route taking the right fork which heads straight up to the cliffs. At the cliff, it disappears into an improbable looking shaft in the rock – the legendary 'tunnel' shortcut that will take you right through the mountain and out the other side. The tunnel itself is a bit of a squeeze and large packs will need to be passed through, but it's great fun getting through this feature. On the other side, a rope will probably be needed to assist in the clamber down the steep little drop. A rope may already be in place but it's best not to count on this.

Once through the tunnel, clamber down a little further and join the path that heads to your right (now south) along the cliff.

At this point it is vital to start paying attention to little signs that indicate the correct track: arrows scraped on the rocks indicate the way, crosses or sticks or stones laid across the track warn of wrong turns. Some of the myriad side tracks appear (and are) well-travelled, but can lead you to precarious and dangerous positions. If any track starts getting narrower and more rugged, it is worth backtracking to look for an arrow. One commonly taken incorrect track leads countless people straight up a steep ascent when the real route (marked with arrows) veers diagonally left across a tricky boulder section.

The main route takes you up a gully and then goes almost directly up the tail end of The Castle, not up the cliffs on the eastern side. If you find yourself on an exposed cliff on the eastern side, with no fixed ropes in place, it is probably the wrong way.

If you are on the correct route, you will, near the very top, reach a tiered section of rock, which will probably have fixed ropes in place. Always tug on these ropes first, to check they are secure, and the first person up should also verify that they are a suitable aid. If in doubt, replace them with your own rope. If there are no fixed ropes in place, the best climber should clamber up and set a rope for the rest of the party.

The little scramble up here – on ledges initially, and then up a chimney – is quite exposed and some people may struggle with the height, but urge them on as you are nearly up to the stunning views at the top. Just take time and extreme care.

Clamber up the last little rock face (you can climb up through the half circle), and you will be standing on the plateau, 800 m above sea level, and 700 m above your starting point. On the eastern side are stupendous views over Byangee Mountain, Pigeon House and the Clyde Gorge.

You may be content to stop here, but if you have time, it's worth clambering the extra kilometre through the heath, sedgeland and rock platforms to the southern end of the plateau. It will take about half an hour each way and you'll be rewarded with even more views.

Enjoy the summit for a while, but remember it will probably take four hours or so to return down the mountain the same way, assuming nothing goes wrong.

DURRAS MOUNTAIN AND SNAKE BAY

SOUTH COAST

WALK: 12.5 km return

TIME REQUIRED: 4 hours

BEST TIME: Any time of year: in summer you can have a swim at the end, and in winter the seas can pound dramatically into the coastline, driven by fierce southerlies

GRADE: Moderate

ENVIRONMENT: Rainforest, rocky bays, dramatic coastline, eucalypt woodland, mountain

BEST MAP: www.environment.nsw.gov.au/NationalParks

TOILETS: Eco-toilet at the start of the walk

FOOD: Bateman's Bay, 30 minutes drive away, is a large town with takeaway outlets, restaurants and supermarkets

TIPS: Don't expect superlative, panoramic views from the top of the mountain – you will get snatches of vistas, rather than one great lookout

[above] *Murramarang National Park*

With a bit of everything, this walk has some lovely
coastal scenery, rainforest, a mountain and
wildlife, including lots of kangaroos.

There are two main walks from the delightful South Coast treasure
of Pebbly Beach, in Murramarang National Park, and this walk
combines them both into a mixed half-day adventure taking the
shape of a 'Y'. If you only have time to do one half of the walk, stick
with the flatter walk out to Snake Bay, which has lovely rainforest
pockets and an interesting coastline.

To begin, head north from the camping area (where eastern grey
kangaroos and wonga pigeons are often seen). The single large
track ducks through a gate and behind some rental cabins, then up
a rise into the start of the forest.

Two of the obvious dark-green rainforest plants you'll see along
this walk are cabbage palms (growing up to about 15 m in height

Cycads and thick forest on the flanks of Durras Mountain

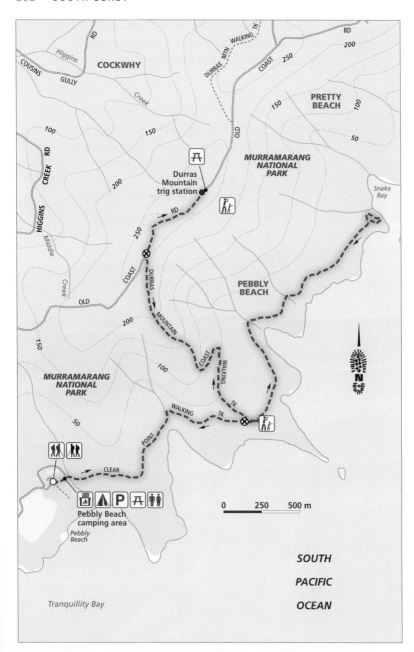

Snatching views from the summit

and with multi-fingered leaves like massive fans], and cycads, usually growing to 1.5 m or so.

The track potters along the coast for 1.6 km, with gentle rises and falls. Ignore the track diversion off to the right and you will come to an obvious, marked fork in the track. You can choose to do just one of the forks, but this description covers both.

The track to the left snakes up Durras Mountain, and if you are keen for a longer walk along the ridge, drifts along to Pretty Beach.

It rises 250 m over a couple of kilometres through some lovely forest with marble gums, cycads and vine forest. The gradient is fairly consistent and the track is relatively easy to walk, but it's worth stopping regularly and enjoying the views through the trees of the coastline far below.

Towards the top of the mountain the track flattens out and meets a larger track from the left. Turn right here through a grassy section with kangaroos to a picnic table and the Durras Mountain trig station. There is no single spot to gain a panoramic view, so it's worth exploring the vicinity. For example, turn right at the water tank, and head downhill a hundred metres or so to a spot offering a view of the coast to the south including Montague Island. There are other unmarked places near the summit to look west towards the distinctive shape of Pigeon House Mountain.

After a well-earned break, return back down the mountain to the fork by the coast and then head left. Almost straight away you'll see a sign and a small track to Clear Pt on the right. This beautiful peninsula has large open grassy areas (often with kangaroos) and few trees, so views up and down the coast are plentiful. It's a great spot for a break, or to explore some rock platforms where you might see sooty oystercatchers (black birds with carrot-like long bright orange beaks) and other waders.

Follow the track for another couple of kilometres, as it winds through some beautiful rainforest patches with prolific birdlife. A bench seat in a cool spot underneath some cabbage palms and a well-made wooden bridge indicate you are nearly at Snake Bay. The track peters out at the bay, with a tangle of small footpads leading down to the rocky foreshore. Enjoy exploring this interesting little cove for as long as you like, before heading back to the fork, and then along the coast back to Pebbly Beach for a swim or a barbecue.

Eastern grey kangaroo

BIG HOLE AND MARBLE ARCH

WALK: 12.5 km return

TIME REQUIRED: 3 hours

BEST TIME: Dry mornings, to give you more time to explore the canyon system

GRADE: Mostly moderate, but the end is steep and the canyon is tricky

ENVIRONMENT: Eucalypt forest, canyon, cave

BEST MAP: Deua National Park Visitors Guide, *National Parks and Wildlife Service*

TOILETS: Pit toilet at the start and finish of walk

FOOD: Braidwood has service stations, a pub, general stores and some takeaway shops

TIPS: The most spectacular feature on this walk is the Big Hole, after just 1.5 km, so you can turn around there if you don't have much time

[above] *Glorious heathland*

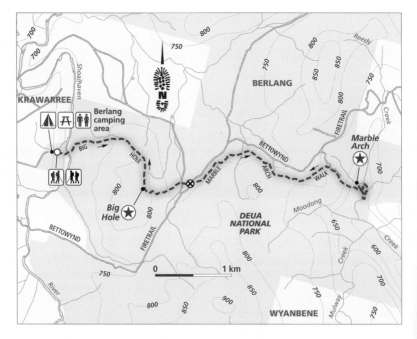

This walk is interesting rather than spectacular. Much of it is flat and through closed-in forest, but you'll wade across the Shoalhaven River, and discover two remarkable features: a giant sinkhole, 100 m deep and approximately 35 m across, and a canyon and cave with attractive marble bands.

Deua National Park is 100 km south-east of Canberra, and covers 1220 sq km of rainforest, eucalypt forest, swamps, heath and rocky scrub. This walk starts at the Berlang Camping Area, which is 40 km south of the small town of Braidwood. Most maps advise taking the Krawaree Rd from Braidwood, but all signs in the area seem to call it the Cooma Rd.

The entrance off the road to the camping area and the Big Hole is well marked, and you'll trundle along a dirt road for 1 km, turning sharply to the left at one point. The camping area is very, very simple, with a few picnic tables, a pit toilet and a self-book-in

Walking through the canyon

Common wombat

system. There is no tap water, but the Shoalhaven River is nearby. Boiling or other purification is recommended. There is only one track from the camping area, and it leads straight down to the river. Although there are stepping stones, most of the time you will have to wade across, along the slippery and uneven stones. Beware: the water can be surprisingly cold, and the crossing is long enough to make it potentially painful on cosseted toes.

The track from here is a little uneven and rises through a forest to a small heathland. Catch your breath at this point and take a look around at the views behind and to the side of the deep green mountains and open farmland.

After a few hundred metres more, you'll see a sign warning that you are approaching the Big Hole. There is a well-constructed lookout at the Big Hole, but it would be easy for excited children to find themselves precariously positioned on the wrong side of the fence, on the edge of a 100 m drop.

The hole itself is very impressive, being round, about 35 m across, and seemingly in the middle of nowhere. Its walls are composed of sandstone and conglomerate, but it is believed to have formed when surface rock collapsed progressively into a cavity formed within limestone. There is now a rich fern forest growing at the bottom.

The track (less defined from here) continues past the left of the lookout. Less-enthusiastic walkers might want to turn back here, but those who continue will find little things of interest along the way. Note how the termite mounds get bigger and bigger, until they are the size of small cars, and how they change colour with the underlying soil. You'll see plentiful signs of wombat activity and, if you're lucky in the early morning or late afternoon, a wombat moving around outside its burrow. There are bound to be swamp wallabies and eastern grey kangaroos among the banksias, acacias, stringybark and creamy gum trees. Relatively early on, the thin track crosses a fire trail – keep going straight over the trail (and remember to do the same on the way back).

It takes about an hour at a fast pace to finish the flat section of the walk, before reaching the short but steep downhill to the creek. The forest here is more diversified, with a variety of tree species, shape and age. At the bottom of the stairs (be careful in wet conditions) the track dives down into the creek on the right. The rocks in the creek are likely to be slippery.

From here be careful if it there has been recent rain, and check water levels. Do not enter the cave and canyon if very heavy rain is expected while you are there.

The limestone cave, or arch, is initially unimpressive, but keep your eyes open for bats and the bands of white and red marble. A torch may be helpful. Make sure you go right through the cave – the dark section at the back is only about 10 m long, and then you'll be out into the sunshine again. From here, turn right into the creek and within another 10 m or so, you'll be entering a very narrow slot canyon. Those who have been canyoning in the Blue Mountains may not find it spectacular, but it is a cute little canyon, and has the unusual bonus of marble streaks through it. Unless the canyon is completely dry, you are likely to get wet shoes through this section as the polished walls are extremely slippery, and there is not much room to move but in the pools of water.

Travel down the creek as far as you like – the marble band continues for about 1 km, but the best sections are near the beginning. Return the same way to the campsite. If your shoes are still wet from the canyon by the time you reach the Shoalhaven again, then you might as well just keep them on when you wade back across.

WOLUMLA PEAK

SOUTH COAST

WALK: 8.5 km return

TIME REQUIRED: 2.5 hours

BEST TIME: Clear days, cooler weather

GRADE: Moderate to hard

ENVIRONMENT: Thick gum forest, views over mountains and farmland

BEST MAP: Exploring the South East Forests National Park, NSW National Parks and Wildlife Service

TOILETS: Pit toilet at the Myrtle Mt picnic area, 1 km north of the start

FOOD: The walk is halfway between the small towns of Wyndham and Candelo, both of which have limited shops

TIPS: Non-walkers can still enjoy the great view at the top of Wolumla Peak by dropping walkers off, then driving around to Wolumla Peak Rd (most of which is unsealed), and parking at the top of the climb

[above] *A woolly trunk, clothed in a coat of many colours*

A very steep fire trail, through rich, changing forest types, leads to a fire lookout with panoramic views over the Bega Valley, towards the Snowy Mountains, and out to sea.

A great workout for heart, lungs and legs, this steep trail starts on Myrtle Mountain Rd, halfway between Candelo and Wyndham. Official national park guides say the walk starts in the Myrtle Mountain picnic area, and then follows the road south for 1 km, but you can avoid the walk along the road by parking in a spacious area on the west side of the road, opposite the Yurammie Link Fire Trail (1 km south of the picnic area).

The walk starts out on the Yurammie Link Fire Trail (take care when crossing the road to start the walk, as it is on a bend). You'll quickly gain about 150 m in elevation while moving through a forest of stringybark, grey box, maidens gum and tall monkey gums. In the 1950s koalas were prolific here, and there is still a

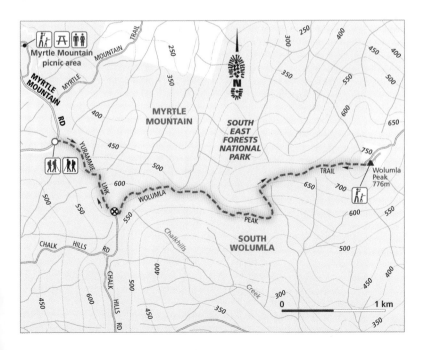

Koala

small population, so remember to look for them when you stop for a breather.

After 1 km you will reach a fork with another fire trail. Turn left, through an area of moist forest, with tree-ferns and other lush species. The trail soon heads down a very, very steep and slippery slope to a saddle.

The final 2 km rises 300 m, passing through a range of drier then wetter forest types, with tantalising views towards the mountains to the south and the farming country to the north. Look out for lyrebirds lurking on the forest floor and wedge-tailed eagles roosting in the canopy. There

Tall, moist forest

View from the fire-spotting tower

are also a variety of flowers and plenty of big trees in some superb old-growth forest. It is easy to see why the much of this region was logged until protests began in the 1980s, leading to the formation of the South East Forests National Park.

In the final few hundred metres, the trail becomes quite rubbly, steep and awkward to walk on, but you will soon be at the top, at an elevation of nearly 800 m. Beside the trig station is a fire-spotting tower. The stairs up to the narrow balcony around the cabin are usually open for visitors (just ask permission if the tower is manned). On a clear day the views are impressive – from rugged mountains (possibly capped with snow) to the west and south, the coastline near Merimbula and Tathra to the east, and the expansive dairy country of the Bega Valley to the north. It's a fantastic reward for a solid climb.

If a non-walker hasn't driven around to collect you at the top, then take the same journey, all the way back downhill.

LIGHT TO LIGHT

SOUTH COAST

WALK: 32 km one way

TIME REQUIRED: 2 days

BEST TIME: Late spring, when the water is inviting and the wildflowers are out

GRADE: Easy to moderate: generally flat, but with some rock-hopping and stairs

ENVIRONMENT: Beautiful coastal scenery, remote beaches and coves, coloured rock platforms, heathland, forest

BEST MAP: Light to Light Walk, NSW National Parks and Wildlife Service

TOILETS: Pit toilets in the major camping areas and at the start and end of the walk

FOOD: Eden, the nearest major town from either end, has plenty of options

TIPS: At the time of writing there is no reasonable option for transport between the two ends of the walk. So, it's best to have at least two cars to the walking party so one can be left at the far end

[above] *Beach at Saltwater Creek*

With some of the most colourful coastline in NSW, and a wealth of wildlife, this relatively flat walk is an absolute treat. Combine that with some great camping spots, and the opportunity to stay in a lighthouse keepers' cottage, and you have the makings of a NSW classic, although it is still only walked end-to-end by a few.

Right near the bottom of the state, Ben Boyd National Park can be wild and windy, or sedate and stunningly radiant, dressed in multicoloured robes of orange, maroon, green and sapphire. The rocks along the coast here – some of the oldest coastal rocks in NSW – have multiple layers and rich colours, and are set beside a sparkling sea that changes colours from aqua and turquoise to azure, navy and the legendary sapphire for which this stretch of coast is named.

Due to poor organisation by locals, this one-way walk has no easy transport option, making life difficult if you have one car. But with a few friends and a couple of cars, it is a dream. Allow about 1.5 hours to drop a car at one end and to stash a water drop in the bushes at Saltwater Creek (the halfway campsite). If you don't feel like carrying a full pack the whole way, it's also a good idea to leave

Mowarry Point

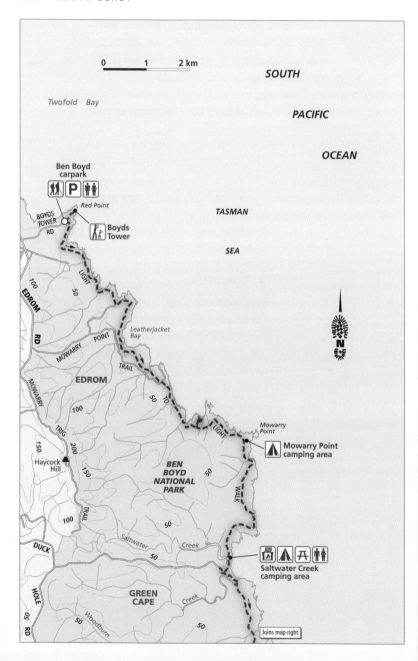

Joins map right

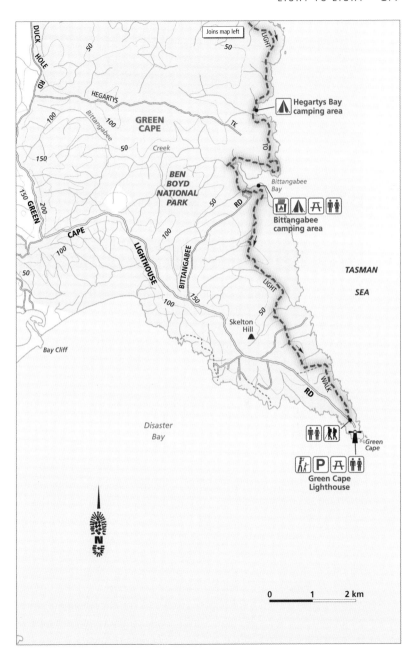

Colourful beach boulders

tents and other heavier gear here. Tent sites cost $10 per adult per night, with a self-registration system. Bookings will be needed during the Christmas and Easter school holidays.

You can walk the track in either direction. The text that follows describes the route north to south.

DAY ONE: 14 KM

From Eden, drive 18 km south along the Princes Highway then turn east on to Edrom Rd. Drive another 16 km then take the turnoff to Ben Boyd carpark.

Start by wandering around the surprisingly beautiful and well-maintained sandstone construction called Boyds Tower. Originally intended to be a lighthouse, it instead served as a lookout for the whaling industry and, poignantly, there are a couple of lookouts near the base of the tower that provide great vantage points for today's whale watchers. Humpbacks are most commonly seen here in late winter or early spring on their southerly migration. Keep an eye out for other marine life, including turtles and dolphins.

The Light to Light track south is well-marked the whole way, with posts and regular large signs. Occasionally other unmarked tracks or fire trails will cross it, but just keep following the signs.

It initially drifts through thick tea tree forests that have been battered and bashed by coastal storms and strong winds. Occasionally it meanders through forests of woollybutt, ironbark and other solid gums before breaking out into delightful Leatherjacket Bay. The rocks here are rich in iron oxide, giving them vibrant crimson and maroon hues, and the water is gin-clear, allowing you to see deep into rock pools.

You are bound to spot eastern grey kangaroos on the next stretch to Mowarry Pt, as the tall forests and banksia woodlands give way to more open grass country. You'll see the gorgeous, cream-sanded beach at Mowarry Pt well before you reach it. It's a marked detour of a few hundred metres off the track and a great spot for a swim, some lunch and to just enjoy life for a while. Camping is permitted at Mowarry Pt, but there are no toilets or other facilities, and fires are not permitted.

When you can peel yourself away, it's only another 4 km or so to your overnight spot at Saltwater Creek. The track takes you pleasantly through more thick tea tree and woollybutt forests

Rock-hopping at Leatherjacket Bay

Southern brown bandicoot

before coming out onto the beach at Saltwater Creek, beside a lagoon.

The excellent campsite – with a dozen sites or so – has toilets, gas barbecues, a great beach, and is frequented by all manner of wildlife, including wrens, kangaroos, southern brown bandicoots, massive brush-tailed possums and some very crafty currawongs determined to share your dinner.

DAY TWO: 18 KM

Starting with a stroll along the beach, then a tricky hop (or wade) across the creek, this day's route takes you a little way inland for long stretches and doesn't quite have the spectacular coastal scenery of the previous day. However, it initially takes you into some spectacular waist-high heathland that blooms with all manner of flowers, including yellow and orange peas, pink correa bells, white hakeas and multi-coloured orchids. After a few kilometres you'll even get a glimpse of the Green Cape Lighthouse, which will seem much closer than it is.

The track migrates through a changing tide of ecosystems, including a native pine forest, and a tall forest where towering white-trunked gums stand like masts in a sea of lime-green bracken. Peeking through the undergrowth you're bound to see swamp wallabies, more kangaroos, goannas and, if you're particularly lucky, a wombat or two. Off the coast, you might see sea-eagles soaring and a seal splashing in a bay. It's even possible to see albatross out to sea.

You'll pass another little hike-in camp spot called Hegartys Bay before crossing a cascading creek on your way to Bittangabee Bay. This is a great option for lunch, with pit toilets, barbecues and a lovely little beach. (It also has a large camping area, with more than 30 sites.)

The bay was used as supply port for the Green Cape Lighthouse (with goods transported the last 7 km to the lighthouse overland by

The heathland blooms in all shades of the rainbow

a horse-drawn tram). The ruins of a stone storehouse can be seen by the bay. An extra hundred metres or so up the hill there are more ruins, in this case, of a farmhouse that was partly constructed in the 1840s but probably never completed.

The final stretch to Green Cape again deviates a fair way from the coast, through more lovely heathland, dry woodland and thick banksia woodland. The walking is easy and you have a good chance of seeing rare ground parrots and a host of other birds. Within a couple of hours you'll find yourself nearing the end.

You'll pass a small cemetery just before you get to the 29 m lighthouse (which was the largest concrete structure in NSW when it was built in 1883). Buried here are many of the 71 people who perished when the steamship *Ly-ee-moon* crashed onto nearby rocks in 1886 (despite the lighthouse being there).

For walkers today, the lighthouse provides an exclamation mark at the end of this superb coastal trek. You can take a tour of the lighthouse, or those keen for a special treat can stay at the lightkeepers' cottages on the headland. Book at the Merimbula office of the National Parks and Wildlife Service: (02) 6495 5000.

Alpine meadow and Mt Jagungal

SYDNEY

CANBERRA

ACT AND SNOWY MOUNTAINS

The alpine areas of the ACT and NSW provide fantastic bushwalking opportunities, particularly in the early summer when the alpine meadows erupt with wildflowers and the tarns and lakes sparkle like jewels. The air up here is clear and inviting, and the views from the roof of Australia are some of the best to be had in the country.

BLACK MOUNTAIN VIA BOTANIC GARDENS

ACT AND SNOWY MOUNTAINS

WALK: 9 km loop

TIME REQUIRED: 3 hours

BEST TIME: A clear, cool day

GRADE: Moderate

ENVIRONMENT: Botanic gardens, eucalypt forest, extensive views

BEST MAP: Black Mountain Summit Walk, available from the Botanic Gardens Visitor Centre at the start of the walk

TOILETS: At the Australian National Botanic Gardens Visitor Centre, elsewhere in the gardens and at Telstra Tower

FOOD: Canberra shops or the Telstra Tower cafe

TIPS: Bring a picnic and spend some extra time enjoying the botanic gardens

This walk starts in the magnificent Australian National Botanic Gardens, then climbs through lovely eucalypt forest to reach Telstra Tower on Black Mountain, one of the most prominent landmarks in Canberra, with extensive views on a clear day over the ACT.

Plenty of people drive to the lookout on Black Mountain, but in doing so miss two of the ACT's great botanical wonders: the stunning Botanic Gardens, perhaps the most beautifully laid out of all our botanic gardens and featuring only native plants from around the country; and Black Mountain itself, which has the greatest diversity of plants in the ACT.

[above] *Rainforest Gully in the Australian National Botanic Gardens*

Unlike many of the granitic surrounding mountains, the bulk of Black Mountain consists of sandstone.

The network of tracks up and around the mountain can be joined at various points, but the most interesting spot to start the walk is at the Botanic Gardens (although it will cost you to park your car there). Pop into the visitor centre to get a copy of the Black Mountain Summit Walk map and the visitor guide to the gardens.

The route up the mountain starts from the 'back gate' at the opposite end of the gardens, so you start off with a lovely walk through the Rainforest Gully and past the Rock Garden and Eucalypt Lawn. Keep high up the gardens, and clear signage will point you towards the Black Mountain walk.

It's more than a kilometre through the gardens, and once you reach the Black Mountain Gate, the shortest route to the summit and back is 5.4 km. The gate is locked at 4.30pm each day.

Once through the gate, cross to the fire trail marked 'Black Mountain Summit Walk'. After about 100 m, the route leads to a thinner walking track, and climbs steadily through lovely woodland with scribbly gums, drooping lime-coloured cherry ballart and red stringybark. The track is obvious and offers very pleasant walking. Ignore one small track that comes in from the right.

The walk starts in the lush environment of the Australian National Botanic Gardens

As you near the top of the mountain, you will reach an X-junction, with the yellow concrete Summit Track continuing straight ahead, and the Forest Track (not signposted) crossing it. The Forest Track loops around the mountain, keeping to approximately the same altitude, and has some excellent information signs. Turn right and follow this track through patches of much thinner eucalypts on the more exposed western side of the mountain. The track is a little rougher than what you have been walking on, and after about 1 km

Telstra Tower opened in 1980

pops over a little creek before encountering Black Mountain Drive. Cross over the road and you'll see the continuation of the Forest Track ahead. Instead of taking this, head up the mountain, on the track to the left, which will bring you to the 812 m high summit and the 192.5 m Telstra Tower in about five minutes. You can pay to go to the viewing platforms inside, visit the cafe or restaurant, or endeavour to ignore the whole thing and just enjoy the views over Canberra from the ground-level viewing areas.

To return a different way, head back down to the spot where the Forest Track meets the road. Proceed about 20 m into the carpark, and then take one of the small tracks down to the left. Most of the network of tracks and picnic areas here join one rough track that descends quite sharply downhill, back through the eucalypt forest and down to a large water tank. Walk past the tank, and you'll join a slightly larger track. When it swings very close to the road, you'll join a large management trail that roughly follows the fence line of the Botanic Gardens, still taking you through quite lovely woodland. The management trail rises slightly before swinging around to the right, back down to the botanic gardens gate you left through, after about 1 km.

Take a different route back through the 40 ha of gardens, dallying for as long as you can. There are 74 000 individual plants here, representing 6200 species, making it the world's most comprehensive living display of Australian plants, and any nature lover will find plenty to love here.

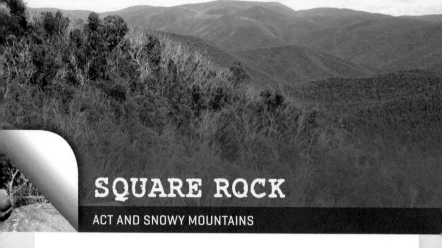

SQUARE ROCK

ACT AND SNOWY MOUNTAINS

WALK: *9 km return*

TIME REQUIRED: *3.5 hours*

BEST TIME: *A clear day*

GRADE: *Easy*

ENVIRONMENT: *Snow gum and alpine ash forests, granite boulders and cliffs*

BEST MAP: *Square Rock Walking Track brochure, available from Namadgi National Park Visitor Centre and usually in a box at track head*

TOILETS: *At Gibraltar Falls, 6 km back on Corin Rd*

FOOD: *Canberra suburbs such as Tuggeranong have plenty of options*

TIPS: *Bring some lunch and enjoy a long break at the surprise at the end*

Although a pleasant journey through a wildlife-rich forest, the beauty of this walk is the stunning surprise at the end – an exciting jumble of huge granite boulders on the edge of a cliff, providing a glorious natural playground with awesome views.

Few people realise that about half of the ACT is taken up by Namadgi National Park, an alpine wilderness with snow-capped peaks, ranges, camping areas and large tracts of forest. There are some very special

[above] *Views over Tidbinbilla Nature Reserve and Namadgi National Park*

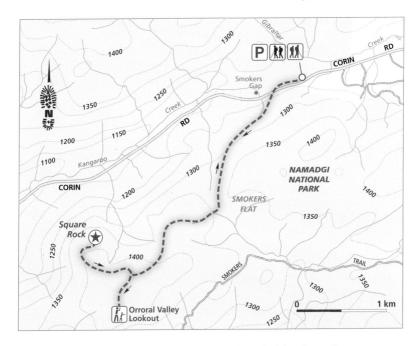

spots that can be reached in less than an hour's drive from the centre of Canberra, and this little gem is one of them.

Take Corin Rd off Tidbinbilla Rd in the south-west of Canberra, and travel along it for 13.5 km. You will pass the lovely Gibraltar Falls picnic area 6 km before the start of the walk (it has barbecues, toilets and a very short walk to the lovely falls) and an area on the left-hand side of the road marked 'Smokers Carpark'. Travel just past Corin Forest Mountain Retreat on the right-hand side to the little carpark marked 'Square Rock Walking Track'.

The signposted and easy-to-follow track initially runs parallel with Corin Rd for a few hundred metres, before crossing the road (the track continues on the opposite side about 10 m to the right). There is abundant wildlife through this area, particularly reptiles, so keep an eye out for a huge variety of skinks, little dragons and snakes such as eastern browns. There are also wallabies and kangaroos, and myriad birds such as olive whistlers twittering among the alpine ash and other gum trees. You might even

Spectacular summit of Square Rock

spot a wedge-tailed eagle soaring overhead. There is also a rich collection of colourful fungi.

The track ascends from about 1200 m to 1350 m, so there are a few steps and gentle rises, but they shouldn't trouble most walkers. Along the way you'll see some stunning collections of rounded granite boulders, formed by erosion over the past 400 million years or so.

At Smokers Flat, you're bound to hear the calls of multiple frogs in a pretty little wetland on the right-hand side of the track. There are stepping stones through the boggy grass. A track on the left leads to Smokers Fire Trail – ignore it and continue straight through the snow gums, mountain gums, peas and other thick vegetation.

About 2 km past Smokers Flat it's worth taking a 1 km return detour to Orroral Valley lookout. The small boulders and view aren't nearly as spectacular as what is to come, but it's a nice place to stop and have a drink.

Back on the main track, it's less than a kilometre to Square Rock (some of which is downhill) and the end of the track. About 50 m before the end, there is a sign warning of cliffs ahead, and if you have young children, it would be good to keep a close eye on them from here.

There is a short steel ladder up to the rocks, which provide a fantastic playground for the adventurous, with tunnels to crawl through and huge boulders to clamber onto. The cliffs are quite vertiginous and overhanging, and you are advised to take care as you enjoy this stunning spot and its 180-degree views. In close you'll find multiple skinks, large and small, sunning themselves on the granite.

Take the same route back to the car.

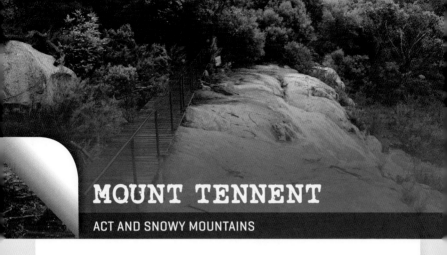

MOUNT TENNENT

ACT AND SNOWY MOUNTAINS

WALK: 15 km return

TIME REQUIRED: 4 hours

BEST TIME: A clear day in autumn

GRADE: Moderate

ENVIRONMENT: Snow gum forest and alpine grasses, mountain views

BEST MAP: Rooftop's Namadgi - ACT South Activities Map

TOILETS: Namadgi Visitor Centre has flushing toilets

FOOD: Canberra shops or Tharwa general store

TIPS: The visitor centre closes at 4pm on weekdays and 4.30pm on weekends, so it is best to park just outside the visitor centre gates

This is a relatively gentle walk to the summit of a major feature in the south-west of the ACT. It takes you through some lovely terrain, including snow gum forest.

Few of us have time to complete the 650 km Australian Alpine Track, even though it is one of the premier long-distance walks in the country. However, most people can at least do the first part of the walk from its northerly starting point, the Namadgi National Park Visitor Centre, to the looming 1384 m summit of Mt Tennent, which is the dominant mountain seen from Canberra's southern suburbs. Originally called Tharwa by the Indigenous inhabitants, it was later named after an early bushranger, John Tennent, who frequented the area in the late 1820s.

[above] *Boardwalks over polished granite*

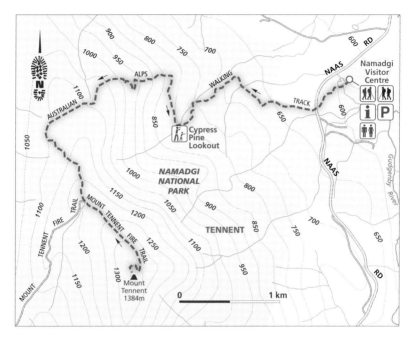

It's a long, constant ascent to the summit from an altitude of about 600 m, but it stays relatively gentle the whole way, and there are plenty of opportunities to take a break and enjoy the views back over productive grazing land if it is a clear day, or, if the mist is swirling, in close at the rich vegetation and bird life.

Start by parking just outside the Namadgi National Park Visitor Centre gate (in case you are late back). You can walk straight out the back door of the centre to the start of the walk. The path winds past the waterhole to the road, then crosses the road and starts heading up the hill.

Through this low, forested section, you'll cross a few bubbling mountain creeks, see a variety of twittering birds, such as grey fantails, and admire a range of fungi, from chunky, dinner-plate-sized bracket fungi through to standard mushrooms and delicate coral fungi. Large granite boulders magically appear around corners, in fantastic shapes and forms.

It will take fit walkers about half an hour to get to Cypress Pine Lookout, which has a cut-out bench for a quick rest. Continue on the well-defined track, but if it is wet, be careful on the slabs of granite, as they can be slippery. Some have extra steps cut into them and it's wise to use them. You'll cross (on bridges) a couple of excitedly bubbling creeks along the way.

After nearly 5 km of constant ascent, you'll reach a fork. The track to Booroomba Rocks, to the right, is well worth taking if you have a car at the other end, or are camping, but otherwise head left toward the summit of Mt Tennent. If you are walking to the summit and back, it will take at least an hour from here (2.5 km each way).

The forest opens out past this point, with tussock alpine grasses between the resplendent gums, and there is a small downhill stretch (the only one). You are bound to see eastern grey kangaroos and swamp wallabies in this section and at times hundreds of orange and black butterflies lift up from the grasses. Much of the mountain was burnt in the 2003 fires, but wattles and other vegetation are now well and truly covering the scars.

Alpine grasses and multi-hued gums

Flush of fungi

After about a kilometre through some open grassland, you'll reach a well-defined fire trail. Head left up the fire trail, which will become steepish, past some magnificent trees and more grazing kangaroos. As you approach the summit, keep an eye out for lyrebirds.

The top of the mountain has the ubiquitous telecommunications tower, but also a fire tower that may allow access to the first level, where you can enjoy tremendous views over southern Canberra, all the way to the city.

Return the same way, enjoying the extensive views east on the way down.

MOUNT JAGUNGAL

ACT AND SNOWY MOUNTAINS

WALK: *45 km loop*

TIME REQUIRED: *2–3 days*

BEST TIME: *Summer*

GRADE: *Hard*

ENVIRONMENT: *Remote alpine wilderness, with meadows, snow gum forests, alpine streams and valleys, and a mountain over 2000 m*

BEST MAP: *Rooftop's Kosciuszko National Park Forest Activities Map Jindabyne–Khancoban*

TOILETS: *Pit toilets at track head and at Derschkos, O'Keefe and Round Mountain huts*

FOOD: *Khancoban, 44 km away from the head of the track, has a few shops and takeaways*

TIPS: *Personal locator beacons (often called EPIRBs) can be hired quite cheaply from Kosciuszko National Park offices. The huts are fantastic places to stay a night, but you must travel with a tent and be well prepared for all weather conditions at any time of year. In winter this area is likely to be completely covered in snow. Those with mountain bikes could tackle Mt Jagungal in a day by riding the Round Mountain Trail to the Tumut River, then walking to the summit and back. Keen and experienced cross-country skiers would also enjoy this in winter.*

[above] *Alpine meadows on the way to Mt Jagungal*

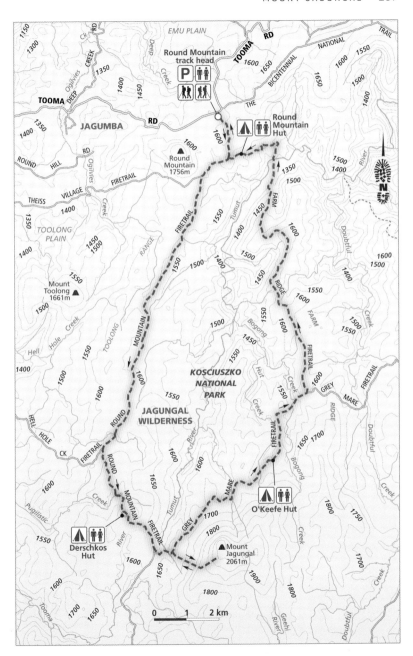

At the heart of Kosciuszko National Park, this wilderness area is visited by far fewer people than other areas of the park, and you will barely see another soul. However, the excellent huts and well-defined tracks mean you can have a remote alpine experience while still staying relatively safe and untroubled. Mt Jagungal itself stands on its own, some 500 m above the surrounding plain, and is Australia's most northerly and easterly mountain over 2000 m, so has far-reaching, 360-degree views. Unlike some other peaks in the Snowys, it has a classic mountain shape, so you actually get a sense of climbing something substantial.

This walk can be done in 2 long, hard days, but those with more time are encouraged to do it over 3, allowing more time to just enjoy the serenity of this beautiful place. There are plenty of hut and camping options, and abundant fresh water in alpine streams, meaning you don't have to carry more than a few litres at any time.

Park at the Round Mountain track head, which is 44 km east of Khancoban along Tooma Rd. There is a 'trip intentions' book at the start to document the date and time, and your proposed route.

The first day takes you quickly along the easy-to-walk, well-maintained Round Mountain Trail, past 1755 m Round Mountain.

Yellow everlasting daisies

The bulk of this day is across alpine grasslands, abundant in wildflowers in spring and summer. Because it is such open country, wildlife isn't obvious, but you will see evidence of feral deer, alpine foxes, abundant eagle nests in the dead snow gums, and birds such as Richard's pipits (groundlarks), magpies and stunning flame robins.

After just 1.5 km, a track will come in from the left, which is the way you will be coming back. Round Mountain Hut is less than a kilometre down this track and is a good place to stay or camp if you have arrived late in the day.

You will need to jump across a couple of the streams along the way, but others have sturdy concrete bridges across them. The walking is very easy, and you will make good time, even with a heavy pack. Mt Jagungal looms over the track ahead, an unmistakable landmark in this relatively flat country.

Nearly 12 km from the start, the Hell Hole Trail comes in from the right. Ignore this and continue another 2.3 km to Derschkos Hut. This surprisingly good refuge has stacked firewood inside and out, a loo with a view, three rooms inside, a bush saw and other tools, and a large wall map. It can provide respite from bad weather, or a place to stay the night.

If you have the time, energy and good weather, you might want to leave your packs at the hut and make a lightweight afternoon assault on the summit which is about a 9 km return hike from here. On any walk in this area though, all walkers should, at a minimum, take rain gear and warm clothes.

Another option is to continue walking across flat terrain another 2 km to the headwaters of the Tumut River. There is a junction along this section where the Round Mountain Trail joins the Grey Mare Trail which comes in from the right. Your way to the bottom of the mountain is clearly to the left.

After a short forested section on Jagungal's skirt, you will reach the lovely headwaters of the Tumut River – a great place to fill up water bottles for the ascent. There are a few possible campsites here, but if you do camp, be extremely careful not to pollute the water.

Derschkos Hut

The little footpad of a track begins beside the stream and goes almost straight up. It can be hard to follow in places among the thick, hip-high vegetation (long pants are advised) but basically it goes up the most obvious treeless section towards the ridge that extends south-west from the summit.

The track becomes steeper and steeper in the last section before the ridge, and if you are still carrying a full pack (because you are planning on camping on the ridge), the going will be very tough. However, the rewards begin as soon as you reach the ridge, with widespread views in the direction from which you have come, and some lovely trees unravaged by the 2003 fire. The snow gums up here are bent over by the wind, and there are pink triggerplants and long, lush alpine grasses among the granite boulders. A flat section sheltered among the trees would be a great place to camp, although there is no water on the ridge.

The footpad to the summit might look like it's going to skirt round the mountain, but it eventually swings around and takes you scrambling up the lichen-covered boulders from the south. From the top, the view extends unimpeded in every direction, across rugged terrain to distant mountains. It is completely exposed and the weather at this altitude can change in minutes, but if you are prepared, it's a great spot to just sit, rest and enjoy the unbroken horizons of wilderness.

On the way up to the ridge, you will have noticed a handful of rock cairns which help mark the way down if the weather closes in. There are also some wooden posts. Still, it is most advisable to be off the ridge well before the weather turns nasty.

Once back down on the main track, continue in a north-easterly direction, with the mountain on your right. You'll travel through some lovely forest and spy Round Mountain in the distance, which is now your guide home.

About 6 km from the Tumut River headwaters, having passed an automated weather station, you'll reach the delightful O'Keefe Hut, with an open fireplace, comfy furniture and decorated with 1930s newspapers. Many maps point out that O'Keefe Hut was burnt down in 2003. It was, but a hut was rebuilt here in Jan 2011. This is an excellent place to stop for the night – either after a long first day on a two-day trip, or after an easy second day on a three-day trip. There are great camping areas around the hut as well.

A couple of kays after leaving the hut, the trail descends steeply to the freezing Bogong Creek, which may have to be waded without shoes. Be careful walking along the creek with packs because hidden holes will jump out and grab legs. This is your last chance to fill up water bottles before reaching the Tumut River close to 10 km distant, and you have a few steep hills to cover.

The first is straight after the creek – one of the few nasty steep pinches on the whole walk. At the top, as you are recovering

Contorted gums

your breath, keep an eye out on the left for the Farm Ridge Trail signposted just off the track. It isn't as well defined as the Grey Mare Trail, but you won't miss it as long as you remember to look for it.

Take the Farm Ridge Trail, which immediately ascends again to a ridge, where there are some lovely spots among large trees for a break. This trail is not as easy to walk along as the going thus far, and you will travel considerably slower than you have been. You will walk along the ridge through forests and open country before the long descent into the large Tumut River Valley. You will see the river and at times it will feel as though the track is taking the longest possible route to get down, but it does follow a fairly strict northerly route.

The river is more than 7 m wide at this point and will have to be waded. The rocks may be slippery. On the other side, another harsh ascent awaits up slippery clay, then the track veers sharply west. It is only about 4 km from the river back to the car, but the first 3 km are uphill and at this stage that will feel extremely taxing. A lovely cascading stream provides some distraction, as does Round Mountain Hut.

When the track rejoins the Round Mountain Trail, turn right and the carpark will reappear in 1.5 km.

Summit of Mt Jagungal

MOUNT KOSCIUSZKO VIA BLUE LAKE

ACT AND SNOWY MOUNTAINS

WALK: 22 km loop

TIME REQUIRED: 9 hours

BEST TIME: Early summer, when the wildflowers are usually at their best and there is some snow on the ground; in winter this walk is completely under snow

GRADE: Moderate but long

ENVIRONMENT: Glorious high country above the treeline, alpine lakes

BEST MAP: Rooftop's Kosciuszko National Park Forest Activities Map Jindabyne–Khancoban

TRANSPORT: Car to Charlottes Pass

TOILETS: Eco-toilets at Charlottes Pass trackhead at the start of the walk and at Rawsons Pass near the summit of Mt Kosciuszko

FOOD: Jindabyne, 40 km from track start has many options; cafes at Charlottes Pass and Perisher may or may not be open in the off-season

TIPS: Start early and be prepared for all conditions, including snow in summer

[above] *Track down to Snowy River*

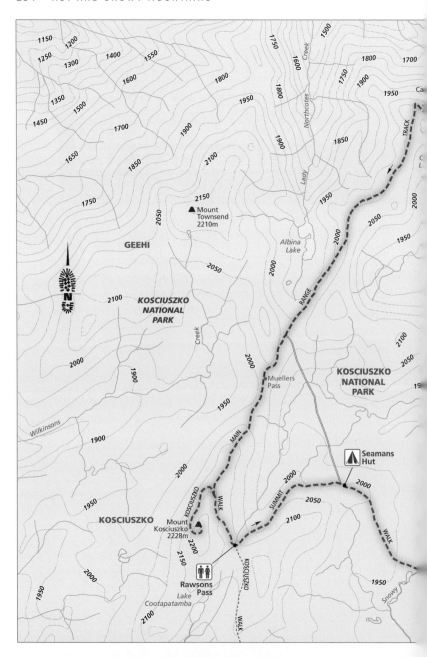

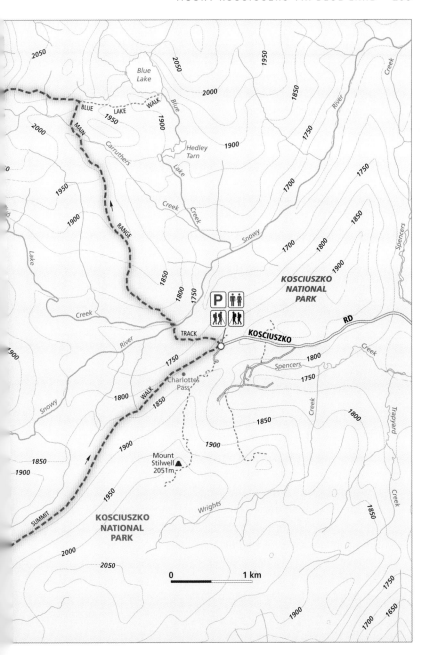

There are several ways to get to the summit of the highest mountain on the Australian mainland (there are much loftier mountains in subantarctic and antarctic Australian territories), but this is the best route, taking in some glorious high country scenery and Australia's largest and deepest glacial lake.

As if there is a list of things to 'achieve', many people just want to 'tick' the fact they've been to the summit of Mt Kosciuszko. The easiest way to do that is the 14 km return walk from Thredbo, where you can get a chairlift to the top of the range, then take a stroll along a steel mesh track to the summit and back. 'Kozzie' itself is not a spectacular mountain – more of a hummock really – and so some people leave feeling a little disappointed.

You won't risk disappointment taking this route, as it's a stunning walk in its own right, and while it has the potential to offer some surprises, it is all on marked tracks. The final section of the walk takes the direct route back to Charlottes Pass along the relatively flat Summit Rd (dirt, now closed to vehicles, but open to bikes) which is easy to follow, even if you've dallied too long and darkness is falling. In fact, many people walk the road at night in order to be on top of Australia for dawn.

Start early at the carpark at the end of the road above Charlottes Pass. Unfortunately day-long parking means positioning your vehicle precariously on the side of the road, as the carpark is limited to 20-minute stops.

Once on the track, head down to the right, away from the gorgeous snow gums (the last you'll see of them for a while), down the paved walking track marked 'Main Range Track (to Blue Lake)'. At the bottom of the valley, you'll ford the headwaters of the Snowy River, and after the spring melt your feet may get wet. Generally, though, the large stepping stones make for a fun crossing.

Keep following the track up the long hill on the other side. About 45 to 60 minutes after starting you'll get to a point offering a great view over Hedley Tarn to the right (a tarn is a small mountain lake), which is a top spot to grab a drink and take a breather.

Above the treeline, looking over Hedley Tarn

Further on you'll reach a fork. Your route heads left, but first duck along to the right for a little bit to get a great view of Blue Lake – Australia's largest and deepest glacial lake. If you have the time and the inclination, head right down to the lake, which often has large pockets of ice and snow sitting around it, even in summer. Take off your shoes and enjoy the icy-cold water. Further on, this track takes you to Hedley Tarn, but you probably don't have time to visit that today, so turn aound and head back the way you came to the fork, then continue west on the Main Range Track towards Carruthers Peak. At 2142 m, this will give you an amazing view over much of the terrain, including lovely little Club Lake below, Mt Sentinel due north, Victoria to the west, Mt Townsend (the second highest mountain on the mainland, at 2209 m) to the south-west and Kosciuszko beyond it. It's a great spot for a morning tea break after the tough little climb.

The route forward is obvious, and takes you down past delightful Lake Albina. Highly capable and prepared bushwalkers who want an extra challenge often veer off-track here, passing to the north of the lake, to climb Mt Townsend (which includes a rock scramble at the top). The view from it is better than from Kosciuszko, but there is no formed track and navigation skills are essential, particularly if the weather closes in. From Townsend, those who have done the detour can head SSE to meet the track back at Muellers Pass.

Most people, however, should just stick to the track – this walk is long enough without adding such a tough detour. Ignore a small track that comes in from the right at Muellers Pass, and continue about another 2 km to the next obvious track on the right which is the 1 km track to the 2228 m summit of Mt Kosciuszko. Take this and enjoy a well-earned rest at the top, finding some protection among the boulders if it is windy and cold. Often there is quite a crowd at the summit, but remember most people haven't had the great experience getting here that you have!

On your descent, turn right towards Rawsons Pass, where toilets were built discreetly into the mountain in 2007, in order to help protect the area from the 100 000 or so people who visit the mountain each year. Here the track forks again. You want to turn left towards Charlottes Pass. The other way is the 5 km route straight through to Thredbo chairlift, which could be a nice alternative if you have organised transport. It is about an hour's drive (70 km) back to Charlottes Pass.

It's about 8 km down the old Summit Rd back to Charlottes Pass, and mountain-bike riders may share the track. It is probably the least interesting part of the walk, but you will pass the lovely little Seamans Hut, which has provided life-saving shelter to people caught out in bad weather. If your timing is good you'll also spy meadows of stunning alpine flowers, such as big yellow billy buttons and silver snow daisies.

Over the last couple of kilometres before Charlottes Pass you'll pass along the lower western flank of Mt Stilwell (2051 m).

You may still have energy and inclination to walk the very short snow gum loop at the end of the track. If you have any water left, splash it on the trunks to bring out the myriad colours in the bark.

If you and your companions are very fit walkers, and think you would like the option to spend more time at Blue Lake and Hedley Tarn, consider doing this walk in the other direction. This way, by the time you arrive near Blue Lake, you can assess how much time you really have to dally with these alpine delights.

Remember to be prepared for all conditions – weather can change rapidly in the high country – and if you are not acclimatised, you may find that the altitude slows you down a bit, making breathing harder than usual. But you can always blame that on the breathtaking scenery.

Paved track down to Snowy River headwaters

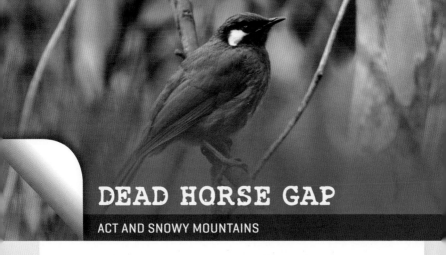

DEAD HORSE GAP

ACT AND SNOWY MOUNTAINS

WALK: 9 km loop (including chairlift)

TIME REQUIRED: 3.5 hours

BEST TIME: Early summer, when the wildflowers are usually at their best and there is some snow on the ground; in winter much of this walk is completely under snow

GRADE: Moderate

ENVIRONMENT: Alpine environment above the treeline, snow gum forest, river walk

BEST MAP: Rooftop's Kosciuszko National Park Forest Activities Map Jindabyne-Khancoban

TRANSPORT: Car to Thredbo

TOILETS: At the bottom and top of the chairlift

FOOD: Thredbo shops and restaurants or the cafe at top of the chairlift

TIPS: Bring an extra layer of clothing

This is a very fine introduction to alpine walking. As well as enjoying one of Australia's most spectacular chairlift rides, you will experience alpine herb and flower fields above the treeline, then snow gum forest and a river walk, and it's almost all downhill.

Several factors can affect some people's enjoyment of the high country in summer. One is the weather – getting uncomfortably cold, and not being able to get warm again. Another is the altitude. If you haven't acclimatised, walking at close to 2000 m can leave you short of breath.

[above] *White-eared honeyeater*

With this walk you avoid both of those potential problems: you start at the coldest, most exposed point, then gradually come down into more protected, warmer areas; and secondly, the walk is primarily downhill and not overly long, so the thin air should not be an issue.

This walk starts with a fun chairlift ride from Thredbo village, at 1300 m, up to about 1850 m. Try to park somewhere near the Kosciuszko Express Quad Chair (in summer it is the only chairlift running). The best carpark is near the playground, slightly past the chairlift (if coming from Jindabyne). Put on an extra layer of clothing before getting on the chairlift – the approximate temperature at the top of the lift is listed on a signboard at the bottom, and the difference can be more than 10°C.

The chairlift is hideously expensive (around $25 one way), so make sure you enjoy the rare treat of riding effortlessly over some of Australia's most spectacular ski terrain. Be sure to look back towards the village and watch for mountain-bikers hooning downhill.

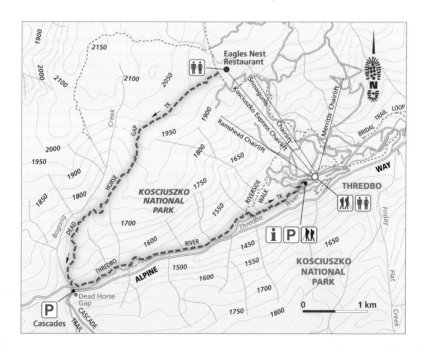

Thredbo River

At the top, you can either duck inside the large cafe and enjoy a hot chocolate or two, or veer around the left and start heading up the track towards Mt Kosciuszko. This is the most popular way to reach the summit.

After about 350 m, a sign indicates the start of the Dead Horse Gap track which veers sharply off to the left. The track does not look like much compared to the main track, and in fact can be a little difficult to follow over its first few hundred metres, but it does become clearer again. Just keep heading towards the ski-tow equipment, as the track passes right under it.

The track through this section heads slightly uphill and then across the ridge, and is quite rough, so watch your step. There's plenty to distract you, including alpine bogs, meadows of paper daisies and billy buttons, and beautiful granite boulders either rounded by wind and rain or split into jagged shapes by water freezing and expanding in fissures inside the rock.

With great views ahead and to the left, you'll soon come to one of the outposts of the ski fields, the head of a valley called the Golf Course Bowl. A little further on, the track winds its way down into the tree line. The first few snow gums are very gnarled and twisted by the strain and stresses of living at this high altitude. This is a very pretty section of the track, with flowers at the base of many of the beautifully shaped and coloured trees. Keep an eye out for a divine little picnic spot on a rare flat spot between snow gums on the left of the track.

Then you'll come to the snow gum graveyard, the bleached skeletons of thousands upon thousands of trees still standing after the inferno of 2003. This eerie sight is offset by sections of living trees such as the olive-trunked black sallees, alpine flowers and gurgling creeks. The bushes get chest-high here, in contrast to the low herbs found above the treeline, and the temperature should become warmer as you descend into the shelter of the thicker forest.

Soon you'll hear the cascading Thredbo River, still a fair way below. Silver and bronze skinks sit like mascots on almost every step, and you'll probably see some greenish parrots: in summer they are most likely young crimson rosellas that haven't earned their full colours yet. The Alpine Way comes in sight, and the track feels like it is heading in the wrong direction, almost parallel to the road, but eventually it swings back and meets the river near the Cascades carpark, about 500 m east of Dead Horse Gap proper (a watershed on the Great Dividing Range).

Skink warming itself on a rock

The high country flowers profusely in summer

The 5 km route back to Thredbo is clearly marked to the left on the flat before you reach the river. The track stays relatively flat, and crosses the river on sturdy bridges a couple of times. Unfortunately the first section of this track doesn't get close to the river, but be patient and some wonderful rest stops will appear after the first bridge. There are bubbling cascades and attractive beetles, some beautiful snow gums and a small lookout with a bench by a waterfall.

A mountain-bike track joins the track from the left, and then you'll be walking between the golf course and the river. Keep following the river and you'll eventually come to a road. Turn right, across the bridge, then left, and you'll be back at the car within a few hundred metres.

If you want to do this walk without paying the hefty chairlift fee, consider parking at the Cascades carpark, and doing it in reverse. The ascent from this point is more gradual than the steep hike up from Thredbo. You'll need an extra hour or so.

Gloucester Tops Circuit

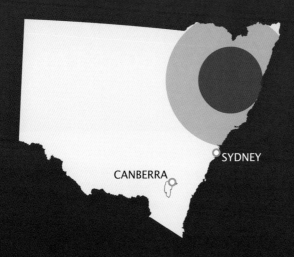

CANBERRA

SYDNEY

NORTH-EAST

Volcanic landscapes, subalpine areas, heathlands abounding in native wildflowers and beautiful walk-in beaches are just some of the natural treasures ready for bushwalkers to discover in the north-east of the state. Pay particular attention to the fragmented, but vast, World Heritage–listed Gondwana rainforests in this region.

ANGOURIE COASTAL WALK

NORTH-EAST

WALK: 12 km return

TIME REQUIRED: 3 hours

BEST TIME: Summer

GRADE: Moderate

ENVIRONMENT: Isolated beaches, coastal heath

BEST MAP: Yaraygir Coastal Walk, available at www.environment. nsw.gov.au/resources/parks/ brochures/20100479Yuraygir CoastalWalk.pdf

TOILETS: At the start of the walk and at the picnic area at the end of Pacific St, Angourie

FOOD: Yamba, 6 km away, has plenty of takeaways, cafes and supermarkets

TIPS: Take the whole day and enjoy a swim or three

This crackerjack summer walk is along the most northerly section of the longest stretch of undeveloped coastline in NSW, and offers lonely beaches, rock platforms, views and wildflowers. Overnighters may wish to camp at the walk-in Shelley Beach camping area, but there are no facilities.

The Yuraygir Coastal Walk is a magnificent four-day route, linking 65 km of walking tracks, beaches and rock platforms through the longest stretch of protected and undeveloped coastline in NSW. This out-and-back day-walk

[above] *Back Beach, Angourie*

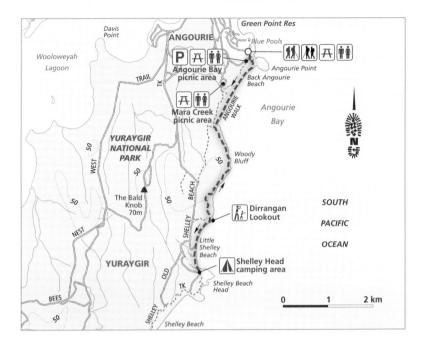

is the most northerly section of the route, and will give you a taste of the rest. Even in the busy summer school holidays you can quickly get away from the beach crowds, and feel quite alone in this stunning wilderness.

The little settlement of Angourie is some 18 km off the Pacific Highway north of Grafton, via the township of Yamba. Angourie is renowned among surfers but its relative isolation and long distance from Sydney has kept its development and profile very low key. It is on a beautiful stretch of coast and the hinterland has some lovely intact rainforest.

This walk starts at the end of the most southerly road in Angourie, Pacific St, where there are toilets, a picnic area and a sign describing the whole 65 km walk. Head down the track through a cool forested section, ignoring tracks up to the picnic area to the right. The track will bring you onto and along the length of Back Beach, a long and pretty stretch of sand. You will need cross a creek on the way, so you might as well take off walking shoes straight away.

Note the interesting eroded coffee rock formations at the back of the beach near the start of the walk.

At the end of the beach, a set of steep stairs leads up onto the Angourie Walk. Turn left at the top, along the coast. As it meanders along the cliff top, you'll pass spiky pandanus trees and wildflowers, including the lovely soft white flannel flowers. The whole time you'll hear the sound of the surf surging against the rocks below.

The track continues through a variety of coastal ecosystems, including tunnels of coastal banksia, low heathland and wet marshy areas where the track is raised on boardwalks. A high point is the Dirrangan Lookout, with extensive views south down the coast, including Lake Arragan, and the conical Clarence Peak inland.

Away from the crowds on the southern end of Back Beach

Coastal pandanus

Keep an eye out too for dolphins in the water and humpback whales during their yearly migration between Antarctica and northern Queensland. The best time to spot them on this stretch of coast is during Aug and Sept.

In the air you'll almost certainly see the majestic white form of the sea eagle. With a wingspan up to 2 m across, it is Australia's second largest raptor (after the wedge-tailed eagle). A similarly shaped brown bird in this area, with a brilliant white head, is the Brahminy kite.

Soon the track descends down to Little Shelley Beach, which may well be completely deserted. You will usually find a colourful collection of stones and shells across its surface, inviting some gentle beachcombing. Shelley Headland campground is down the far end of the beach, and although there are no facilities there, it's worth walking the full length of the beach and exploring the point. The camping area has plenty of shady spots, and it's a nice place to stop for a swim and a lunch break before heading back, unless this taste of the Yuraygir Walk beckons you on further.

Brahminy kite

MINYON LOOP

NORTH-EAST

WALK: 7 km loop

TIME REQUIRED: 2.5 hours

BEST TIME: During or immediately after rain, when the waterfall thunders off the escarpment

GRADE: Moderate to hard

ENVIRONMENT: Plunging waterfall, Bangalow palm rainforest, eucalypt forest

BEST MAP: www.environment. nsw.gov.au/nationalparks/ parkWalking.aspx?id=N0062

TOILETS: Pit toilet at the start of the walk and at Minyon Grass, three-quarters of the way through

FOOD: Although you will pass a few little hamlets with general stores on your way to Nightcap National Park, your safest bet for food is Lismore, a large town 45 minutes drive away

TIPS: For a fantastic and unusual night bush walk in Nightcap National park, join a guided tour using special night-vision goggles in order to see possums, tawny frogmouths, bandicoots and other animals. The company also does guided day walks and wildlife tours through the park. Vision Walks: (02) 6685 0059, 0405 275 743; www.visionwalks.com

[above] *Thick and lush canopy*

**The premier walk in Nightcap National Park,
this steep route starts at the top of the dramatic
Minyon Falls, plunges 150 m down into a dark
Bangalow palm forest at the base of the falls, then
rises sharply again.**

Nightcap National Park is on the southern edge of the giant
Mt Warning volcano caldera, and has the highest annual rainfall in
NSW. Those travelling here from the south will find the subtropical
and warm temperate rainforests have a distinctly Queensland feel.
The park is part of the vast fragmented Gondwana Rainforest World
Heritage Area that ranges from Barrington Tops in the south to Main
Range, Lamington and Mount Barney national parks in Queensland.

The park can be tricky to find, but the national parks visitor
centre at Lismore has a helpful mud map that points the way via
Bexhill and Rosebank. Make your way to the Minyon Falls picnic
area, where there are gas barbecues, picnic tables and a grand
view from the top of Minyon Falls. About 100 m high, it tumbles
spectacularly over a multicoloured rhyolite cliff.

The loop starts along the boardwalk, then crosses the creek
on some concrete stepping-stones. You'll follow the precipitous
escarpment but in most areas a fence prevents you from getting
too close to the edge. There are some beautiful scribbly gums,
flooded gums and tallowwood and an unlogged stand of brushbox.

Fig and palm forest

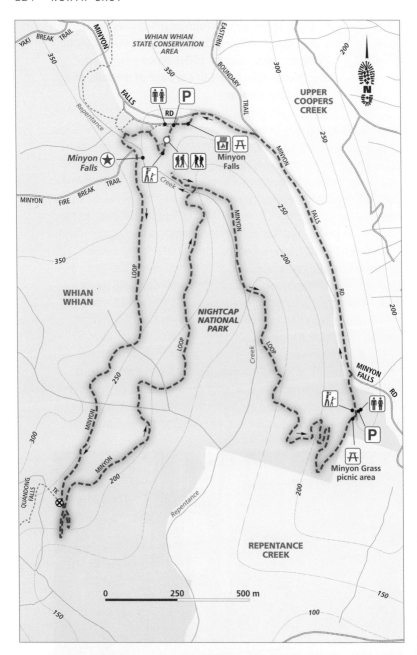

An unmarked track comes in from the right, which is the way to Quandong Falls. It's about a 15-20 minute return trip to the falls and is worth taking if Minyon Falls is flowing well. Otherwise you can score a distant view of Quandong Falls through the trees a few hundred metres along the track.

Tawny frogmouth

The main track zigzags down into the rainforest, with figs, vines and battalions of beautiful Bangalow palms. Look up to admire their bright red fruits and umbrella fronds forming a canopy.

Birds in this area (perhaps more seen than heard) will include wompoo pigeons, olive-backed orioles, green catbirds and – if you are especially fortunate – colourful noisy pittas on the forest floor.

At the lowest point, you'll cross the creek, where a tricky track that requires a little rock scrambling leads left to the base of the falls. There you can see the multicoloured rhyolite cliff and the large pool at the bottom of the falls. It's a lovely spot to cool off before the climb out.

The track zigzags up the steep valley side to Minyon Grass where there is a lookout with a view across the rainforest to the falls, a picnic area and toilet.

The last stretch of this walk is a fairly unpleasant climb along the narrow, unsealed, dusty road back to Minyon Falls. You might consider leaving most of your party at Minyon Grass, while the driver retrieves the vehicle.

Campers can stay at the pleasant Rummery Park area a few kilometres up the road.

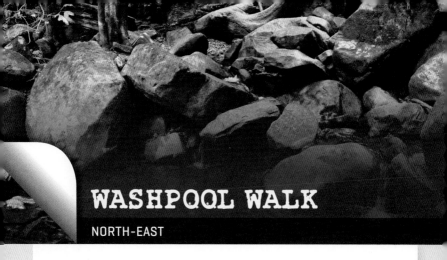

WASHPOOL WALK

NORTH-EAST

WALK: 8 km loop

TIME REQUIRED: 2 hours

BEST TIME: Summer, so you can swim or wade at the end

GRADE: Moderate

ENVIRONMENT: Rainforest, open eucalypt forest

BEST MAP: www.environment.nsw.gov.au/nationalparks/parkWalking.
aspx?id=N0061

TOILETS: Pit toilet at the start of the walk

FOOD: Washpool National Park is halfway between the large towns of
Glen Innes and Grafton

TIPS: This is the sort of walk that suits a fairly quick pace, as you pass
through various beautiful vegetation communities, with little need for
long stops, as there are minimal long views

[above] *A jumble of boulders amongst lush forest*

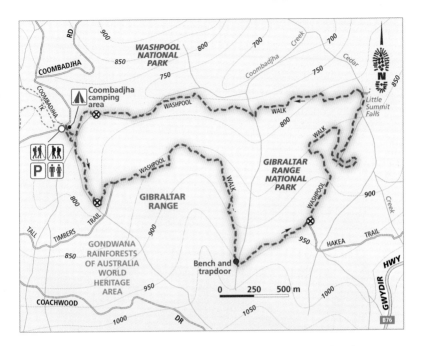

This quiet spot promises a wonderful introduction to some different vegetation communities at a relatively high altitude (almost 1000 m), including beautiful rainforest and tall eucalypt forest.

Washpool National Park abuts the Gwydir Highway, between Grafton and Glen Innes, and contains a quarter of Australia's rainforest species and the largest area of coachwood forest in the world. An easy 5 km drive off the highway on a signposted gravel road leads to the Coombadjha camping and picnic area.

There are a few different walks here of various lengths, including the 80 km World Heritage Walk that links Washpool with Gibraltar Range National Park across the highway.

On the Washpool Walk you'll see plenty of coachwood, as well as crabapple, sassafras, ferns, vines, epiphytes, and the Methuselahs of the forest, 1000-year-old red cedars that are 50 m high and more than 2 m across.

This is a loop walk with two halves – a long uphill, and then a long downhill.

From the carpark, at the end of the road, take the track to the right (near the toilet), along the creek, through a dark vine and lilly pilly forest, then turn right at the junction (rather than taking the 'short loop' to the left). The track heads upwards, and soon reaches a management trail where you should turn left (signposted). There are some excellent interpretive signs along the track.

Towering red cedars, the apartment blocks of the forest

Summit Falls

Birdlife is quite prolific, and you'll no doubt hear whipbirds and see white-browed scrubwrens darting across the track. A short detour on the left takes you to the towering red cedars – like giant apartment blocks, their huge trunks teem with lifeforms, including ferns, mosses and lichens. Other trees around here include strangler figs, walking stick palms, yellow carabeen and black booyong.

As you approach the highest section of the walk, you'll cross Cedar Creek, where there is a bench and trapdoor. Open the trapdoor and a cup on a string invites you to taste the crystal-clear water.

Soon the route breaks into open, drier forest, where you should notice increased light and a sudden change of plant species – now forest oak, banksia, wattle, hakea and tall eucalypts. This section includes a lookout (with restricted views to the south-east) before the track descends towards the little Summit Falls (a short, steep detour off the track).

Once you cross Cedar Creek again, you'll be back into the thick of the rainforest, following Coombadjha Creek increasingly closely until you cross it. In the final few hundred metres before you reach the picnic area and campground, you'll find a couple of deep waterholes that could be good for a swim before you pop back up at the carpark.

WONGA WALK

NORTH-EAST

WALK: 6.5 km loop

TIME REQUIRED: 2.5 hours

BEST TIME: During or immediately after rain, when the waterfalls flow bigger and the forest glistens

GRADE: Easy to moderate – the track is nearly all paved and has gentle gradients

ENVIRONMENT: Pure subtropical rainforest, waterfalls

BEST MAP: Dorrigo National Park Walking Tracks, NSW National Parks and Wildlife Service, available at visitor centre, and on signs around the track

TOILETS: Flushing toilets at the visitor centre at the start of the walk and at The Glade Picnic Area, one-third of the way through

FOOD: The Canopy Cafe at the visitor centre has excellent lunches, desserts, pastries, free-trade coffee and a delightful range of special herbal teas: (02) 6657 1541; canopycafedorrigo.com

TIPS: As this track is paved and relatively short, it is ideal to walk in the rain (which may wash away some of the crowds) and you can dry off and reward yourself afterwards in the cafe

[above] *Skywalk Lookout*

Very popular, this paved, gentle walking track takes you through spectacular old-growth World Heritage–listed rainforest, alive with birdsong and the sound of waterfalls.

Like Minnamurra Falls down the south coast, the Wonga Walk provides a showcase of unlogged rainforest, and is very popular with school groups and travellers. It is unlikely to be a quiet, contemplative experience, as there will be plenty of fellow walkers at any time of year – particularly in the sections near the visitor centre.

Tristania Falls

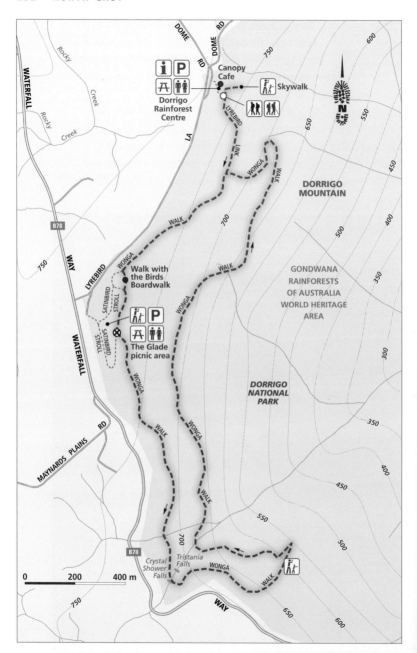

However, the rainforest here is so deliciously beautiful it is definitely worth the couple of hours it will take to walk the Wonga Walk circuit. The track is nearly all sealed or on raised boardwalks, is gentle in gradient, and has only one small staircase, which will be downhill if you do the loop anti-clockwise. Going in that direction also splits the uphill into two parts. There are lots of interpretive signs (perhaps too many) that will introduce you to many plants and other aspects of this subtropical rainforest.

Straight out of the back of the excellent Dorrigo Rainforest Centre, you will find a cafe on the left, the Skywalk lookout straight ahead, and the start of the walk (marked Lyrebird Link) on the right. It would be hard to resist checking out the view from the Skywalk, which juts out 21 m above the forest floor, over a valley with 140 tree species and more than 50 types of vine.

When you've satiated your long-distance vision, start down the track. You'll almost immediately be aware of birds in the forest around you. More than 120 species have been recorded. Many can't be seen, but little birds (scrubwrens, logrunners, grey fantails) will dart across the track in front of you, larger birds will call from high in the trees, and brush turkeys or lyrebirds may strut around on the ground. If you're particularly fortunate you may see the stunning

The Skywalk Lookout juts out 21 m over the forest floor

male regent bowerbird, in plumage of black and gold.

Signs early in the walk warn of the abundant giant stinging trees here. Most are set back from the track, but even the fallen leaves can cause major irritation. Stinging tree leaves are light-green, can be as big as dinner plates and are often quite damaged by insects.

Once you reach the Wonga Walk circuit, turn right, and you'll be introduced to the various giant trees here that stretch 30–40 m above you. There are native tamarinds, crabapples, yellow carabeans with buttress roots, thick reddish-trunked tallowwoods, black apples and rosewoods. You'll hear the unmistakable call of the whipbird and, if you are quiet, the deep 'wom-poo' of wompoo pigeons high in the trees. Although a large green and purple pigeon up to 50 cm long, they are hard to spot in the foliage unless they move. The loud, 'strangled baby' cry is the green catbird, a rainforest specialist.

Regent bowerbird

Before you reach The Glade picnic area, you'll veer left on the Walk With the Birds Boardwalk which takes you quite high above the valley floor. The boardwalk has a couple of places to sit and observe some of the avian life.

Veer left at the intersection after the boardwalk, keeping to the Wonga Walk track. Soon you will come to a suspension bridge in front of Crystal Shower Falls. Once off the bridge, you can take a short deviation to stand behind the falls, with a curtain of water falling into the pool at the base.

The track then continues downhill to Tristania Falls, the lowest point of the walk, and the site of the only stairs, which lead down to a bridge across the water.

From here it's gently uphill all the way, passing more plant types, including strangler figs, Bangalow palms, walking stick palms, and pothos vine clinging in dense green fronds to nearly every tree trunk. Eventually you'll get back to the Lyrebird Link, turn right and you'll be sitting in the cafe in almost no time at all.

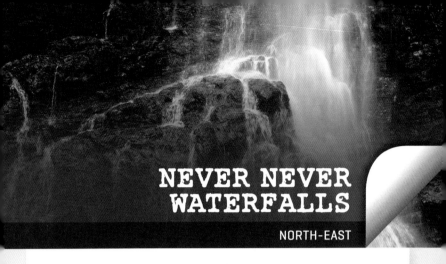

NEVER NEVER WATERFALLS

WALK: *11 km loop*

TIME REQUIRED: *4 hours*

BEST TIME: *Mornings, all year round*

GRADE: *Moderate to hard*

ENVIRONMENT: *Warm temperate rainforests, waterfalls, canyons, views*

BEST MAP: Dorrigo National Park Walking Tracks, *NSW National Parks and Wildlife Service* – available at Dorrigo Rainforest Centre and also on signs around the walk

TOILETS: *Pit toilet at the picnic area at the start of the walk and flushing toilets at the Dorrigo Rainforest Centre 10 km away*

FOOD: *The Canopy Cafe at the visitor centre has excellent lunches, desserts, pastries, free-trade coffee and a delightful range of special herbal teas: (02) 6657 1541; canopycafedorrigo.com*

TIPS: *Diamond pythons are large rainforest-loving snakes that may lie in the track and refuse to move. They are not poisonous and unlikely to be aggressive towards people but if you are nervous about stepping over them, don't try to move them (they can still bite), just walk through the bush around them.*

[above] *Red Cedar Falls*

Combining the 'best of the rest' of Dorrigo National Park, this circuit joins sections of several tracks to take in a series of beautiful waterfalls in warm-temperate forest.

The Dorrigo Rainforest Centre (see previous walk) is the focal point of the most-visited area of Dorrigo National Park. The Never Never picnic area, 10 km away, is the other main point of access in the park. It offers a range of walks, which can be linked in this 11 km loop that offers three major waterfalls and lots of smaller ones. The forest is dense and beautiful but, unlike the Wonga Walk, has been logged (the route follows some of the logging tracks).

The access road leads left from the visitor centre, initially through farmland. The last 8 km is on a slippery and winding gravel road, finishing at the Never Never picnic area.

Starting at the very first carpark you come to, take the small track that heads north-east. This is the start of the Rosewood

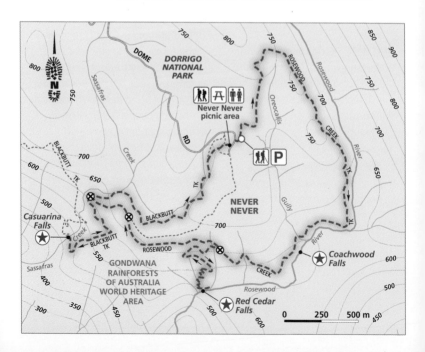

Creek Track that will take you through sassafras, coachwood and crabapple forest as it swings around to follow the course of Rosewood Creek. You'll also find the endemic rainforest trees Dorrigo plum and crimson-flowering Dorrigo waratah (only distantly related to the NSW state flower *Telopea speciosissima*). At first it is difficult to get a good view of the creek, even though at times it will seem maddeningly close as it bubbles and gurgles below; but rest assured the track does descend to creek level eventually. If you really can't wait that long, a few short and steep, unofficial footpads lead off to the left to mini waterfalls, gullies and swimming holes.

Dorrigo waratah

Almost 3 km into the walk, you'll come to Coachwood Falls, which has views at the top and a footpad to the bottom. Always be careful on the rocks as they can be treacherously slippery.

As you walk along the track, you'll see more and more evidence of the park's logging history. Giant stumps sit beside the track with steps cut into them, but there is no shortage of grand trees – particularly the rust-red tallowwood and enormous brushbox soaring 30–40 m above the forest floor – and at times you'll wonder why some trees were left while others were taken.

Head left at the first major intersection you'll come to and walk 1.3 km down to the base of Red Cedar Falls. These have the greatest drop of any accessible falls in the park. Even very fit walkers will take almost an hour to descend the 200 vertical metres to the base of the falls and back up again. However, the track isn't particularly steep as it is designed with lots of switchbacks, and the view down the gully at the end is definitely worth the effort. Once the track spills out into the open beside the falls, climb the little rocky knoll in front of the falls for the best view.

After you have sweated back up to the top, turn left onto the Rosewood Creek Track, left again onto the Link Track and then another left on the Blackbutt Track for an 800 m downhill section

View down the gully from Red Cedar Falls

A reminder of past logging operations

to Casuarina Falls. The track here is narrow, slippery and quite fun as it winds along the steep edge of the Sassafras Creek Valley.

You'll come to Casuarina Falls halfway up the valley. It offers some gentle falls into a pool above the track, and a big drop below. There are also some distant views to be had of McGraths Hump and Dorrigo Mountain.

From the waterfall, the Blackbutt Track continues across the creek and then off to Callicoma Falls, eventually reaching the road. Those wanting to extend the walk can follow this route and then walk 4 km back along the road to the Never Never picnic area, but instead it is recommended that you turn back here, turning left at the first intersection. The track will wind back up to the Never Never picnic area, where your car awaits. On the way up, you may well encounter a few lyrebirds.

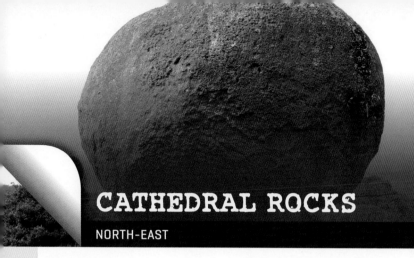

CATHEDRAL ROCKS

NORTH-EAST

WALK: 6 km loop

TIME REQUIRED: 2.5 hours

BEST TIME: Winter, when you could get a dusting of snow or misty conditions. Alternatively, a few days after a rainy period, because the bush here can look a little tired after a dry spell

GRADE: Moderate – some gentle stairs and fun rock scrambling is involved

ENVIRONMENT: Exciting maze of granite torrs and boulders, tall eucalypt forest, marshland

BEST MAP: On signs at the start of walk, and at every junction

TOILETS: Pit toilet between the picnic and camping area at the start of the walk

FOOD: Armidale is a large town, a one-hour drive away

TIPS: This is an exciting walk for teenagers or others with a sense of adventure, but younger children should be watched carefully at the top

[above] *A massive pink granite boulder sits like a giant's marble*

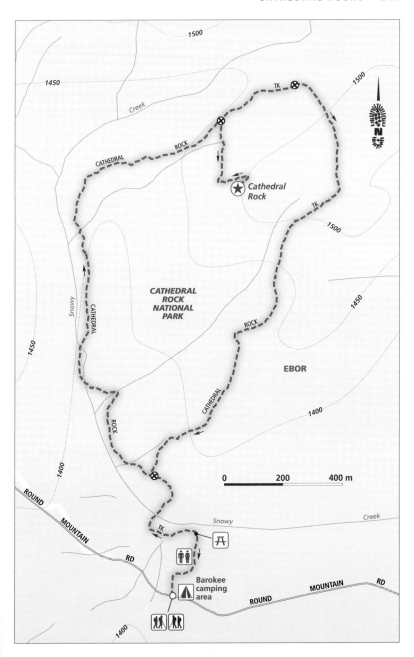

*This fun and relatively gentle route through
a subalpine landscape culminates in a three-
dimensional maze of giant pink granite boulders
through which you crawl, squeeze and climb over
to get to a vantage point with extensive views. It is one of the
highest points in New England, some 1500 m above sea level.*

The Waterfall Way between Armidale and Dorrigo is one of the
classic natural drives in NSW: an ebony necklace winding through
a string of jade and emerald treasures – Oxley Wild Rivers, New
England, Dorrigo and Cathedral Rock national parks. There are, not
surprisingly, beautiful waterfalls and lookouts to visit, and a range of
walks. Keen bushwalkers could easily spend a week in this area.

   The most fun walk along the stretch is this 6 km jaunt. It starts
at the Barokee Rest Area, which is the main picnic and camping
area in the park. Turn west off the Waterfall Way about 6 km
south-west of Ebor, on the signposted road into the park. It's an
8 km well-graded but slippery dirt road (unsuitable for caravans)
with a few sharp bends, so take it easy.

   From the picnic area, the track heads across a swampy area that
can be rich with animal life – the most obvious of which are birds
and abundant eastern grey kangaroos in the early mornings and

Chain up to the summit

late afternoons. After rain, this area can be quite wet to walk through and you may get your feet wet.

Eastern grey kangaroo

A few hundred metres after wandering out the other side of the swamp, you'll begin to encounter the pink granite boulders that make this area so unique. They have thick mottled coats of lichens, ferns and mosses, and some have entire plant communities growing on them, but underneath they are a lovely dusty pink. Some of the boulders – as large as cottages – are arranged in ridiculous stacks and precarious positions.

You'll also encounter your return track coming in from the right. You can do the track in either direction, but it is recommended to go clockwise.

Initially the track follows the creek line, through tall eucalypt and banksia woodland. Because of the high altitude, you will also see sub-alpine species such as snowgrasses. At the next junction, where there is a bench, take the track to the right, which winds up to the top of Cathedral Rock. You'll score a view of a large granite feature on the skyline that looks like one of the Easter Island statues. Birds in this section include lyrebirds, scrubwrens and always-laughing kookaburras.

The only point where you could possibly get lost is about 100 m before the main cliff line, where the track braids in several directions. The main track swings right, and then back left directly underneath the towering granite walls.

Then the best bit begins, the last little wander along the ridge. At times you'll have to duck under boulders, squeeze through narrow passages and jump atop the boulders in an other-worldly three-dimensional maze. It feels very much like one of the dreamy scenes from the Australian film classic, *Picnic at Hanging Rock*. But in this case there are occasional arrows to mark the way and bring you back to reality.

Three-dimensional maze of boulders at the summit

So many of the massive boulders take on human characteristics: giant heads, and reclining people enjoying the view. The granite is very coarse and so fairly 'grippy', but you'll want to take care in a few places where a slip could be nasty. In the last few metres before the summit, a chain offers assistance up a rock slab.

The extensive views from the top stretch right over the surrounding farmland and include various other large boulder piles nearby, and Round Mountain, the highest point in northern NSW.

Once you've enjoyed and explored this adventure playground, head back down to the junction with the bench, then turn right up to another junction. The track to the left goes to Woolpack Rocks and Native Dog Creek, but this, shorter walk swings right, back down through lovely tall subalpine forest to the initial track junction. Turn left, back through the swampy area and back to the carpark.

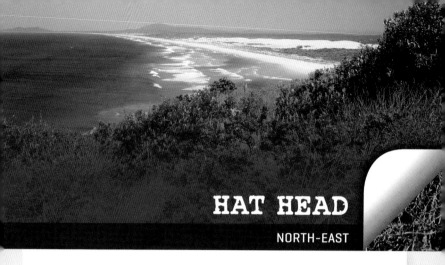

HAT HEAD

NORTH-EAST

WALK: 11 km loop and return (4 km loop plus 7 km return track)

TIME REQUIRED: 4 hours

BEST TIME: Warm but not stifling afternoons

GRADE: Moderate (4 km loop), easy/moderate (7 km Connors Track)

ENVIRONMENT: Beaches, coastal heath and paperbark woodland, dramatic coastal features

BEST MAP: www.environment.nsw. gov.au/NationalParks/parkHome. aspx?id=N0014

TOILETS: Flushing toilets at Hat Head Reserve, a 4 km drive away, or a walk across the Korogoro Creek bridge

FOOD: Hat Head, 3 km drive away, has a takeaway, general store and bowling club

TIPS: Take swimmers and a towel

Short-beaked echidna

[above] Killick Beach

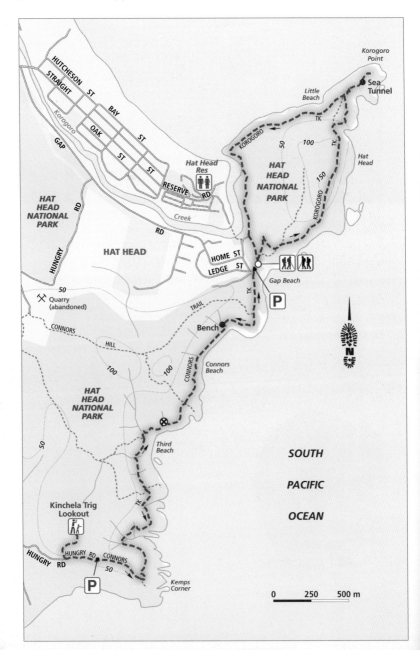

Combining some dramatic coastal features with a couple of walk-in beaches on a quiet stretch of the NSW coast, this route links the Hat Head loop (called the Korogoro Track) with the linear Connors Track, but as the carpark is in the middle, either can be done separately.

Cherished by holidaymakers and rock fishers, Hat Head is on a relatively quiet stretch of the NSW north coast, east of Kempsey. To get there, you drive under the longest bridge in the Southern Hemisphere – the Kempsey Bypass on the Pacific Highway.

Just before you reach a little bridge that leads to the cluster of shacks and holiday houses that make up Hat Head, turn right to 'The Gap', and follow Gap Rd 2 km to the coast. At the carpark, Hat Head (and the looped walking track) will be on your left, and Connors Track on your right. Either of these walks are great on their own, or you can combine them into an 11 km afternoon stroll. The text that follows describes the Hat Head loop first (called the Korogoro Track), walking anti-clockwise.

Pandanus over a divine isolated beach

The track initially heads fairly steeply up Hat Head, as if aiming for the summit, before peeling off to the right and hugging the coastline quite high up. You'll pass through banksias clinging to the mountainside and get great views of dramatic rock features, gulches and coastline, and some wildflowers in close.

A sign warns of a poor track suitable for 'experienced walkers only' but it really isn't that bad – just a little eroded in places. In the late afternoon or early morning you may well see eastern grey kangaroos on the grassy sections, and in the winter months keep an eye out for humpback whales.

The track swings down to a saddle before reaching a T-junction. The track to the right heads further out to the point, while the track to the left is your way back. Initially head right, and within 100 m you'll see a narrow sea tunnel to the right of the track.

On your way back around the north side of Hat Head, you'll enjoy extensive views over coastal pandanus (the spiky palm-tree like plants) down the long stretch of Hat Head Beach towards Smoky Cape Lighthouse at the far end.

The final section of the loop goes through a shaded paperbark forest, alongside the tannin-stained Korogoro Creek. Common throughout eastern Australia, tea-coloured creeks are not a sign the water is polluted (although they may be), but result from rich

Colourful pea

tannins in the vegetation, released as organic matter decays in the water.

Once back at the carpark, take Connors Track south. As you walk through the coastal heath and banksia, keep an eye out for some special treats: echidnas, which are common here, eastern brown snakes and wildflowers, including flannel flowers and the dusky coral pea, which has a low-growing reddish flower. Dolphins are also commonly sighted in the water around this area.

Rounding the first headland you'll pass a bench before moving down onto Connors Beach. It's unpatrolled, but great for a swim.

The track at the far end of the beach scales the rocks beside a post (it may be hard to spot initially). Follow the track (slightly eroded in places) through a few sheltered gullies and you'll come to Third Beach. Access to this beach is via a grassy gully at the north end.

Unfortunately, along this section of track you'll notice some of the introduced weeds lantana and bitou bush. These are regularly poisoned but haven't been eradicated completely.

As you come out of the scrub onto Windy Gap and Kemps Corner, you are likely to see more eastern grey kangaroos. If you want to scale the hill behind you, walk a little way west to a carpark, continue up the road for about 200 m then take a track to the right which leads to Kinchela Trig; but the view from the top is obscured and not really worth the climb. It's better to explore the point. Be sure to get across to the south end for a view over Killick Beach and a long stretch of coast. Head back to the car via the beaches, maybe taking a dip or two.

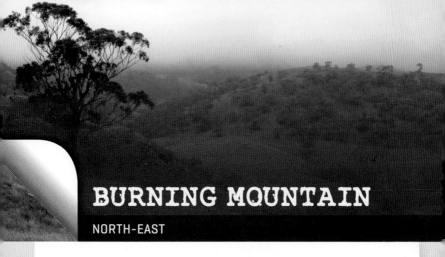

BURNING MOUNTAIN

NORTH-EAST

WALK: 4 km return

TIME REQUIRED: 1 hour

BEST TIME: Spring

GRADE: Moderate – there are many stairs to negotiate

ENVIRONMENT: A smoking mountain that has been burning underground for thousands of years, stringybark and ironbark forest, farmland

BEST MAP: This book

TOILETS: Flushing toilets at the start of the walk

FOOD: Scone, 20 km south has plenty of options

TIPS: Break up a drive on the New England Highway with this unusual little jaunt

One of the most unusual spots in NSW, Burning Mountain has been burning for an estimated 6000 years. Although this route doesn't offer spectacular views or particularly beautiful forest, it is a great walk because of its novelty and fascinating natural history.

Just a couple of hundred metres off the New England Highway, between Scone and Murrurundi is the Burning Mountain Rest Area and Nature Reserve. There is only the one walk, but it is well worth stretching the legs there for an hour or so.

[above] *New England scenery*

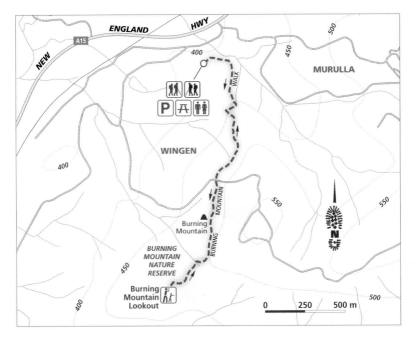

The rest area is on the east side of the highway and well marked with a turning lane. It has picnic tables and flushing toilets, but no potable water.

The main attraction of this walk is to see a mountain that has been burning – underground – for thousands of years: so long in fact that it is incorporated into Aboriginal dreamtime stories. Although the forest isn't spectacular, there is plenty to catch your attention, including some great bird life (particularly rosellas, king parrots, kookaburras and speckled warblers), eastern grey kangaroos (who reportedly like the warm soil) and some unusual plants, such as the kangaroo thorn, a spiky wattle, and the native olive, which has purple fruit.

From the carpark, the route first takes you over a large stile into farmland. There will probably be grazing cattle near the dams and a cowpat or two. Initially the track heads uphill, gaining about 100 vertical metres in the first kilometre, but there are benches and picnic tables along the way and the gradient is never too steep.

It's a fairly well constructed track, but some stairs halfway along the walk are poorly designed to be just at the wrong stride length.

Once atop the ridge, the track winds through pleasant stringybark and narrow-leafed ironbark forest. It crosses a management track, but keep going straight, following the obvious narrower track.

It is believed that the coal seam, about 30 m underground, was ignited about 6000 years ago near the Pages River, about 6 km north, so the burning zone is moving south at a rate of about 1 m a year. As it moves, it weakens the subsurface, so on this walk you will see very recent subsidence and areas where ravines have opened up. It's quite exciting to be in an area where rapid geological change is happening, almost before your eyes.

At one point, you'll notice the hillside on the left side of the track is almost bare of vegetation. This is one of many places where the heat has scorched the earth and killed the plants.

The end of the walk is a vegetation-free zone. A raised walkway takes you over what looks almost like an industrial fill site, with a quite lovely palette of colours – the yellow of sulphur (which you can smell quite strongly in the air), red iron-oxide ochres and white sinter. Look carefully and you can see the heat haze over the surface of the ground, and the wisps of smoke for which the mountain is famous.

Scorched earth at the top of Burning Mountain

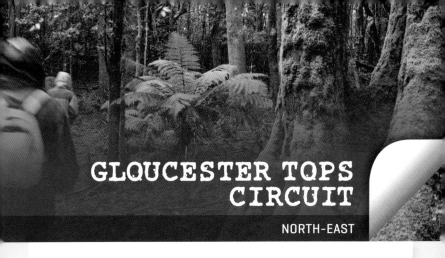

GLOUCESTER TOPS CIRCUIT

WALK: *7.5 km loop*

TIME REQUIRED: *3 hours*

BEST TIME: *Cooler weather, such as winter, with a chance of snow*

GRADE: *Moderate*

ENVIRONMENT: *Snow gums, subalpine grassland, waterfalls*

BEST MAP: *Barrington Tops National Park and adjacent reserves, National Parks and Wildlife Service*

TOILETS: *At the Gloucester Tops picnic area, 18 km before the start of the walk*

FOOD: *Gloucester, 1 hour away by car has many options; locals recommend the coffee at Perenti, 69 Church St, which also serves a range of great food based on local produce: (02) 6558 9219*

TIPS: *Rug up and enjoy!*

[above] *Walking among the moss-covered Antarctic beech*

Perhaps the best introduction to the World Heritage-listed Barrington Tops National Park, this high-altitude loop combines three of the park's smaller walks and includes subalpine grasslands, woodlands, snowgums, waterfalls and the mainland's most southerly Antarctic beech forest.

With altitudes up to 1500 m, it often snows in this subalpine neck of the woods, three hours' drive north of Sydney. Much of the wild 74 000 ha Barrington Tops National Park is included in the Gondwana Rainforests of Australia World Heritage Area, preserving living relics of our planet's evolution when the Australian continent was joined to Antarctica and South America. The area receives some 1200 mm of rain each year and conditions can change unexpectedly, so be prepared for almost anything.

Half the adventure in exploring the national park is in getting to the start of the walking tracks. This sensational loop starts about an

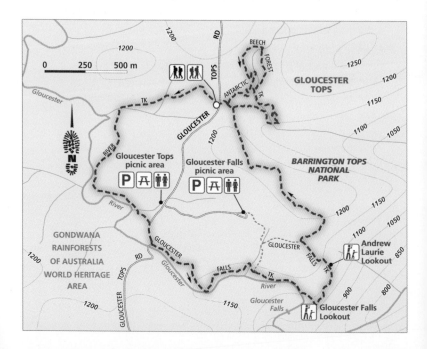

Vibrant mosses on Antarctic beech

hour's drive from the nearest town, Gloucester. First head south of Gloucester down Bucketts Way through rolling farmland, then right onto Gloucester Tops Rd. After about 10 km it will change to a dirt road. A few more kilometres on, it takes a sharp turn to the left at a fork in the road. Take this sharp turn, which should be signposted 'Gloucester Tops'.

The next section of road takes you across the Gloucester River half a dozen times over low concrete fords. After periods of very high rain, the road will be impassable, but during normal periods the water can still be deep enough to cause a considerable splash. It is suitable and great fun for sedans as long as you take care.

After the Gloucester River picnic area (with pit toilets) the winding road will begin heading up the mountain and the temperature may well drop 10 degrees or more over the next 18 km. The road will fork again, and again you will head left, stopping at the first carpark on the right side of the road, marked 'River Track'. The loop walk will finish on the opposite side of the road.

The River Track starts at an elevation of 1150 m, with a gentle meander through subalpine grasslands and woodlands. There are colourful snowgums and mountain gums, with an understorey of snowgrass, mat rush and acacias. Take time to observe the thick growths of lichens completely covering some saplings and to enjoy the quiet and mystery of this special area. A few delightful log crossings mark swampy areas and creeks where you might hear the call of some of the more rugged frog species – there are 18 species in the park, including the rare glandular frog. Other animals in this section include swamp wallabies, eastern grey kangaroos, wombats and the rufous scrubwren.

Soon the walk begins following the Gloucester River as it gushes over rocks and drops. The River Walk officially finishes at a small, unattractive picnic area. An epic 220 km multiday walk, called the Tops to Myalls Heritage Trail, heads across the river from here,

Subalpine woodland

finishing at Hawks Nest on the coast. Those after a real walking adventure completed by few people should definitely consider this classic.

Our walk, however, keeps to the same side of the river. Go across the dirt carpark and onto the Gloucester Falls Track, which keeps tracing the river, although some distance above it. In a couple of places there are steep pads off the track down to the river if you want a closer view, but otherwise you will be seeing the river through the dark canopy of trees. Lovely silvereyes and fairy wrens will probably keep you company. The walk culminates in the Andrew Laurie Lookout, a small fenced area with quite distant views over several falls.

From the lookout, the track ascends fairly steeply up towards the Antarctic Beech Forest Track. An alternative track to the left offers a short cut back to a carpark, but keep on the right track.

Soon you'll come to the Antarctic Beech Forest Track, a 2.5 km loop, with a short additional loop (called the Short Loop). At the time of writing, one section of the long loop was closed, meaning walkers could hike three-quarters of the way around the track, but then had to backtrack. The long loop is definitely worth taking, as it delves past thick tree ferns, towering Antarctic beech more than 30 m tall, brown barrel, sassafras and black olive berry. Roots and trunks and fallen trees are covered in brightly covered mosses and lichens; and the forest can be beautifully moody in mist or drizzle. Cool temperate rainforests like this occupy much of the misty heights in the park above 700 m elevation.

There are a couple of stepping stone crossings, and the track wanders past some more pretty falls before coming back to the main track. The loop finishes only 100 m or so from where you parked your car, so when you rejoin the main track, simply turn right and follow it up the gentle rise back to the road. Once again you can enjoy the adventurous drive back out of the park.

CORKER TRAIL TO CAREYS PEAK

WALK: 20 km return

TIME REQUIRED: 6 hours

BEST TIME: The tall, ancient forests of Barrington National Park are best in moody, misty cool weather, although a clear day will reward you with good views; this walk will be most comfortable in winter but be prepared for snow

GRADE: Hard

ENVIRONMENT: Rainforest, tall eucalypt forests and subalpine woodland, plus views over the ranges to the Hunter Valley

BEST MAP: Barrington Tops National Park & adjacent reserves, National Parks and Wildlife Service

TOILETS: Pit toilets are available at the Williams River Day Area, a 15-minute drive from the start of the walk and at Wombat Flat, a 300 m detour off the route about halfway along

FOOD: Dungog is a reasonable-sized country town, one hour drive away

TIPS: As the walks here are a little out of the way, and this walk is quite long, it is worthwhile staying nearby – either camping, or at the cosy self-contained Barrington Wilderness Cottages 10 minutes drive from the start of the walk. Ph: 1300 731 490, www.barringtonwildernesscottages.com.au

[above] *Male flame robin*

Gaining nearly 1 km in height over 10 km, this challenging walk goes up and up and up through the major ecosystems of Barrington National Park, providing some excellent views.

There are several routes up Careys Peak, one of the highest mountains in Barrington National Park. This is the toughest track to do it in a day, but worth it for the challenge and the opportunity see the changing vegetation at different altitudes. Starting at 657 m above sea level, you'll climb up to 1560 m, and then back down again, passing through stunning Antarctic beech forests, rainforests and subalpine woodland. It's a 20 km return trip, although the sign at the start incorrectly claims it is 12 km each way.

From the Dungog side of the national park, drive to the end of Salisbury Rd, which becomes Williams Top Rd, passing Barrington Wilderness Cottages, and on to the picnic area at Lagoon Pinch, which is at the end of the dirt road (if you keep taking every 'right' option). There is tank water at the picnic area (not advised for drinking) but no toilet.

From here the track goes steeply up, with a heart-starter right out of the blocks. But don't stress: on this walk most of the steep pinches only last a few hundred metres, with lesser gradients

White everlasting daisy

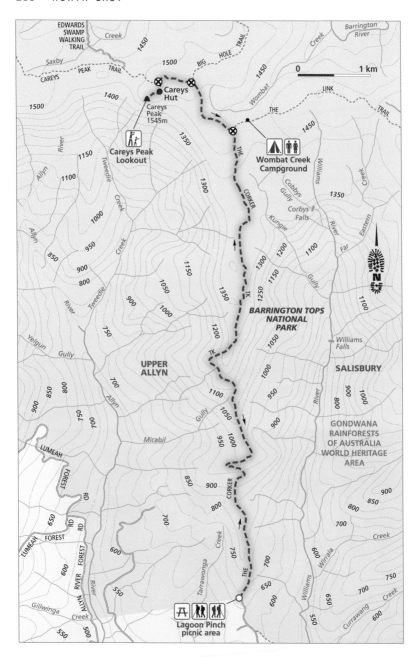

Careys Peak, on the skyline at right

between to help you catch your breath. Most of the climbing is done in the first 6 km, so the second two-thirds of the walk are much easier.

Note the huge trees at the beginning of the walk in the vine forest: turpentines, corkwoods, Sydney blue gums and the occasional red cedar. In a few places you can see where loggers took some of the biggest of the trees, leaving massive stumps, 3–4 m in diameter. There will probably be an orchestra of lyrebirds making music in the shadows and darting across the track like startled chickens, and goannas are relatively common.

Views unfortunately are sparse, and more like glimpses between the trees, but you will see the ridge of the range you are climbing to the right and to the left.

There are alleys of tree ferns and way up high, birds-nest ferns and elkhorns, and trees wearing iridescent lichen shawls.

The first decent views are at the 5 km mark, where a small gap in the trees reveals a range out to the left. You'll see the pointy summit of Careys Peak, and Mt Barrington to the left of it.

Not far past this, the track levels out a little, and you'll be in the thick of a glorious grove of Antarctic beech trees, rising 30 m or so off the forest floor. Standing like comrades beside these relics of Gondwana are messmates and brown barrel, and a host of tree ferns underneath.

Surprisingly, the track heads slightly downhill after this, but when it rises again, you'll quickly be in the sub-alpine woodland, with tussocky snowgrass, mountain gums and mountain ribbon gums. Birdlife through here can be superb, with crimson rosellas overhead and stunning flame robins bobbing along the track.

Crimson rosella

The track becomes a little stony at this point and slightly harder on the feet.

At the signposted junctions with other tracks, just keep turning left and you'll reach Careys Peak. However a right turn at the first junction may be worth your while. It leads to the Wombat Creek camping area 300 m distant, where there is a pit toilet, and water in the creek (probably the only place to fill up water bottles on the whole walk).

As the walk swings around to the west, you'll reach another junction (the right turn of which goes to the Black Swamp camping area), and then not long after, another turn left brings you quickly

Thick forest on the way to the summit

View from the summit

down to the delightful Careys Hut. Not much in the way of shelter, it dates back to 1934, but was modified in the 1970s. Careys Peak summit is only a few hundred metres up a narrow track from here, and as there is nowhere decent to sit at the top, you are best advised to grab your cameras and leave your daypacks here.

The summit has a railing and offers 180-degree views to the south over the forested mountains and the Hunter Valley. Note the 1934 sundial at the summit. A tiny bush bash to the right, of just a few metres, will provide views to the west and the sub-alpine plateau, with its swamps and snow grass plains.

As the summit is small and overgrown, the best place for lunch and a welcome break is back down on the grassy area around Careys Hut. It's a beautiful, peaceful place to sit, and the birds will probably gather around, including whipbirds, honeyeaters, robins and a host of others.

When it's time to head back, remember, it's nearly all downhill!

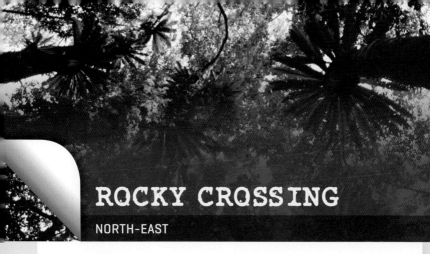

ROCKY CROSSING

NORTH-EAST

WALK: 18 km loop and return

TIME REQUIRED: 5 hours

BEST TIME: The walk is very shaded with stunning swimming holes, so it is a particularly good summer option

GRADE: Easy to moderate – pretty flat most of the way

ENVIRONMENT: Rainforest, huge trees, bubbling cascades and swimming holes

BEST MAP: Barrington Wilderness Cottages walking map

TOILETS: Pit toilet at the carpark and picnic area at the start of walk

FOOD: Dungog is a reasonable-sized country town, 40 minutes drive away

TIPS: As the walks here are a little out of the way, it is worthwhile staying nearby – either camping, or at the self-contained Barrington Wilderness Cottages positioned right near the start of the walk. Ph: 1300 731 490, www.barringtonwildernesscottages.com.au

Brush turkey

[above] *Tall trees support an aerial ecosystem*

This is a truly beautiful rainforest walk along the Williams River as it burbles and cascades downstream, with pools to swim in, towering trees and interesting wildlife.

The Dungog side of the Barrington Tops National Park contains some of the most southerly sections of the World Heritage–listed Gondwana Rainforests of Australia. It takes about 40 minutes from Dungog to drive up close to the end of Salisbury Rd, through rolling farmland.

The walk starts at the Williams River Day Area, just before the road heads sharply up the hill to the left. It's right near the entrance to Barrington Wilderness Cottages, which makes this a great place to stay before or after this walk. Many old maps have 'Barrington Guest House', but this burnt down more than a decade ago.

From the picnic area (which has a gas barbecue), duck across the bridge, and onto the lovely Blue Gum Loop walk. These gorgeous blue and white-trunked trees stand as straight as telegraph poles, but more than twice as high.

The track on the east side of the river crosses over side creeks and gullies while passing through towering tree ferns and dark rainforest. There was once a suspension bridge in this section but they are all solid structures now.

Keep an eye and ear out for lyrebirds, brush turkeys and maybe even the stunning paradise riflebird, which can sometimes be heard tearing apart fallen logs to get at insects.

At all stages on this walk, if you venture at all off the track, be aware of giant stinging trees. They have large, light-green leaves covered in minute barbs that can deliver a very painful and irritating sting. (The best remedy if you are stung is to repeatedly use sticky tape or similar to try to remove the barbs.)

When you cross the Williams River a second time, the track will fork – left is back to the car (the way you will eventually head home) while right is further up into the forest, where you'll walk through a dark forest of turpentine, sassafras and strangler figs. You will come across large tree stumps still showing the steps cut into

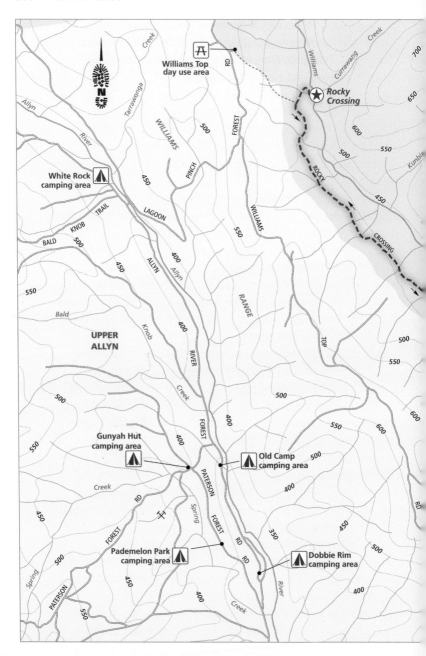

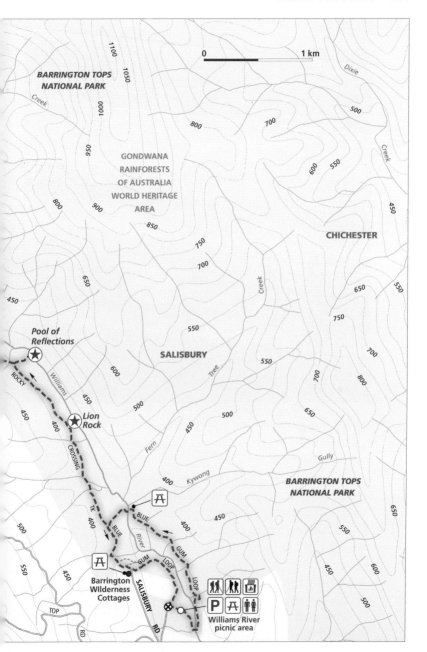

1100
1050
1000
950
900
800
850
750
700
650
550
600
500
450

500
550
600
650
450
550
750
700
800
700
650
550

BARRINGTON TOPS
NATIONAL PARK

Creek

Dixie
Creek

GONDWANA
RAINFORESTS
OF AUSTRALIA
WORLD HERITAGE
AREA

CHICHESTER

Pool of
Reflections

ROCKY

Williams

Lion
Rock

CROSSING

SALISBURY

Creek

Tree

Fern

450

400

TK

BLUE

BLUE

River

GUM

LOOP

Kywong

Gully

BARRINGTON TOPS
NATIONAL PARK

GUM

LOOP

LOOP

Barrington
Wilderness
Cottages

SALISBURY

RD

TOP

RD

Williams River
picnic area

0   1 km

Rocky Crossing

them by axemen who once logged this area. Closer to the ground, just waist high, are plants with very large leaves like elephant ears, called cunjevoi.

The track generally keeps a little away from the river, but there are several great opportunities to head down to the water. The first is Lion Rock, which has a stunning chasm cut into the rock, and a large natural swimming pool beneath. Stand next to the chasm and look right, and you'll see the lion's head near the pool, on the same side of the river.

Another 15 minutes up the track, you'll reach the lovely Pool of Reflections, which again is perfect for a dip.

As the track continues up to the highest point, Rocky Crossing, note the huge number of giant birds-nest ferns and elkhorns high in the trees. Some trees have rich mini-ecosystems of ferns, vines, lichens and mosses growing on their trunks. A short, marked diversion leads to a large strangler fig.

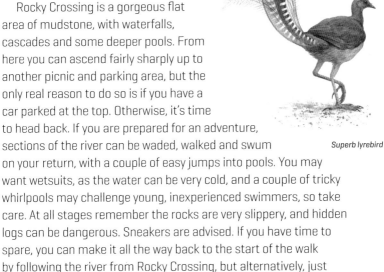

Rocky Crossing is a gorgeous flat area of mudstone, with waterfalls, cascades and some deeper pools. From here you can ascend fairly sharply up to another picnic and parking area, but the only real reason to do so is if you have a car parked at the top. Otherwise, it's time to head back. If you are prepared for an adventure, sections of the river can be waded, walked and swum

Superb lyrebird

on your return, with a couple of easy jumps into pools. You may want wetsuits, as the water can be very cold, and a couple of tricky whirlpools may challenge young, inexperienced swimmers, so take care. At all stages remember the rocks are very slippery, and hidden logs can be dangerous. Sneakers are advised. If you have time to spare, you can make it all the way back to the start of the walk by following the river from Rocky Crossing, but alternatively, just do a section or two, for example, from the Pool of Reflections to Lion Rock.

On the track, when you hit the Blue Gum Loop fork, keep going straight ahead on the same side of the river, and you'll soon pass Barrington Wilderness Cottages on the right, before returning to the picnic area.

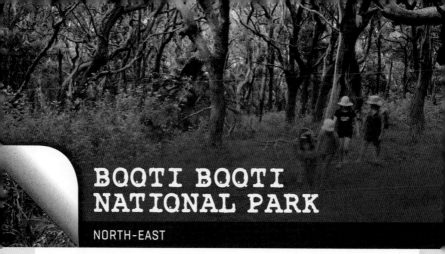

BOOTI BOOTI NATIONAL PARK

NORTH-EAST

WALK: 7.5 km loop

TIME REQUIRED: 2 hours

BEST TIME: Summer

GRADE: Moderate – some steep climbs and rough tracks to negotiate

ENVIRONMENT: Cabbage palm forest, beach, coastal headland, lakeside walk

BEST MAP: The Great Lakes National Parks, *Department of Environment and Climate Change, NSW*

TOILETS: At Elizabeth Beach at the start of the walk and The Ruins camping area, halfway through

FOOD: Forster/Tuncurry, 15 km away, has everything you might need

TIPS: A lovely break from the beach on a summer holiday, this walk is perfect for a cloudy day

[above] *Booti Hill forest*

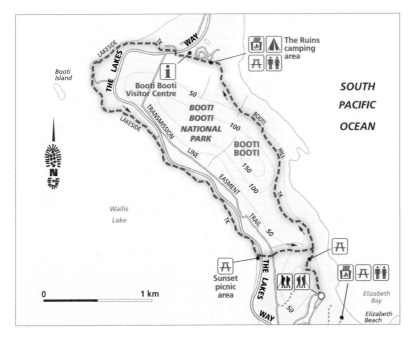

With lovely cabbage palm rainforests, and a combination of steep coastal headlands, beautiful beaches and a flat lakeside walk, this route has a bit of everything, and is just the right length for many people who want an interesting couple of hours in the bush.

The Lakes Way, from the Pacific Highway to Forster, is the gateway to many North Coast delights. There's the tallest tree in NSW, The Grandis (76 m tall), access to Myall Lake, the popular beaches at Seal Rocks, and lovely hidden beaches and camping spots at places such as Smiths Lake and Booti Booti National Park. This 7.5 km loop includes two excellent swimming beaches – Elizabeth (patrolled during the swimming season) and Seven Mile – as well as a walk along part of the shore of 25 km long Wallis Lake.

The camping area at The Ruins is particularly recommended, and this walking loop goes through the campground. However, if you are just doing the walk, it's best to start at the settlement of Elizabeth Beach, about 20 km south of Forster on the Lakes Way. This way, you start with the steepest ascent. Turn east off Lakes Way into Lakeside Crescent, then take the first left into Lethbridge Rd. At the end of this road is a turning circle and parking. The surf club, picnic area and toilets are further down the beach, a few minutes' walk away.

As you face the beach, you will find a track heading steeply up Booti Hill on the left side of the carpark. Take this as it ascends 80 m through cabbage palms and stringybark. There are some lovely dark sections of rainforest, but the track can be rough at times with exposed roots and rocks. Once atop the ridge, there are some colourful orange and pink-barked angophoras and a clearing with a picnic table and great views over the ocean. There is a turnoff to the left (which is the way you will come back) but keep going straight ahead, through tall forests with ironbarks and enjoy more views through the trees. As well as lantana, you are likely to see another very invasive weed in this section, the bitou bush. It has yellow flowers and has taken over huge tracts of eastern Australia's coastline. Still, there are lovely sections here with different native vegetation types. As you start the descent towards

Seven Mile Beach, south headland

Booti Hill

Seven Mile Beach, you will pass through tea tree forest and some coastal scrub.

About 100 m before reaching the beach, a little fisherman's track comes in from the right-hand side. Those with extra time might enjoy the walk along this track. After a while it leads to some lovely wave-washed platforms and rock pools. It's certainly worth just pottering 50 m along it for a good view down the beach.

The track descends to the southern end of Seven Mile Beach, which is a great place for a quick rest and/or a swim. To continue the loop, take the first beach exit track, which leads almost directly to the amenities block of The Ruins campground. Walk straight past this and up the gravel road, past the Booti Booti Visitor Centre on the right-hand side, and out to the road. You'll see the track continuing directly opposite. Be careful crossing as it's something of a blind corner.

After a short grassy section, you'll reach the lakeside, with some thick cabbage palm forest on the left-hand side of the track. The track now follows the winding lake's edge, through some tall gum forest. After a couple of flat kilometres you'll reach a picnic area with tables. It's right beside the road, but is still a nice spot for quick stop.

From here it's just a short stroll back along the road to the starting point, but it is far more interesting to cross the road again and head up the steep fire trail on the other side, through some lovely tall gum forest that includes an endangered ironbark. The track comes out at the top of the ridge near the clearing and picnic table you visited early in the walk. From here you can retrace your steps down the steep track to the Elizabeth Beach carpark.

MYALL LAKE

NORTH-EAST

WALK: 25 km return

TIME REQUIRED: 2 very easy days (recommended), or 1 moderate day walk

BEST TIME: Warmer months, particularly spring or early summer

GRADE: Easy

ENVIRONMENT: Wet heathland, extensive freshwater lake, paperbark swamp, coastal forest

BEST MAP: The Great Lakes National Parks, *Department of Environment and Climate Change, NSW*

TOILETS: There is an eco toilet at the carpark at the start of the walk and at Johnson Beach camping area and Shelley Beach camping area

FOOD: There is a restaurant/bar/kiosk at Myall Shores, a 5-minute drive and punt from the start of the walk

TIPS: Take binoculars for bird spotting

[above] *Shelley Beach*

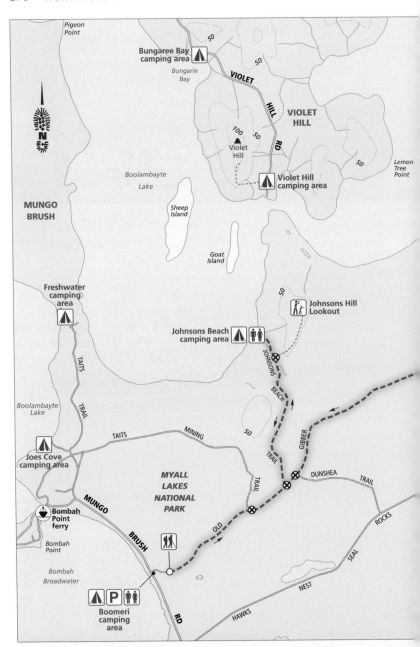

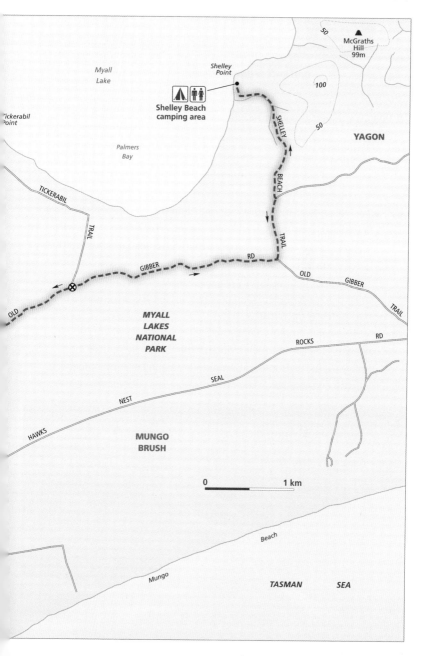

McGraths
Hill
99m

Myall
Lake

Shelley
Point

Shelley Beach
camping area

Tickerabil
Point

Palmers
Bay

YAGON

TICKERABIL

TRAIL

SHELLEY

BEACH

TRAIL

GIBBER

RD

OLD

GIBBER

TRAIL

OLD

MYALL
LAKES
NATIONAL
PARK

OLD

ROCKS

RD

SEAL

NEST

HAWKS

MUNGO
BRUSH

0   1 km

Beach

Mungo

TASMAN   SEA

A bird-lovers dream, this easy, flat walk ends in some quiet isolated camping sites on the shores of a vast freshwater lake, with crystal clear water and soft creamy sands.

This lovely long walk could be nicknamed 'Birdsong Alley' as the vast bulk of it is along a flat fire trail with so many birds zipping around, singing, twittering, squawking and scrawking that at times it is a cacophony. There are 280 bird species in Myall Lakes National Park and if you keep your eyes open, you'll see many of them on this walk. Adding to the bush concerto is the croaking of thousands of frogs in the Moors swamps along the track, and the buzzing of bees in the flowering paperbarks.

Myall Lakes National Park is a 48 000 ha wildlife paradise that has the largest natural brackish lake system on the NSW coast. The 10 000 ha of wetlands are so important to many bird species that they have been placed on the Ramsar list for wetlands of international importance.

The walk is mainly along the Old Gibber Track, which can be accessed by driving 25 km north from Hawks Nest on Mungo Brush Rd to the Boomeri Camping Area and carpark on the right. If you are coming from the north, drive in from Buladelah, turning left

Darter

Cabbage palm forest near Johnsons Beach

at Crawford St, which turns into Bombah Pt Rd – a mostly excellent dirt road. After 15 km you will reach the car ferry at Myall Shores. There is a fee to use the ferry, but the service is fast (leaving every half hour or so), and it is a lovely spot. Once across the water, it's only a couple of kilometres down the road to Boomeri.

The walking track (actually a wide vehicle track) leaves from the far end of the carpark. Don't be put off by the fact that the first kilometre or so has some sharp gravel sections – after that the surface becomes one of hard-packed sand, which is one of the nicest possible surfaces to walk on, providing cushioning and support for your feet. It's also some of the easiest walking you'll find anywhere, being almost dead flat the whole way. It would make an easy mountain-bike ride, and that could be an excellent way to carry camping gear to Shelley Beach.

In the carpark and along the first section of the walk, there are some stunning, large xanthorrhoeas. Once upon a time these spiky plants were called 'black boys' in the Australian vernacular, as their trunks are nearly always black. Fire is very important to their reproduction. They are also called grass trees, but as they are not closely related to either grass or trees, many people are now calling them by their Latin name, xanthorrhoea.

In spring the heathland is coloured with wildflowers, but at any time of year there is something flowering – acacias, paperbarks or gums. There are some lovely pink-skinned angophoras (red gums) along the walk, and other large trees provide some degree of shade along most of the route. Occasionally you will come across a section of low heathland with little to no shade. Be warned: there are no views of the lake along the track – you need to take one of the side tracks to get down to the lake.

The birds along the route are too many to mention, but include the snapping sounds of restless flycatchers, friarbirds, wattlebirds,

Myall Lakes National Park

yellow-tailed cockatoos, pheasant coucals and the very friendly red-browed finches, little greenish birds with a red racing stripe across their eye, and a flash of red at their rear. Some of the more colourful species include eastern yellow robins, which have a vibrant yellow front, and turquoise parrots, elegant small parrots with a mixed plumage of grass green, brilliant blue and yellow.

There are plenty of other animals to be found along here, including dingos and goannas, myriad butterflies and colourful dragonflies. Myall Lakes National Park contains nearly a third of all the plant and animal species found on the NSW coast.

After about 1 km, a small unmarked track comes in from the left. The next track is the well-marked Johnsons Beach turnoff, which we will visit on our return. A couple of other signposted tracks meet the Old Gibber Track along the way, but just keep going for about 9 km until you see the well-marked track to Shelley Beach. This track will take you through a few new vegetative communities. First there are some towering banksias, then a paperbark swamp with dark ruby-brown tannin-stained waters, then a beautiful section of tall gum forest, followed by coastal scrub.

Don't expect a 'beach' when you get to Shelley Beach, but the paperbark-fringed lakeside does have creamy sand and beautiful fresh water to swim in. The lake is shallow and flat so you can wade out for a long way just enjoying the serenity while looking across the vast lake at the undulating hills of McGraths Island, Swan Pt and Pats Head. Near the water's edge you may see cormorants, darters, pelicans and sea-eagles overhead, and fish can be quite clearly seen in the clear water.

There are 18 campsites here, and houseboats occasionally pull up, but out of peak times you will probably have the whole place to yourself. There is an eco toilet. All water should be boiled.

Return the same way, but this time take the 4 km return trip detour down to Johnsons

Australian pelican

Beach, which is even prettier than Shelley Reach, with a small 'beach' area. In fact, those pressed for time or after a much shorter walk will enjoy the 8 km return walk to Johnsons Beach, which also has camping sites and an eco toilet. As well as some stunning angophoras with huge girths near the start of the track, this side route reveals yet another vegetative community – a littoral rainforest with cabbage palms and lots of mozzies. More than halfway along this track you will see a turnoff to the right to a lookout, but at last check it was overgrown, infested with weeds and the view was miniscule at best. Better to just keep going down the small hill to the water. If there is no one around, this is a perfect place to swim au naturale and enjoy the beauty of the water, the trees and the lake environment.

Turquoise parrot

STOCKTON BEACH SAND DUNES

WALK: Approximately 7 km

TIME REQUIRED: 2 hours

BEST TIME: Almost any time except very hot summer days and very windy days

GRADE: Moderate – it can be tough walking up dunes through soft sand

ENVIRONMENT: Sand dunes, beach

BEST MAP: Woromi Conservation Lands, *Department of Environment, Climate Change and Water, NSW*

TOILETS: Birubi Point Surf Lifesaving Club at the start of the walk

FOOD: There is an excellent kiosk at the Birubi Point Surf Lifesaving Club

TIPS: Bring something to slide down the sand dunes – an old body board, cardboard boxes, etc.

[above] **Horseriding on Stockton Beach**

This unusual walk will help you explore one of the natural wonders of NSW – the enormous shifting sand dunes of Stockton Beach. There is no defined track, so your walk can be as long or as short as you like.

Just north of Newcastle, Stockton Beach is a most unusual 32 km strip of sand. It includes not just the highest shifting sand dunes in NSW, but the largest continuously mobile coastal sand mass on the east coast of Australia. As well as walking the dunes, you can traverse them by camel, 4WD, horse, 4-wheeler or sand boards. If you face away from the lapping waves and look at these towering cream sand dunes, with a train of camels in the foreground, you could easily imagine being in the Middle East.

This may not be a true 'bushwalk' but it is an interesting walk and the sand is soft and pleasant to walk on, with very few rocks or sticks.

Start your sandy adventure by finding Anna Bay, at the north-eastern end of the beach, along the Nelson Bay Rd, about 35 km off the Pacific Highway. Turn down Gan Gan Rd, then James Paterson St, passing the 4WD access to the beach (on your right). Park in the large circular parking area at the end of the street, near the Birubi Point Surf Lifesaving Club. This club, in an excellent spot with a glorious overview of the beach, includes a good kiosk with a variety of hot and cold food and beverages.

Pacific gull

From the club you will see the dunes stretching away to the right, some distance behind the beach. If time is short, you could just head straight for the nearest dunes, but a better option if you have the time is to walk down the beach for a couple of kilometres, then head inland, up some high dunes, then back along the highest peaks to the carpark. With the clubhouse as a beacon and the vast blue ocean on one side, it is almost impossible to become lost, even if you do find yourself down in a sand valley between several large dunes for a while.

The walk along the beach is fascinating, with camel trains and horses, dogs, trailbikes, wave jumpers and 4WDs to entertain you. The latter can be quite dangerous as they zoom along the beach or over sand dunes, and they can be hard to hear on approach, so keep an eye on small children. Along the beach you may also see pied oystercatchers, gulls and terns, and a variety of pippis underfoot.

Just behind the beach, some small dunes can hold ephemeral wetlands, where you might see wading birds such as ibis, or other hunters such as ravens and crows. The area is called the Worimi Conservation Lands after the Worimi people, whose traditional lands include the dunes. As the wind moves the sand about, many Aboriginal sites have been uncovered in the dunes, including middens, campsites and burial sites. There are also more than 20 threatened plant species in the conservation area.

After the wetlands, it's time to head up into the high dunes. Pick the largest one you can see and aim for the top. The sand in

Stockton Beach sand dunes

Between the beach and the towering dunes

places is hard-packed and easy to walk on, but at other times it is lusciously soft, and you will sink up to your knees. The dunes can be up to 40 m above sea level and the summits provide a great view of the sharp lines and curves of other dunes, and the unending blue of the Pacific Ocean.

Even if you haven't brought a board, some dune faces are so steep you can easily slide down them anyway, or jump into the soft sand.

It's great fun climbing the peaks, but the walk back along the tops of various dunes is much more tiring than the stroll along the beach. Keep this in mind when you are deciding where to turn inland and back to Anna Bay. After a couple of hours you will probably have covered 7 km or so and be ready for a swim at the patrolled beach near the clubhouse, or just a few quiet moments at the outdoor kiosk enjoying the view.

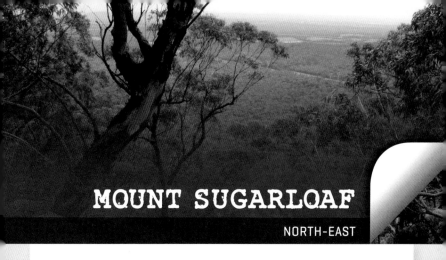

MOUNT SUGARLOAF

WALK: 3.5 km

TIME REQUIRED: 30 minutes to 1.5 hours

BEST TIME: Breaking up a road trip north of Sydney

GRADE: Easy

ENVIRONMENT: Moist gum forest, mountain with panoramic views

BEST MAP: 1:25 000 Wallsend, NSW Land and Property Information

TOILETS: Flushing toilets at the carpark and picnic area

FOOD: Newcastle shops

TIPS: Take your time and enjoy the serenity in some lovely forest

One of the easiest walks in this book, this is a great walk partly because of its location. It is only 5 minutes from the Sydney–Newcastle freeway, and about 1.5 hours from Sydney, so perfect to break a journey north or south. The view from the summit is great, but the best bit is the forest.

There are a couple of loops around Mt Sugarloaf, in increasingly large circles as you go down the mountain. Most people seem to just walk the bitumen track to the summit, but it is definitely worth doing one or both loops. This route covers both loops and the summit in an easy stroll.

[above] *Summit views*

Snow was recorded on the 412 m mountain in 1965. Its prominent position near the coast means Captain James Cook described it on 10 May 1770 as 'a remarkable hill shaped like the crown of a hat'. Local Aboriginal people called it 'Warawollung', meaning 'human head', because it resembles one from some angles.

From the Sydney–Newcastle Freeway, turn west onto George Booth Drive near Newcastle. After about 650 m, turn onto Mt Sugarloaf Rd, and follow it 3 km to the top. If it's not too crowded, park at the top carpark, near the fishpond with beautiful water lilies. Alternatively, there is plenty of parking lower down or across the road in the vast picnic area.

Lily pond near the carpark

Gymea lily and forest

From the top carpark, walk straight ahead into the forest (not up or down the hill) and you will find a track (the Red Track). Within a few metres, you will see a red arrow pointing straight ahead, and a track veers sharply left. Take this left track, down to the lower, longer track (which used to be marked as the Green Track, but all the markers seem to have disappeared). This 1.8 km track now travels around the mountain, through lovely spotted gum forests. This beautiful tree is one of only a few winter-flowering eucalypts that occurs near the coast, making it an important nectar tree for many species. There are also loads of Gymea lilies, which produce massive red flowerheads in spring and summer. Clouds of mozzies can be merciless in the forest after rain, so take insect repellent. Keep an eye out for beautiful diamond/carpet pythons – large, non-aggressive and non-venomous snakes that are often kept as pets (but, as with all wild snakes, you should not interfere with them as they can still deliver a nasty bite).

Under the canopy there are boulders with interesting features, tussock grasses, lime-green bracken and a rich collection of lichens and mosses.

Avoid the unmarked fire trail that heads sharply left, and keep travelling around until the track forks. Either of these wide tracks will take you back to the top of the picnic area. However, it's best to take the left fork, then a small, unmarked foot track (sometimes called the Cliff Track) that comes off it to the left and goes to a lovely lookout, before continuing along the escarpment offering great views. After another 10 minutes, keep your eye out on the right for a bitumen road in a large cleared area, which is the bottom of the picnic area. (The small track keeps going along the escarpment and down the mountain at this point.)

Walk up the bitumen road through the picnic ground and back to your car, grab a quick drink, then head out on the Red Track, straight out from the carpark. This shorter loop takes you to a lovely section of xanthorrhoeas (grass trees) set among many more Gymea lilies. The track comes in on the high side of one of the large telecommunications towers, and joins the steep bitumen road to the summit. There are a couple of flights of stairs at the end, but it is only about 250 m to the top.

Tree growth means it's no longer a true 360-degree view from the summit, but there are lovely long views in almost every direction.

BOUDDI COASTAL WALK

WALK: 9.5 km one way or 19 km return

TIME REQUIRED: 3 hours one way, all day return

BEST TIME: A warm, sunny day in early spring

GRADE: Moderate to hard one way, hard if taken both ways – although the ascents are not big, the track is constantly undulating, and there are a lot of stairs

ENVIRONMENT: Stunning beaches, cliffs, flower-rich coastal heath, woodland

BEST MAP: Bouddi & Wyrrabalong National Parks, NSW National Parks

TOILETS: Flushing toilet at MacMasters Beach at start of walk and at Putty Beach campground; there is a pit toilet halfway through at Little Beach campground

FOOD: Gosford, a 20-minute drive away, is a thriving metropolis with everything

TIPS: This is another walk that you can easily access small sections, so don't be put off by the distances if you do not want to walk far. Bouddi National Park is such a special area, and it is well worth exploring Maitland Bay and its surrounds, even if you don't do the whole walk.

[above] Maitland Bay

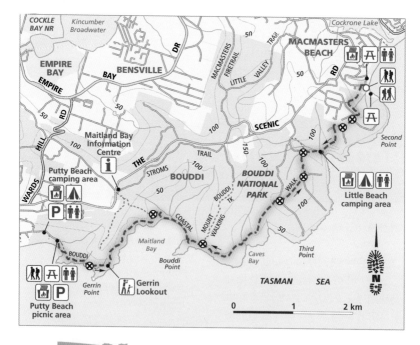

A surprisingly tough coastal walk, this takes you along sea cliffs, through stunning flowering heathland, and to some of the best undeveloped beaches on the coast.

For many people, the Central Coast is Sydney's summer playground. It's only a bit over an hour's drive from Sydney and the beaches are clean and beautiful, although many of them are hemmed in by development on three sides.

Bouddi National Park is a welcome green space in this busy stretch of coast, with undeveloped bushland and absolutely stunning beaches that require just a little effort to get to. Most of the beaches have carparks about 1 km away – enough to deter large crowds. This walk joins a few of those beaches. It's a lovely half-day walk in one direction, or a tougher full-day walk in both. Although the track rarely rises more than 100 m above sea level, it undulates almost constantly, and that, plus a few sections of sand, makes it quite tiring. But the reward of a swim at a sparkling, unadulterated beach takes any sting away, and there are great swimming/surfing beaches at each end.

Start the walk at MacMasters Beach, on the northern edge of Bouddi National Park. Out of summer there should be parking down by the surf lifesaving club. In summer it will probably be street parking only. MacMasters has a divine sea pool, is patrolled in season, has barbecue facilities, and is renowned as one of the most attractive beaches on the Central Coast.

Between the surf lifesaving club and the toilet block 100 m up the road, a set of stairs leads up to the next street, Macmaster Parade. Follow the steps up and turn left, to the end of the road, where you will enter Bouddi National Park on a shady track through cycads, xanthorrheas and bloodwoods. Within a few hundred metres this track reaches the back of a row of houses. You can either continue straight to the road and turn left, or turn left behind the houses and follow them around and then up to a fire trail. There is usually plenty of active and noisy birdlife around this interface between gardens and the bush, with rainbow lorikeets, kookaburras, cockatoos, honeyeaters and other species.

Tessellated pavement, naturally formed

In spring, the next section of sandy fire trail can be some of the best anywhere for coastal wildflowers. It can be like walking down the aisle of a large flower shop, with flannel flowers, peas, native iris and bouquets of colour on either side.

A couple of junctions offer tracks down to the coast, but our route heads inland slightly. Keep following the signs to Little Beach. There are no signs at this stage indicating you are on the Coastal Walk, but don't worry, they begin to appear south of Little Beach. The track changes from a wide fire trail to a narrow, eroded track for the descent to the beach.

Little Beach has a walk-in campground with six sites and a pit toilet, but no drinking water. This lovely beach offers good snorkelling, but its rocky nature may make it unsuitable for swimming when the tide is out.

From here the way forward is not obvious. It doesn't head across the campground as you might expect, instead, walk about 250 m up the access road (past the toilet); with a towering eucalypt forest on your left-hand side. A marked track then darts steeply into the forest, and you will be on one of the mercifully shaded sections of the track, before emerging into an open banksia heathland on a

Seaside pool at McMasters Beach

wide sandy track that heads downhill to Caves Bay. Ignore a track to your left that goes to Third Pt (aka Bombi Pt) and take the narrow track down to the creek. At the bottom of the hill, when you reach the creek (pulsing with frogs and wattlebirds), you can rock-hop along the boulders to your left for 30 m to get to Caves Bay, an interesting rocky inlet.

The route climbs sharply again, into an area where you may see anything from bouncing butterflies and superb fairy-wrens to soaring sea-eagles. As the track meanders along the edge of the sea cliffs, you'll get great views out to the northern outskirts of Sydney and to Barrenjoey Lighthouse on the end of the Palm Beach isthmus.

Soon the track swings around to the right, and you'll be above the biggest jewel of the walk, Maitland Bay – a glorious crescent of yellow sand set against a sparkling sea. The shape of the bay protects the beach in almost all winds and the waves are consistently gentle and curling. It's a prime spot for a long break and a well-deserved swim. If you ever want to reach this beach directly, it's just a 1 km walk from the Maitland Bay Information Centre on The Scenic Rd, Killcare Heights.

At the far end of the beach, a paved track travels up towards the information centre, and then offers a fork left to Putty Beach. Take this track, which heads up to a great lookout with sensational views back over the route you've just travelled. It's also a great spot to look for whales, particularly as they head north May through to Aug.

From this high point, it's all downhill, and mainly on raised walkways. Another fork left offers a 100 m detour to the little Bullimah Beach where an excellent sign explains a geometrical tessellated pavement on the cliff edge.

Keep following the track around to Putty Beach, which is another delightful long stretch of sand. The nearest carpark, toilets and picnic area, are about 100 m along the beach. There is also a large camping area.

If you haven't arranged a car pick up, then you'll get to experience the whole walk again on the way back. Make time for a few more swims on the way.

MOUNT GOWER, LORD HOWE ISLAND

NORTH-EAST

WALK: 10 km return

TIME REQUIRED: 9 hours

BEST TIME: All year

GRADE: Moderate to hard – the steepness makes this a strenuous walk, but you can only do the track with a guide, who travels at a moderate pace

ENVIRONMENT: Rocky coast, steep semi-tropical mountain, rainforest, mist forest

BEST MAP: Australian Geographic map of Lord Howe Island

TRANSPORT: A lift to the start of the walk can be arranged from your Lord Howe Island accommodation, or hire a bike (which is how most people get around the island)

TOILETS: None – go at your accommodation before you leave

FOOD: Lord Howe Island settlement

TIPS: Bring a camera!

[above] *The 875 m summit of Mt Gower*

Positioned 600 km east of NSW's north coast, Lord Howe Island has a sheltered coral lagoon, dense rainforests, beaches, birds galore and two towering mountains that rise up from the sea. The highest of these is Mt Gower, a solid 875 m climb. The walk can only be done with a local guide, takes 8–9 hours, and requires the use of some ropes.

Although it may seem unnecessary for experienced walkers to be compelled to pay for a guided walk, you will not be disappointed with this stunning adventure on this World Heritage–listed wonder, or the quality of the guides. One of the two guides, Jack Shick, has been guiding people on the mountain for 20 years, completing more than 1350 climbs. His tours are Mondays and Thursdays, leaving from the south end of the island at 7.30am. The other guide, Dean Hiscox, is a naturalist and was an island ranger for 16 years, so is intimately acquainted with the Lord Howe Island woodhen recovery program and other aspects of the fauna and flora. His walks are on

Starting at sea level

The summit often has a halo of clouds

Wednesdays. Book early as there are limited places. Because of the altitude attained you should not attempt the walk if you have been scuba diving in the previous 24 hours.

The start of the walk involves one of the few flat sections, towards the hulking presence of the mountain. The climb then begins, at first through a lush palm forest. There are some ropes to help pull yourself up, but it isn't too steep at this stage. On the walk, you'll see Lord Howe's four species of palm, the most famous of which is the kentia.

The next section, called the Lower Road, is a narrow track with a steep drop below and a cliff above. Again there are ropes to help steady yourself, but make sure you take the time to enjoy the view and take photos. The top of the mountain, when you reach it, is often covered in cloud, so it's best to take advantage of any views you get.

Next you'll travel through the Erskine Valley, with occasional glimpses of Mt Lidgbird, the island's second highest mountain at 777 m. There is a walking track to its summit, which you can do without a guide.

Drink freely from the untainted waters of Erskine Creek, and fill up your water bottles, as the track only gets steeper from here. First there's a sharp rise to the saddle between Lidgbird and Gower, with great views over the coral lagoon and the whole island. You are now about halfway up the mountain. From the saddle the track heads ever upwards, with more ropes for assistance, but the rocks have plenty of grip and good hand holds. If you are finding it hard-going, the rest of the party will always wait for you to catch up.

Once the gradient decreases, you'll find yourself in a moody, dripping mist forest, with tangled timber, and lichens and moss over everything. It seems other-worldly – reminiscent of Tolkien's Fangorn Forest.

Keep your eyes peeled for one of the rarest birds in Australia – the Lord Howe Island woodhen, found only on this island. Also, at the summit in autumn and winter, the guides will 'call in' providence petrels, which will almost fall at your feet.

If it is clear at the top, the stunning views should include the impressive sight of Balls Pyramid, a towering 600 m sea spire 23 km away.

There is time for a leisurely lunch break, before the journey back the way you came, finishing around 4.30pm.

The Lower Road

The Breadknife, Warrumbungle National Park

SYDNEY

CANBERRA

WESTERN NSW

Red dirt, emus, soaring volcanic plugs, koalas, rare species, Indigenous sites and views across the vast plains of inland Australia: bushwalking in western NSW may not have a huge quantity of great bushwalks, but it makes up for it in diversity and spectacle.

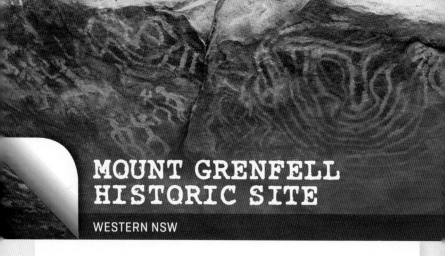

MOUNT GRENFELL HISTORIC SITE

WESTERN NSW

WALK: 5 km loop

TIME REQUIRED: 1.5 hours

BEST TIME: Cobar's tourist season is considered to be Easter through to the October long weekend (cooler months)

GRADE: Moderate

ENVIRONMENT: Stony arid country with open woodlands and grasslands

BEST MAP: National Parks Back O'Bourke, *National Parks and Wildlife Service*

TOILETS: Pit toilet at the start of the walk

FOOD: Cobar (an hour's drive away) is a thriving mining town, with large supermarkets, service stations, takeaways, cafes, bakeries and restaurants

TIPS: To take good photos, look for the camera holes in the cages that protect the artwork

[above] *Intricate designs in white ochre*

This site has perhaps the densest area of Aboriginal rock art in the state, with an extraordinary 1300 motifs within a few hundred metres.

Formerly a sheep station, the Mt Grenfell Historic Site was hidden from most white eyes until the 1960s. It is an amazing concentration of Aboriginal rock art.

This little loop walk passes the three caves with their layer upon layer of art, and is well worth the hour-long drive from Cobar. There is no camping at Mount Grenfell though, so be prepared to travel back again at the end of the day.

First travel 40 km along the sealed Barrier Highway, west of Cobar, then turn right onto the marked dirt track. This road should be open to sedans for most of the year, but can become deeply rutted or impassable after rain. As in all western parts of the state, take particular care if driving in the early morning or late afternoon, as red kangaroos may well bound in front of your vehicle. Female reds are more of a bluey-grey, and are often called 'blue flyers'.

Rocky landscape near the artworks

Other animals you are likely to encounter include feral goats, gnawing many of the trees to head height or higher, gaily coloured mulga parrots, emus and butcherbirds. The long grasses are also home to many snakes.

After 32 km of dirt, you will come to the carpark, and a pit toilet. There is no reliable drinking water here, so make sure to bring your own.

Previously, the road went another kilometre closer to the artworks, but it has been gated off, so the walk starts with a very easy stroll along the old road to the old parking area, with a picnic table and some interpretive signs.

The Ngiyambaa Walkabout track leads off to the left here, and ascends slowly through the sandstone country to the top of the ridge. You will walk through a woodland with red and yellow box trees, wilga, mulga, white cypress, grey mallee and spear grass.

Emu

Emus in yellow ochre

The top of the ridge provides views of the 73 500 square kilometre Cobar Peneplain, stretching out in all directions. You should be able to pick out some mining infrastructure in the distance.

From here the track winds down to the creekline, and the first of the three caves that are covered with paintings, in red, white and yellow ochres. There are emus, kangaroos, dancing figures, handprints and some intricate abstract designs thought to relate to the Brewarrina fish traps, some 200 km away.

You will immediately notice that the ambience of the area has been destroyed by the installation of large cages over the artwork. This has been done primarily to protect the artwork from the goats that would otherwise use the caves for shelter, but also as protection from vandals. Thankfully the builders installed some camera holes along the fences, for those who want a clear shot.

A dripline of rubber sealant has also been installed to prevent water from affecting the painted surfaces.

As in large art sites in Arnhem Land, the 1300 motifs have been painted on top of each other over time, and it is worth spending some time looking deeply into the art in each cave before moving onto the next. The caves are all within a 300 m stretch.

Just nearby (on a marked, short deviation) is a little permanent waterhole. Although filled up with silt now, it would have been maintained by hand for thousands of years, providing a sure supply for countless generations of Ngiyampaa who used this area.

Once you have finished your contemplations at this special spot, it is just a short stroll along the track back to the old picnic area, and then down the old road back to the car.

MOUNT GUNDERBOOKA

WESTERN NSW

WALK: 6 km return

TIME REQUIRED: 2 hours

BEST TIME: Bourke's tourist season is considered to be Easter through to the October long weekend (cooler months)

GRADE: Moderate

ENVIRONMENT: Arid zone rocky mountain, white cypress forest

BEST MAP: National Parks Back O'Bourke, National Parks and Wildlife Service

TOILETS: Pit toilet at the start of the walk

FOOD: Bourke (an hour's drive away) has supermarkets, service stations and a pub

TIPS: Take the day to explore the other parts of this national park, including some excellent Aboriginal art at the Mulgowan precinct; bring plenty of water

This arid-zone walk is in a stunning red-dirt national park, and with such flat land around, it doesn't take long to get a great view. The walk climbs to the summit at 500 m, from the surrounding plain at an elevation of about 200 m.

This is one of the walks in this book where the destination isn't as important as the journey. Gundabooka National Park is a stunning combination of bright-red dirt and mulga avenues off the sealed

[above] *The well-defined track to the mountain*

Kidman Way, about 50 km south of Bourke, and is well worth visiting. It goes from the banks of the Darling River, across vast plains to the Gunderbooka Range. You will almost certainly see emus, red kangaroos and the bright green flashes of mallee ringnecks, as you head to the imposing Mt Gunderbooka.

 From Bourke, the national park is situated just beyond the black soil country on the Kidman Way. If you are watching for it as you drive, you will notice the vegetation very clearly change from open plains, to thicker, higher vegetation when you hit the red soil country. The turn-off to the national park is clearly signposted. Once off the highway, it is all dirt road, but it should, with care, be manageable in sedans as long as it hasn't been raining. (The sandy soils can become very slippery after rain.) Higher clearance vehicles are preferable.

About 7 km off the highway, you'll see the turnoff to Mulgowan, which is an excellent Aboriginal art site. The Ngemba people have visited this area for many thousands of years, eating wild oranges and limes, bush bananas and the seeds of nardoo. The outstanding art here connects both to Mt Grenfell further south, and Brewarrina to the east.

Views of the long, flat plains

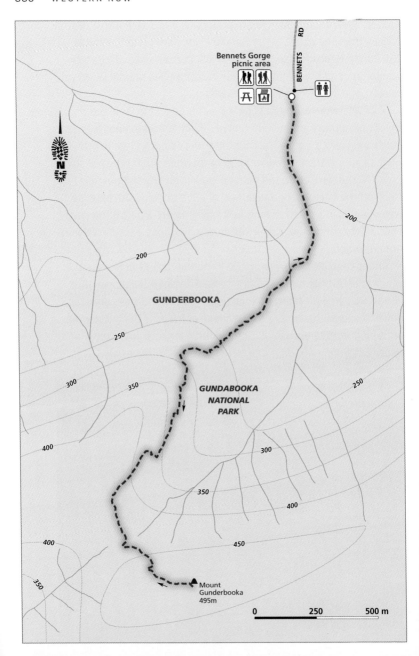

Bennets Gorge
picnic area

BENNETS RD

200

GUNDERBOOKA

200

250

300

350

GUNDABOOKA
NATIONAL
PARK

250

300

350

400

400

450

350

400

Mount
Gunderbooka
495m

0   250   500 m

Keep going along the main track for another 35 km, passing the turnoff to Dry Tank. Most of this road is excellent to drive on, although there can be some corrugations on the corners. Keep an eye out for emus, running with their feathered skirts bobbing up and down.

Turn left towards the signposted Bennets Gorge, which is a 12 km rough track to the picnic area. Along the track you will get some views of the magnificent massif that you are about to climb, with its orangey sandstones. There is a pit toilet and two gas barbecues at the carpark. If you are keen to have a picnic before you start and don't need the barbecues, then walk a few hundred metres up the track, and there is another picnic table under a large shady tree, which has uninterrupted views of the mountain and the plains.

The walk starts with a wide track that heads up a slight rise for about half a kilometre up to two bench seats and interpretive signage. You'll walk through yellow arid-zone grasses, and later pass box trees and bloodwoods towards the base of the mountain.

Past the bench seats and signage, the track can become a little vague, so it's worth remembering where the route goes: to the base of the rounded hill to your right, then up over the saddle at the top of the gorge, and to the top of the mountain. It can look a little daunting, but it isn't that difficult and most people should be able to manage. Whenever you need a breather, take a rest under one of the twisted white cypress trees and enjoy the vast vistas behind you.

The track initially crosses a creekline and across to the base of the mountain. It then winds up the rounded hill like a mulga snake. Because the surrounding country is so flat, you get great views from very early on in the climb. The path is literally a goat track, and feral goats will probably accompany you at least some of the way. Graziers in the district round up the goats for meat.

Every 50–100 m there is a track marker (an eagle), which can be reassuring. It is quite easy to deviate off the track, particularly on corners, but most of the dummy paths peter out after a few metres, so it is easy to retrace your steps and find the main track.

At the top of the ridge the track flattens out considerably and heads through a thicker cypress forest. There are a few clearings here that provide excellent views, particularly to the other side of the mountain.

The track keeps winding gently up to the actual summit. Unfortunately the summit itself is a little disappointing. It has a large cairn, but because it is quite flat, and the trees are 3–4 m high, there are no panoramic views. It's worth sitting for a few minutes and having a drink though, and you may see a whole variety of birds, including wedge-tailed eagles overhead, inland thornbills in the trees, splendid fairy-wrens on the ground and the gorgeous painted honeyeaters in the shrubs.

Return the same way, but it is worth deviating a little from the track on the way down to get to some of the obvious rocks near the edge of the gorge, as they provide a much clearer view.

As you cross the saddle and along the ridge, have a look down to the gully floor on your right, where a large boulder has been split asunder and is standing upright like an opened mussel.

The walk isn't particularly long, but as you will need to take care on the jagged, slippery and winding path on the way down, you will need at least two hours.

The sandy track into Gundabooka National Park

JACKS CREEK

WESTERN NSW

WALK: 2.5 km loop

TIME REQUIRED: 1 hour

BEST TIME: Cooler months, particularly spring

GRADE: Moderate

ENVIRONMENT: Rocky intermittent creek gully, cliffs with views, sparse pine woodland

BEST MAP: www.environment.nsw. gov.au/nationalparks/parkHome. aspx?id=N0008

TOILETS: Pit toilet at the start of the walk

FOOD: Griffith, about 40 minutes away, is a large town with many options including lots of fresh produce, with roadside stalls in season

TIPS: Take a half-day to explore the rest of the unusual Cocoparra National Park and keep your binoculars at the ready

This attractive little gorge is dry for much of the year, but can have pools that provide an oasis for a host of birds and other animals. The walk wanders through the gorge, with its towering red cliffs, then finishes on top of the cliffs, looking down at the gorge and across the plains.

The ranges of 13 000 ha Cocoparra National Park sit prominently above the irrigated farming country near Griffith. It's the sort of national park that needs a bit of time to be appreciated, as its

[above] *Views of farmland from the rocky escarpment*

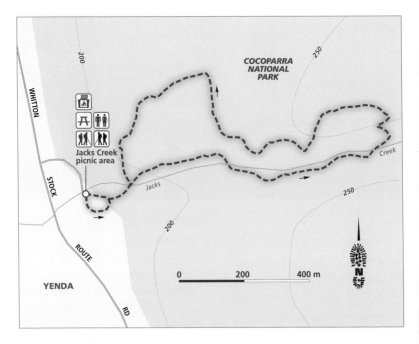

beauty isn't immediately apparent when you arrive. Much of the park was used for cropping and grazing before it was declared in 1969. This is one of several short walks in the park.

To get there, head out past De Bortoli Wines towards the ranges. The easiest way is to take Myall Park Rd from Yenda, and follow it until you reach the Mount Bingar Road, a well-graded dirt track that heads off to the right (signposted to the national park). It will turn sharply left, then right, then left and right again before running into a T-intersection at the Whitton Stock Route. Here there is a park map and information board, and if you turn left you'll soon find the turnoff to Jacks Creek. There is a picnic area with free gas barbecues and a pit toilet, but no fresh water.

There are some more information signs at the beginning of the walk, which heads directly out from the carpark. You'll go through groves of tea trees, acacias and grevilleas, and if you're observant, may spot nodding blue lilies and orchids and some of the park's other 450 plant species.

Waterholes can be a magnet for wildlife

Some 140 bird species have also been spotted here, so keep your eyes peeled and binoculars out, and you may spot species as diverse as budgies, grey fantails and enormous wedge-tailed eagles.

The track can be walked in either direction, but it seems sensible to go straight through the gorge early on, walking the loop in an anti-clockwise direction. Fairly soon the track becomes very rocky and sandy as it winds through the gully, which will almost certainly be dry. The track can become a little hard to follow at times, but it basically follows the bottom of the gorge. Either side of you, stunning orange cliffs, up to 44 m high and made up of sedimentary rocks formed 400 million years ago, hold kurrajong trees and wonga vine.

Feral animals have made the area a bit of a home, so as well as kangaroos, you're likely to see mobs of goats, and maybe even foxes.

After about 700 m, the track heads sharply up to the left, up among the cypress pines. Other trees on the ridge include currawang (an acacia), Dwyer's mallee gum and hill tea tree.

At the highest point, the track is 100 m above the carpark. Once up the hill, the route heads along the edge of the gorge, and there are three great spots to look down into it, and then over the trees to the wide open plains beyond. There's also a bench beside a little

Wonga vine

Orange canyon walls

soak in some grassy woodlands that is reportedly a good bird-watching spot.

Soon the track winds back down the hill, and you'll rejoin the original track just near the carpark.

THE ROCK

WESTERN NSW

WALK: 6 km return

TIME REQUIRED: 2 hours

BEST TIME: Cooler months

GRADE: Moderate

ENVIRONMENT: Arid zone mountain with views over vast plains, cypress forest, rare vegetation

BEST MAP: This book

TOILETS: There is a flushing toilet at the start of the walk

FOOD: The Rock township, about 3 km down the road, has a general store

TIPS: The walk is longer, but not nearly as steep, as it looks

Punching more than 300 m above the surrounding plains south-west of Wagga Wagga, this mountain offers outstanding views. As a bonus, you'll encounter the world's largest stand of a rare and unusual plant species.

About half an hour's drive south-west of Wagga Wagga, you'll find the cute little town of The Rock. In one of the great legends of Australian idiom, it was once called Hanging Rock, but the bit that was hanging supposedly fell off, and the town changed its name to The Rock.

On the drive from Wagga, through low-lying sheep country, you'll see the mountain called The Rock looming more than 300 m over the plains. It has been a special Wiradjuri site for many thousands of years, used for male initiation ceremonies.

[above] *Butterfly leaves woolly ragwort*

Turn into the township and then past it for another 3 km to the signposted turnoff to The Rock Nature Reserve. The short dirt road to the carpark was in poor condition at last check, so take care in sedans.

At the carpark you'll find gas barbecues, picnic tables and flushing toilets. The start of the walk is signposted and obvious.

Although the route up the mountain looks steep and short, track planners seem to have worked hard to take you the easiest way up possible. The walk, called the Yerong Nature Trail, goes along the base of the mountain, then slowly up the front side and finishes right around the back, and the rise is rarely strenuous.

As you walk through the cypress forest at the base of the mountain, keep an eye out for the spectacular glossy black-cockatoo with its fire-engine-red tail feathers. Other birds to look for include babblers, red-capped robins, tree creepers, as well as the ubiquitous currawongs and peewees (or magpie larks). Orange and black butterflies will no doubt flit around, and you may even be lucky enough to spot a yellow-footed antechinus – a small mouse-like marsupial – darting through the scrub.

View from the summit of The Rock

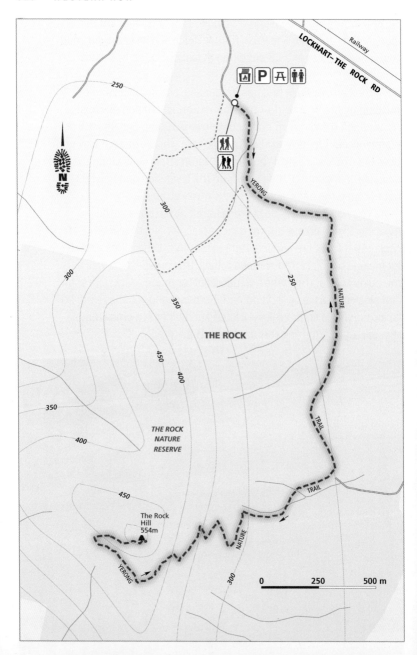

Woolly ragwort flowers

You'll walk about 1.5 km before the track starts climbing, and then it is a fairly steady rise to the top, with some views over the plains. There are stairs and occasional short-cuts through the switchbacks, but try to stay on the main track.

Towards the start of the main cliff line, you'll encounter one of the great treats of this walk – the largest stand of woolly ragwort anywhere in the world. This unusual, yellow-flowering shrub is found at the base of the cliffs and has large leaves that are woolly on the underside. Make sure you stop and feel them. The woolly texture is an insulating layer that minimises water loss.

Towards the top, the primary track makes a U-turn to the right, and is slightly hidden by a large boulder. It is a little confusing as another track goes straight ahead. However, if you miss the turn, it doesn't really matter, as from here you should be able to pick your

Echidna

way to the summit. The straight-ahead track goes to a rocky spine on the back side of the mountain, with lichen-covered rocks, and it is easy enough to follow this to the top.

At the top you'll find a bricked in fire-ring, and although the trees prevent a full 360-degree view, it is a gorgeous place to wander around and admire the vista to the horizon on every side. Enjoy a drink and some food and a break, before heading back down.

MOUNT EXMOUTH

WESTERN NSW

WALK: *20 km return with short loop*

TIME REQUIRED: *6 hours*

BEST TIME: *Spring*

GRADE: *Hard*

ENVIRONMENT: *Volcanic lava mountain, wildflowers, big xanthorrhoea forest, 360-degree views from the highest mountain in Warrumbungle National Park, and a rock arch*

BEST MAP: Warrumbungle National Park, *National Parks and Wildlife Service*

TOILETS: *There is a pit toilet at the start of walk; the park visitor centre, about a 5-minute drive away, has flushing toilets*

FOOD: *Coonabarabran, a 30-minute drive away, is a large town with restaurants, supermarkets, pubs and takeaways*

TIPS: *Mt Exmouth is an awesome destination, but the walk in and out is mainly on a very long and fairly uninteresting fire trail. Therefore, walkers may prefer to add an out-and-back addition to the Grand High Tops loop [see pp 329–34], which avoids the bulk of the ascent [as you will already be up fairly high].*

[above] **Summit of Mt Exmouth, with view over Warrumbungle National Park**

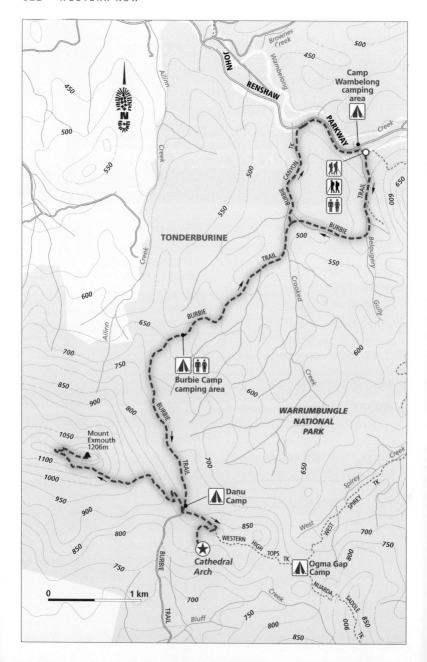

The highest mountain in Warrumbungle National Park at 1206 m, Mt Exmouth sits slightly to the west of most of the other topographic features; a hulking, looming presence. Home to wedge-tailed eagles and an extensive forest of xanthorrhoeas on its south side, it provides an incredible view over the park and the plains beyond. The walk in ascends nearly 800 m, most of it on a fire trail.

Done the Grand High Tops? Belougery Split Rock? Looking for another Warrumbungle challenge? After testing the resolve and dedication of walkers, this epic route will reward a thousand times over with the views from the top and the delightful surprise on the southern approach.

Start at the Split Rock carpark, taking the main fire trail that leads south. Ideally you will do this walk in spring, which will provide lots of wildflowers to look at as you climb steadily upwards – in particular bright yellow wattles. The Warrumbungles are at the junction of wetter eastern and dryer western vegetation communities so have quite diverse plant life. Apart from the flowers, the birdlife and the chance of seeing a koala, there isn't much to break the trudge, and the hulk of Mt Exmouth on the right of the track may even appear to grow higher.

About halfway up the fire trail, you'll come to the Burbie Spring campsite. There is a pit toilet and even a tap here (connected to the spring). Lots of Aboriginal artefacts have been found in this area, but all must be left in situ.

At the top of the Burbie Fire Trail, you'll find another small campsite, Danu Gap. From here the management trail continues straight ahead, the small Mt Exmouth foot track goes right (to the west) and the Western High Tops track goes to the left. It is well worth popping along the Western High Tops track for a kilometre or so, across a scree slope, and then ducking up to see Cathedral Arch – a huge rock archway, with a glorious white gum standing on top.

Head back to Danu Gap and then up the Mt Exmouth track. From here the walk is increasingly interesting as it skirts right around the southern side of the mountain before coming up it on the western side. You'll soon encounter the extensive and beautiful xanthorrhoea forest, with the shaggy-haired trees almost covering the steep hillside on either side of the track. There are a couple of tricky ledges to walk along before the track curves around and up to the ridge line.

A false summit invites exploration on the left, but the main track continues right, past some spinifex and more xanthorrhoeas to the summit cairn and the spectacular views in every direction.

Retrace you steps until the final few kilometres, when you can detour along the Burbie Canyon track to the left. Although not a high-walled canyon, it is a lovely spot, with abundant birds, kangaroos and, unfortunately, feral goats. This track meanders across grasslands before bringing you out to the main road. Then turn right and walk along the road for a bit over a kilometre to get back to the Split Rock carpark.

Cathedral Arch

BELOUGERY SPLIT ROCK

WESTERN NSW

WALK: 4.6 km loop

TIME REQUIRED: 2.5 hours

BEST TIME: Late afternoon, clear weather, spring

GRADE: Hard

ENVIRONMENT: Volcanic lava mountain, wildflowers, black cypress pine woodland, 360-degree views

BEST MAP: Warrumbungle National Park, National Parks and Wildlife Service

TOILETS: There is a pit toilet at the start of walk; the park visitor centre, about a 5-minute drive away, has flushing toilets

FOOD: Coonabarabran, a 30-minute drive away, is a large town with restaurants, supermarkets, pubs and takeaways

TIPS: The peak is a great place to see the sunset, but you will need to carry a torch and be careful getting down after dark

Blue-faced honeyeater

[above] *View from the carpark*

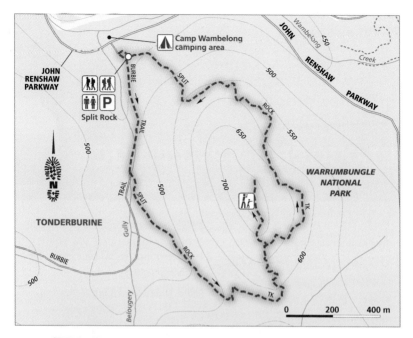

This fantastic walk takes you 350 m up from a grassy woodland area where kangaroos graze, through black cypress forests to the top of a dramatic, split volcanic feature with impressive views on all sides, including of the rest of the Warrumbungles. The top section is listed as 'dangerous with rock-climbing involved' but don't let that scare you off, as it is mostly easy rock scrambling with the route marked well with reflective markers.

Belougery Split Rock towers over the Split Rock carpark, its twin volcanic spires separated by a vegetated area. This loop walk reaches the top of the higher spire, and you can do it in either direction. Anti-clockwise (as described) gets you to the summit fastest, but if you are going to be out after dark, it is recommended you do it in the other direction.

Take the fire trail south out of the carpark. It stays flat for a little while, passing some glorious western golden wattle with flowers the

Volcanic rock

iridescent colour of canola. The dominant tree species here is black cypress pine.

After a few hundred metres, the track splits, with the main fire trail continuing to Burbie Spring and up to Mt Exmouth (the highest mountain in Warrumbungle National Park), and a smaller track heading left, up the creek line to Split Rock. Take the little track which snakes steeply up to the saddle, and then up the ridge to a steel stairway. A gate and sign warns that the track above is steep and dangerous, but as long as it isn't wet, most people should find it a fun adventure: the climbing is not difficult, steps have been cut into the rock and there are reflective markers to follow. It's only a few hundred metres up this section to the summit, and the views over the rest of the national park, and then out to the surrounding district, just keep getting better and better.

Summit view over Warrumbungle National Park

As you climb to the summit, you'll enter a heathland that in spring is alive with wildflowers, including golden and knife-leafed wattle, fringed heath myrtle, kunzia and a garden of smaller flowers. To the east you will see the Siding Spring Observatory, and the long jagged features of the Warrumbungles stretching out magically. It will be hard to pull yourself away.

The return part of the walk is slightly longer. Climb carefully back down to the steel stairs, then turn left along a fairly eroded track along the base of the cliff. Where it comes to the other half of the split rock, a small track wanders onto the face for those who want to climb a second time. The main track, however, continues down, through some tall, shaggy xanthorrhoeas, offering views back out to the west as it descends into the cypress pine forest, and then down to the carpark.

GRAND HIGH TOPS

WESTERN NSW

WALK: 16.5 km loop

TIME REQUIRED: 6 hours

BEST TIME: Cool, clear days in spring

GRADE: Hard

ENVIRONMENT: Dramatic volcanic landscape, wildflowers, black cypress pine woodland, 360-degree views, eucalypt woodland

BEST MAP: Warrumbungle National Park, National Parks and Wildlife Service

TOILETS: Pit toilet about 100 m into the walk and at Balor Hut, halfway through the walk

FOOD: Coonabarabran, a 30-minute drive away, is a large town with restaurants, supermarkets and takeaways

TIPS: Those keen to extend this walk into a very long hike can go from Ogma Gap out to Mt Exmouth, the highest point in Warrumbungle National Park. Balor Hut, near The Breadknife, can be hired for $5 per person per night, and is a great base to stay for a night. You will need to carry sleeping gear, but no tent, and there is usually water in the tank.

[above] *Crater Bluff from Grand High Tops*

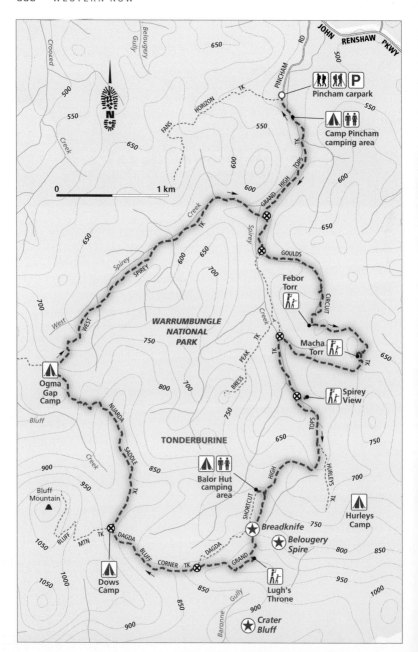

Point Wilderness

A NSW classic, this is the best known walk in Warrumbungle National Park, offering close, stunning views of all the park's volcanic icons: The Breadknife, Belougery Spire, Crater Bluff and Bluff Mountain.

When this part of the continent passed over a volcanic hotspot about 13 million years ago, it formed a massive volcano, towering about 1000 m above the surrounding plains, and lava rose up from many subsidiary vents. Over eons, much of the volcano was eroded away, leaving the hardened volcanic plugs and features that rise up spectacularly – in particular the narrow feature of The Breadknife, the prominent Belougery Spire and Crater Bluff.

Some 60 years ago, bushwalkers and rock climbers were so taken with this impressive landscape, they set about ensuring it was protected as a national park. Very popular during the 1970s and 1980s, it has fallen out of the public eye a little in the past two decades, but has excellent, cheap campsites (powered and unpowered), extensive wildlife (including koalas, emus, and kangaroos), dramatic scenery, fantastic rock-climbing and a brilliant mixed bag of different length walks.

Belougery Spire

Justifiably, the best known walk in the park is the Grand High Tops, which goes up to and around the iconic features making for an absolute classic day out. You can walk it in either direction, but going clockwise means you have the tough climbs at the beginning and finish in the relatively shaded gully of West Spirey Creek.

Start at Pincham carpark in the centre of the park, and take the marked track, ignoring the track to the right. After a kilometre or so, your return route will come in (across a bridge) to the right, but keep going straight ahead. The first half of the track is well made, with paved areas and wooden bridges. In the early morning you're more than likely to see eastern grey kangaroos, and a range of birds.

A diversion left, on Gould's Circuit, is highly recommended. It adds a couple of steep climbs, and a few kilometres, but will give you two great vantage points, in particular the second high point, called Macha Tor. Unfortunately, after this high point, you have to descend all the way to the valley floor again on an eroded track. But you will have the pleasure of passing through a cypress pine forest with flowering peas and other wildflowers.

Once back on the main track, turn left, through a lovely section of the gully that has xanthorrhoeas, wildflowers and lots of birdlife. Spirey View, just 150 m off the track, won't offer as good an overall view as you've seen on Macha Tor, but does have a slightly better vista of The Breadknife, showing how narrow it is.

Soon the track starts climbing again with some awesome views of Belougery Spire on the left. Keep an eye out for rock-climbers high up on the face. The track has long paved sections (a bit of a yellow brick road) and a large, well-made set of steel and timber stairs that take you up steeply to the turn-off to Balor Hut (about 100 m away). The hut has a pit toilet outside. If you don't require the toilet, stay on the track that veers left (not the short cut past the hut to Dagda Gap) and you'll climb up directly below the Breadknife, with more close views of Belougery Spire. Once you reach the ridge line, at 992 m, some 500 m above where you started, you'll get an absolutely crackerjack view of the towering Crater Bluff over the back, and there is plenty of room in among the rocks to take

Koala

a well-earned break. Take this opportunity, because there's a lot more of this walk to go (although mostly downhill from here).

The route continues along Dagda Gap, and then you'll find one of the few confusing signs, pointing back to the right to the carpark. This is the short-cut route and would take you back to Balor Hut and the way you came up. It is much better to complete the slightly longer loop, even though the views aren't as spectacular in the second half.

Continue along, and you'll begin to get a great look at Bluff Mountain on the left, with its cubic rock structure on the lower section of the north face. Some interesting rock climbs go up this feature too.

Turn right at Dows Camp (named after the bloke who built this track), down to another great vantage point called Point Wilderness, and then Ogma Gap. Those who want a really long day out in the bush can deviate here along the Western High Tops to Mt Exmouth. Otherwise, head down into the lovely shaded eucalypt forest along West Spirey Creek. The route crosses the creek several times. Keep an eye out for birds, koalas, goannas, other lizards and snakes.

After a lovely hour or so along the gully, you'll cross a bridge and be back on the original track. Turn left and head back to the carpark.

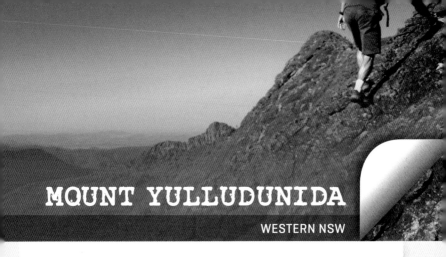

MOUNT YULLUDUNIDA

WESTERN NSW

WALK: 4 km return

TIME REQUIRED: 2.5 hours

BEST TIME: Cooler months, mornings

GRADE: Hard and potentially dangerous

ENVIRONMENT: Volcanic ring dyke, cliffs, forest and scrub

BEST MAP: Mount Kaputar National Park, NSW National Parks and Wildlife Service

TOILETS: Toilets are located 10 km up the road at Bark Hut camping area

FOOD: Narrabri (45 minutes' drive away) has supermarkets, service stations, restaurants and pubs

TIPS: Possibly avoid if you are scared of heights

A dramatic and exhilarating walk, this starts in some pleasant forest, climbs nearly 400 m in altitude and culminates in an off-track scramble up the steep and jagged rocks of an ancient volcano.

Some 21 million years ago, this part of the continent drifted over a volcanic hotspot, 7 km underground. For the next four million years, a spectacular volcanic landscape was formed above the hotspot. It is estimated that at times the volcano was more than 2000 m high. The continent continued to drift and later the same hotspot gave

[above] *Precarious walking up the volcanic remnant*

rise to the Warrumbungles, which you can see on the horizon from the summit of Mt Yulludunida.

Over time, what was left from the violent volcanic eruptions eroded into a series of dramatic features, including volcanic plugs, the upthrust Nandewar Range, and a large ring dyke, where the middle of a caldera has gradually sunk. This walk takes you to that ring dyke, and to a peak on its outer edge. At times those with a fear of heights may find it perilous, and care should be taken, as a tumble down the rock face would be potentially fatal.

The walk begins at Green Camp, 1.5 km after the dirt road into the park changes to bitumen. It's the first turn-off after the information sign near the park entrance. There is no toilet or water at Green Camp, but there is a picnic table. The start of the track is obvious.

The first section of the walk is through a very peaceful woodland of scattered xanthorrhoeas. Keep your eyes roving from the smallest things on the forest floor, such as beautiful coral fungi, wildflowers or the legendary pink slug; up to the profusion of birds above. There are 180 bird species in this park, including

Volcanic plugs and dykes abound in Mt Kaputar National Park

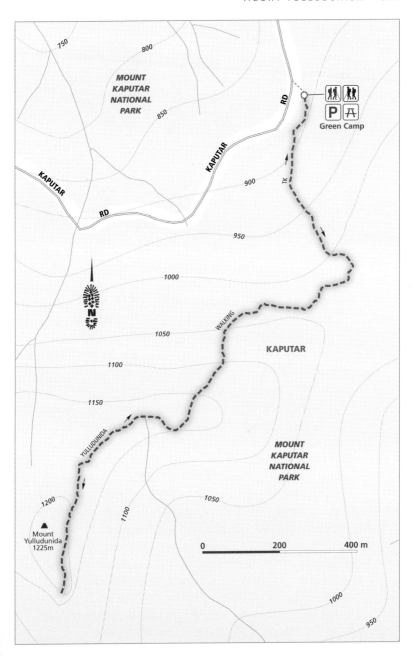

View along the spine

crimson rosellas, raucous cockatoos and the haunting grey goshawk (though in this forested section, you'll have only the accompaniment of small twittering birds to disturb your reverie).

Soon you'll hit the first lot of stairs, and the walk climbs solidly from here up to the 1225 m peak. At one point early in the climb, when the track turns sharply left, there is a little rocky area straight ahead with your first great views. If you miss this, there are other opportunities a few hundred metres further on.

The track is quite eroded and difficult to walk along in places, with some high steps. At the saddle, the track flattens slightly and powers through montane heath, with plants such as kunzeas, before rising again through the last bit of forest.

About 1.5 km from the carpark, the track suddenly stops as you pop out at the rock face. Although the ring dyke is no longer complete, you can see the basic shape of it, and the bald Mt Yulludunida rising straight ahead of you. There is no track from here – initially there are a couple of fence posts and some cairns, but you may lose track of them. The main route, with the most obvious cairns, heads slightly down to the left before rising up close to the summit. This is a great way to come back, but a more exciting way to get to the summit is to head diagonally upwards (not immediately to your right) towards the ridgeline. You'll have to make your way through a few trees, and do a bit of rock scrambling that will tend towards rock climbing at times, but the rock is solid and there are usually excellent handholds. Occasionally you'll find slightly smoother bits of rock, or areas where edges have been knocked off, and you'll know that others have been here before.

Once you reach the jagged ridge, you'll get a great view over the other side. Walking along the ridge isn't as easy as it looks from the ground though, as the spine is jagged and you'll need to pick your way through the rocks and occasional waterholes.

The final hop up to the summit is on smoother, slightly steeper rock, but if you've made it this far you'll have no problem with the exposure. There is a large summit cairn (which may be full of flying ants that will take exception to your presence) and great views all round.

On the way back down, there may be times when it is easier to go carefully backwards, facing the rock and keeping your hands on it.

Xanthorrhoeas and other vegetation clinging to the cliff

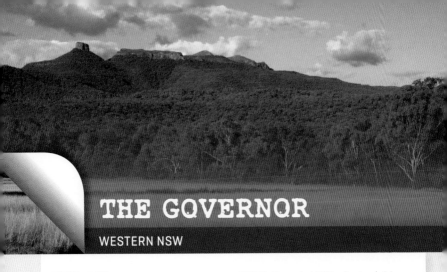

THE GOVERNOR

WESTERN NSW

WALK: 2.5 km return

TIME REQUIRED: 1 hour

BEST TIME: Clear days any time of year

GRADE: Moderate – some steep stairs and rock scrambling at the top

ENVIRONMENT: Volcanic cliffs, subalpine forest

BEST MAP: Mount Kaputar National Park, NSW National Parks and Wildlife Service

TOILETS: Pit toilet at Bark Hut camping area, 2 km down the road

FOOD: Narrabri (45 minutes' drive away) has supermarkets, service stations, takeaways, cafes and pubs; for top-quality fare in a contemporary atmosphere, with indoor and outdoor eating areas, try the Crossroads Hotel: 170 Maitland Street, (02) 6792 5592

TIPS: Allow some extra time to see some of the park's other highlights

[above] *Mt Kaputar National Park*

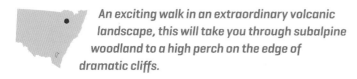

An exciting walk in an extraordinary volcanic landscape, this will take you through subalpine woodland to a high perch on the edge of dramatic cliffs.

Mount Kaputar National Park, near Narrabri, is one of the most underrated national parks in NSW. Its towering jagged outline, with volcanic plugs and pointy peaks, can be seen from many kilometres away, and with heights up to 1500 m above sea level it can get snow on its subalpine summits. There are 13 listed walks in the 54 000 ha park, and keen bushwalkers could easily spend a few days here.

It's an adventure just getting into the park with a 45 minute drive east of Narrabri through low-lying farmland. The road is unsealed and rough once you enter the park, and care needs to be taken as it winds up the hill, with a perilous unfenced drop on the left side. There is an excellent information bay about 2 km past the park entry with information on everything from the volcanic geology of the park 21 million years ago to the rare 15 cm long pink slug that can be found on rocks and trees after rain.

In the mornings, to make the drive even more adventurous, you will probably encounter common wallaroos and dark swamp

Views stretching to the horizon

wallabies hopping across the road. Boulders may also tumble down the steep mountainside onto the road.

The dirt section of road finishes after about 6 km, and then you are back on a sealed, narrow and winding road that continues ever upwards, providing some excellent views, including of the impressive castle-like Euglah Rock to the south, all the way to Warrumbungle National Park on the horizon.

You will pass the signposted turnoffs to Green Camp, Coryah Gap and Bark Hut before getting to the Governor turnoff on the left-hand side of the road. The carpark is only 50 m off the road. When you get out of the car you will notice that the temperature is probably about 10°C cooler than in Narrabri, keeping this walk relatively cool, even in the height of summer.

The walk starts out with a flat wander through a gum woodland, on a sealed track suitable for wheelchairs, to an excellent

The summit offers extraordinary vistas

Well-constructed boardwalk between the lookout and The Governor

lookout on the edge of the cliff. From here you can easily see The Governor to your immediate left, and past it to Mt Mitchell, then right around to Mt Grattai in the distance on your right.

The track continues through lovely subalpine woodland, with some vibrant green mosses growing virulently on the rocks. A series of well-constructed wooden boardwalks and steel stairs then take you down the saddle between the lookout and The Governor. There is a thick tea tree forest here, and you will start to see some of the yellow reflectors that will guide you the rest of the way. If there is water around, be careful on some of the smoother rocks as they can be extremely slippery. There may be some lovely sub-alpine flowers about, such as everlastings.

After ascending steel stairs up to The Governor, the track becomes quite rocky, and follows a water runnel. Veer left halfway up this water runnel, rather than going straight up the steepest section of rock, and then wind back to the highest reaches.

Once on the rocky platforms, the track peters out and you can take your time exploring this 1400 m summit, taking in the breathtaking 270-degree views. It's a great place for a picnic lunch. All cliff edges are unfenced, so take care particularly with younger children.

After you have explored the summit for a while, head back the way you came.

INDEX

C

Y

Stunning views of Sydney Harbour are a highlight of the Spit to Manly walk (see pp 47–51)

Acknowledgements
The publisher would like to acknowledge the following individuals and organisations:

Commissioning editor
Melissa Krafchek

Project manager and editor
Lachlan McLaine

Editorial assistance
Alison Proietto

Cartography
Bruce McGurty, Emily Maffei, Claire Johnston,
Danesh Chacko

Design
Erika Budiman

Layout
Megan Ellis

Index
Max McMaster

Illustrations
Guy Troughton (fauna), David Mackay (flora)

Pre-press
Splitting Image, Megan Ellis

Photography
Front cover: Rock-hopping at Leatherjacket Bay, Ben
Boyd National Park, Light to Light walk, South Coast
(Ken Eastwood)
Back cover: Surveying the vista atop Mount Yullundunida,
Mount Kaputar National Park, Western NSW (Ken
Eastwood); Ken Eastwood on the Light to Light walk, South
Coast (Josh Moffitt)
Title page: The Breadknife, Warrumbungle National Park,
Western NSW (Ken Eastwood)
Other images: All images used in the internal pages are
© Ken Eastwood, except for the images on pp. 296–9
(Don Fuchs/GTI Tourism).

Maps in this book
The maps in this publication have been produced by
combining digital topographic data with field-collected
GPS data. They have been specifically designed and drawn
to complement the author's narrative description of each
walk and to enhance the walker's experience. These maps
can be used as a supplement to navigating and identifying
the location of features described, but are in no way
intended to replace authoritative topographic maps that,
at better scales, will show much more of the natural and
man-made features.

Feature walks on the maps are highlighted and are
easily identified among other useful topographic elements.
General relief of the landscape is shown with contour
lines and heights at 50-metre intervals. The maps also
include roads, tracks, rivers and creeks giving the walker an
appreciation of the geography of the area. A wide variety
of points of interest have also been incorporated focusing
on helping the walker identify attractions such as lookouts,
natural features, picnic areas and important facilities.

Explore Australia Publishing Pty Ltd
Ground Floor, Building 1, 658 Church Street,
Richmond, VIC 3121

Explore Australia Publishing Pty Ltd is a division of Hardie Grant
Publishing Pty Ltd

hardie grant publishing

Published by Explore Australia Publishing Pty Ltd, 2013

Concept, maps, form and design © Explore Australia Publishing
Pty Ltd, 2013
Text © Ken Eastwood, 2013

A Cataloguing-in-Publication entry is available from the catalogue of
the National Library of Australia at www.nla.gov.au

The maps in this publication incorporate data © Commonwealth of
Australia (Geoscience Australia), 2006. Geoscience Australia has not
evaluated the data as altered and incorporated within this publication,
and therefore gives no warranty regarding accuracy, completeness,
currency or suitability for any particular purpose.

Copyright imprint and currency – VAR Product and PSMA Data
"Copyright. Based on data provided under licence from PSMA Australia
Limited (www.psma.com.au)".

Hydrography Data (May 2006)
Transport Data (November 2012)

Aboriginal lands, parks and reserves based on data provided under
licence from the following jurisdictions:
Australian Capital Territory Parks and Reserves (2010) – ACT Planning
and Land Authority
New South Wales National Parks and Wildlife Reserves (2010) – NSW
Department of Environment Climate Change and Water

Disclaimer
While every care is taken to ensure the accuracy of the data within
this product, the owners of the data (including the state, territory
and Commonwealth governments of Australia) do not make
any representations or warranties about its accuracy, reliability,
completeness or suitability for any particular purpose and, to the extent
permitted by law, the owners of the data disclaim all responsibility
and all liability (including without limitation, liability in negligence) for
all expenses, losses, damages, (including indirect or consequential
damages) and costs which might be incurred as a result of the data
being inaccurate or incomplete in any way and for any reason.

ISBN-13 9781741173949

10 9 8 7 6 5 4 3 2 1

Printed and bound in China by 1010 Printing International Ltd

Publisher's note: Every effort has been made to ensure that the
information in this book is accurate at the time of going to press. The
publisher welcomes information and suggestions for correction or
improvement. Email: info@exploreaustralia.net.au

Publisher's disclaimer: The publisher cannot accept responsibility for any
errors or omissions. The representation on the maps of any road or track
is not necessarily evidence of public right of way. The publisher cannot
be held responsible for any injury, loss or damage incurred during travel.
It is vital to research any proposed trip thoroughly and seek the advice of
relevant state and travel organisations before you leave.

www.exploreaustralia.net.au
Follow us on Twitter: @ExploreAus
Find us on Facebook: www.facebook.com/exploreaustralia